Otherworldly islands haunt the imagination of the West. From Atlantis to Ys, the peoples of the Atlantic seaboard have dreamt of, searched for, journeyed to and lost several distinctive kingdoms of the sea – all 'into the West', where the sun sets and where the soul is said to go at death. Are they a collective dreaming of a real place, or mere salty yarns spun by ancient mariners?

In *Lost Islands: Inventing Avalon, Destroying Eden* Kevan Manwaring takes you on an adventurous odyssey charting this metaphysical archipelago, drawing upon philosophy, folklore, literature and myth. This voyage encompasses many imaginary Eden-like utopias. Can we ever hope to attain such paradises or are they ultimately within ourselves – states of consciousness and enlightenment to aspire to and fall from? And why do such island Edens seemingly inevitably end in disasters – whether inundated by mythic floods, as with Atlantis, or with all-too-real ecological disasters, as with Easter Island?

In an era of climate change and global uncertainty the myths of inundations are more poignant today than ever. How permanent is our own 'island state' of living on Earth?

Kevan Manwaring is an author (*The Bardic Handbook, The Long Woman, Windsmith*) and teacher of creative writing with the Open University. He won the Bardic Chair of Caer Badon in 1998 and has been a professional storyteller since. He lives in Bath, Somerset, when not island-hopping.

LOST ISLANDS

Inventing Avalon,
Destroying Eden

Kevan Manwaring

Heart of Albion

LOST ISLANDS:

Inventing Avalon, Destroying Eden

Kevan Manwaring

ISBN 978-1-905646-07-4

Published by

Heart of Albion Press
2 Cross Hill Close, Wymeswold
Loughborough, LE12 6UJ

albion@indigogroup.co.uk

Visit our Web site: www.hoap.co.uk

Printed in England by Booksprint

He who invented it, also destroyed it.

Aristotle, referring to Plato's Atlantis

Acknowledgments

My thanks to Marian Anderson for the author photograph on the back cover, Anthony Nanson and Kirsty Hartsiotis, David Metcalfe, Stephen J. Isaac, Svanur Gisli Thorkelsson, Amy Whitehead, Keith Lord and Bob.

Contents

Introduction   1

Part One – *The Allure of the Imaginary*

1. Into the West   8
2. Atlantis to Oz   29
3. Walking on Brigadoon   62
4. To be a pilgrim   84
5. Inventing Avalon   94

Part Two – *The Cold Light of Day*

6. Did the Earth move?   110
7. The island that ate itself   119
8. Stick in the mud   128
9. When the levee breaks   143

Part Three – *When Worlds Collide*

10. Exiles from Eden   162
11. How the West was lost   176
12. This island Earth   194

Bibliography   200
Index   209

Introduction

Otherworldly islands haunt the imagination of the West. From Atlantis to Ys, the peoples of the Atlantic seaboard have dreamt of, searched for, journeyed to and lost several distinctive kingdoms of the sea – all 'into the West'. Are they a collective dreaming of a real place, or mere salty yarns spun by ancient mariners? In this adventurous odyssey we will attempt to chart this archipelago of the actual and the imaginary. Drawing upon philosophy, religion, folklore, literature and myth, as well as geology, ecology, archaeology and socio-political dimensions, we will explore the subjective and objective psychogeographical terrain of this perennial and diverse phenomenon.

So, all aboard on this wonder voyage to these alluring and elusive isles – where healing, inspiration and a perspective upon the vulnerability of our own present civilisation can be gleaned. The myths of inundations and fragile islands are more poignant today than ever in an era of climate change and global uncertainty. How permanent are our own 'island states'? Can we ever hope to attain such paradises or are they ultimately within ourselves – states of consciousness and enlightenment to aspire to and fall from?

Ian Baker in *The Heart of the World* (2006) describes how he spent twenty years in Nepal, studying Tibetan buddhism. One of the teachings he came to understand was 'that to gain access to paradise one must seek out the *beyuls*, or hidden-away lands. The more inaccessible the *beyul*, the more illuminating the paradise it conceals.' This elucidates the intrinsic nature of lost islands. Their obscurity, absurdity or even non-existence, is a quintessential aspect of their allure to many who catch 'island-fever'.

In *The Voyage of Bran*, a sixth century Irish 'immram' or wonder voyage, the plethora of legendary islands is suggested:

> There are thrice fifty distant isles
> In the ocean to the west of us;
> Larger than Erin twice
> Is each of them, or thrice.

Fortunately, some 'lost' islands are easy to get to. On our immram we will stop at actual islands and locations, such as Glastonbury, Bardsey Island, Isle of Man, Isles of Scilly, Iona, Iceland and the not so accessible Galápagos Islands. We will also visit imaginary ones – Atlantis, Avalon, Tir nan Og, Brigadoon, Shangri-La, The Fortunate Isles, The Isles of the Blessed, Thule and Kêr-Ys – all the while looking for clues to

Site of an ancient sunken city – Kekova, Turkey.

these lost paradises. You will be entertained along the way by explorers, poets and storytellers who have ventured to these distant shores.

Our focus, for the purposes of this book, are Western myths – although let it be taken as a given that this is not exclusively a Western phenomenon. There are stories of lost islands all over the globe, in almost every culture. However, cosmologies are often 'place specific', reflecting the geography, climate, ecosystem and cultural practices of a particular area –so it is perhaps no surprise that all along the Atlantic seaboard of western Europe there are legends of lost islands to the west, across the vast ocean, towards the setting sun.

This book is a cluster of paradigms, each chapter an island, each island a world in its own right, or a way of looking at the world, as I attempt to examine 'lost islands' in various ways, mythological, literary, geological, anthropological, ontological, environmental, political, archaeological and metaphysical. This I will call my 'Little Prince' approach, after Antoine de St Exupéry's masterful creation about the lonely world-hopping divine child whose innocence of perception made him wise to humanity's follies. *Le Petit Prince* (published in England in 1945 as *The Little Prince*) was written a year before the author's disappearance on a reconnaissance flight over the Mediterranean and was based on St X's (as he was known to his friends) formative flying experiences over South America and Africa, vividly recorded in *Southern Mail* and *Wind, Sand and Stars*:

We felt ourselves lost then in interplanetary space, among a hundred inaccessible planets, searching for the one true planet that was our own, the only one with

The sun setting between Steepholm and Flatholm, from Clevedon, Somerset.

landscapes we knew, houses we loved, all that we treasured. (St Exupéry 1939 (1995: 14))

Lost Islands differs from other books on Atlantology, Thule and other lost civilisations, as it does not try to find and prove the actual locations of these places, whether they be mythical or otherwise, but instead chooses to see them as salient metaphors offering us consolation and salutary warnings. I will not attempt to prove or disprove this archipelago of the imagination, but to adopt the Keatsian notion of 'negative capability', to accept these mysteries, savour them and perhaps reflect that man's knowledge is finite, his comprehension of the universe can perhaps only ever be subjective and fallible, and that 'there are more things in Heaven and Earth than a dreamt of in most people's philosophies.'

The questions to be examined here are: Why the perennial popularity and allure of lost islands? Why so many along the Atlantic seaboard? How are they created and destroyed? Why will there be more in the future? This book will set out to answer these questions, or at least embark on a voyage of discovery.

As on all good voyages you will be entertained along the way by the bards as King Arthur's bard, Taliesin, accompanied him on his perilous quest to win the fabled Cauldron of Plenty (as recorded in the poem ascribed to him, *Preiddu Annwn*). Each chapter begins with a section of the framing narrative: the Oisín and Niamh (pronounced 'Uh-sheen' and 'Neev' respectively) story, a classic case of what could be called 'lost island syndrome'. The fictional framing narrative serves two purposes: firstly, to provide aesthetic contrast to engage different parts of the reader's brain

3

from the main rhetorical narrative – a structural dialectic between the actual and the imaginary, and secondly to act a reminder to the reader that it is such stories as Oisín and Niamh's that lured people to lost islands initially.

In his famous preface to *The Scarlet Letter*, entitled 'The Custom House', Nathaniel Hawthorne coined a phrase that is useful for negotiating these nebulous territories:

> Thus, therefore, the floor of our familiar room has become a neutral territory, somewhere between the real world and fairy-land, where the Actual and the Imaginary may meet, and each imbue itself with the nature of the other.
>
> Hawthorne 1850

'The Actual and the Imaginary' was the title for a storytelling conference at the Ancient Technology Centre, Dorset, in 2005. The keynote speaker was author Alan Garner who, in his collection of essays, *The Voice That Thunders* (1997) discusses the influence of: 'the actual and imaginary' on his work. Garner explains how in his writing he attempts to combine 'a sense of the numinous and a rational mind'. This is the approach adopted here.

This encompassing of dualities is key to the understanding of lost islands. Nicholas of Cusa postulated: 'The walls of Paradise is built of contraries, nor is there any way to enter but for one who has overcome the highest spirit of reason who guards the gate'. Sometimes you must bypass logic to access wisdom.

However, it is important to have clear parameters. A working definition of a lost island will help. A litmus test for lost islands is their liminality: they should have some kind of marginal status or nature, and be either hard to get to or not exist at all. Real 'lost islands' we will look at are those with nebulous mythic, religious or cultural associations, and those under threat or already decimated. We will encompass the ecological notion of 'island' in our definition. For an ecologist, the word 'island' refers to any ecosystem that is isolated from the wider world (McIntosh 2004: 37) and the effect of 'islandisation' is one of the main causes of species extinction (Attenborough 2000), warning us of the increasing prevalence of ever-dwindling islands of biodiversity in the future. So, a lost island is a zone that is hidden, obscure, inaccessible, endangered or destroyed.

The book is divided into three sections: lost islands created by the imagination (mythical, fictional, folkloric or sacred); actual causes for lost islands (geological, environmental, archaeological, floods and changes in sea level); and finally the convergence of the two in politics, religion and contemporary culture. This could be seen as a discourse between reason and unreason; the logical and lateral; or the left and right sides of the brain.

In Part One, we look at 'The Allure of the Imaginary', taking the right-hand fork into the lateral, charting a wide selection of imaginary islands, and exploring their perennial appeal. In Chapter One, 'Into the West', we look at the appeal of lost islands through a mythological lens. What has called many seekers and dreamers to these places over the millennia? In Chapter Two, 'Atlantis to Oz', we look at the lost islands of literature. In Chapter Three, 'Walking on Brigadoon', we cast a gaze on the actual 'lost islands' of the British Isles. In Chapter Four, 'To Be a Pilgrim', we explore the long tradition of holy journeys. In Chapter Five, 'Inventing Avalon', we look at the major 'brigadoon' of Britain – the Isle of Avalon, and its associations with Glastonbury.

In Part Two, 'The Cold Light of Day', we double-back and take the left-hand fork, exploring logical reasons for lost islands. In Chapter Six, 'Did the Earth Move?' we take a hard look at geological factors. In Chapter Seven, 'The Island that Ate Itself', we visit Easter Island, as an example of extreme environmental denudation. In Chapter Eight, 'Stick in the Mud', we consider archaeological lost islands. In Chapter Nine, 'When the Levee Breaks', we examine the many flood warnings of recent years, which have and will continue to create the lost islands of the future.

In Part Three, we look at 'When Worlds Collide' – when the actual and imaginary combine or clash with devastating effect: in the realms of politics and religion, to create heaven on earth, or hell. In Chapter Ten, 'Exiles from Eden', we consider religious factors. In Chapter Eleven, 'How the West was Lost', we explore the New World and all that it implies, from a political perspective. In the final chapter, 'This Island Earth', we end our exploration by looking at the bigger picture and draw some conclusions.

A work exploring the world of the imagination has to be, by definition, incomplete – for imaginary worlds are as limitless as the imagination, and to attempt to map and categorise them all would be a fool's errand, for, as Alberto Manguel, co-editor of the fecund *Dictionary of Imaginary Places* says in his preface to the revised edition:

> … the imaginary world keeps growing, and countless continents
> of the mind are born between book covers every year.

(Manguel and Guadalapi 1999)

The nature of lost islands is: the more you look, the more you find. This is something Robert M. Pirsig points out in *Zen and the Art of Motorcycle Maintenance* (1974), concerning scientific method, and ultimately rationality itself: about the way one discovers or even creates more hypotheses the more one tests them – the endless experiment. Quantum worlds brought to life by the observer-participant, like so many Schrodinger's cats:

> For every fact there is an infinity of hypotheses. The more you
> look the more you see.

(Pirsig 1974: (1999: 191))

In this respect, the search for lost islands is as Protean as any search for meaning. When the mythic Peloponnesian apiarist Arastaois journeyed to the Isle of Pharos, home of the famous lighthouse – fittingly for one in search of illumination (to establish why his precious bees had died) – he cornered his relative, Proteus, only for the slippery old fellow to shift shape, until exhausted, he resumed his original form

Et in Arcadia Ego. *Arkadian Peloponnese.*

and spilled the beans. In this case the cause of his hive's demise was Aristaois lusting after Eurydice, the upshot of which was her death (she fled from him and was bitten on the heel by a snake – resulting in a one-way ticket to Hades). We must pursue the truth diligently but at the same time not expect it to conform to our expectations. Its shape may change and it may even change us.

Going in search of something that may or may not exist... A fool's errand, perhaps, but it takes a fool's first step into the abyss of ignorance to begin the path of knowledge, to embark on a journey of discovery, to start on the Holy Road of the pilgrim.

In a world threatened by climate chaos there is a genuine urgency to this task. It is timely to look back at what myths and legends can teach us about floods, the destruction of paradises and lost civilisations. More lost islands are occurring every day. And the way things are going, humanity could become an 'islandised' species itself. The sixth mass extinction could be our own. We should strive to preserve, honour and learn from the vast storehouse of what-is-past while we can. To forget is the greatest insult to our ancestors, and to evolution. As T.S. Eliot says in his poem 'East Coker', from *The Four Quartets*, written under the shadow of annihilation in the Second World War:

> There is only the fight to recover what is lost.
> The rest is not our business.

With that in mind, let us embark.

PART ONE

The allure of the imaginary

Chapter one

Into the West

The invitation

Oisín, the poet of the Fianna, that legendary warrior band of Erin, was out hunting with his father, Fionn Mac Cumhail, their friends, and their two hounds, Bran and Skulan. Suddenly, to their surprise, appeared a woman of otherworldly beauty on a moon-white horse. She wielded a branch of silver and gold, and declared boldly that she had come to Erin to take back with her a husband – and she had chosen Oisín, for his famous songs had carried as far as her homeland, Tir nan Og, the Land of the Ever Young. She introduced herself as Niamh of the Golden Hair, and indeed her hair shone like the sun while her beauty dazzled both father and son. She turned eyes full of enchanting promise to Oisín and enticed him with this description of her paradisal shores:

> Delightful is the land beyond all dreams
> Fairer than aught thine eyes have ever seen.
> There all year the fruit is on the tree,
> And all the year the bloom is on the flower.
> There with wild honey drip the forest trees;
> The stores of wine and mead shall never fail.
> Nor pain nor sickness knows the dweller there,
> Death and decay comes near him never more.
> The feast shall cloy not, nor the chase shall tire,
> Nor music cease for ever through the hall;
> The gold and jewels of the Land of Youth
> Outshine all splendours ever dreamed by man.
> Thou shalt have horses of the fairy breed,
> thou shalt have hounds that can outrun the wind;
> A hundred chiefs shall follow thee in war,
> A hundred maidens sing thee to thy sleep.
> A crown of sovranty thy brow shall wear,
> And by thy side a magic blade shall hang,
> And thou shalt be lord of all the Land of Youth,
> And lord of Niamh of the Head of Gold.

> (Rolleston 1911 (1994: 271))

Travel-worn Odysseus was to spend nine years on Ogygia, comforted by the nymph Calypso. The captain would have been greeted by sight similar to this, as he made landfall at Gozo, Malta, location of Calypso's cave.

Oisín's blood was racing – only he had heard the enchanting invitation to the Land of the Ever Young. Once heard, it was impossible to resist. Despite the warnings of his father, which sounded to the spellbound poet like a voice from far away, Oisín mounted up behind Niamh on the white mare. Half in a dream, he turned to smile at his father, his friends and his faithful hounds as Niamh shook her reins, stirring her steed into swift flight. Little did Oisín know then that would be last he would ever see of Fionn, the Fianna, or the Erin he knew – for he had been summoned to a lost island, and his world would never be the same again.

~~~~~~~~~~~~~~~~~~~~~~~~~

This is the archetypal pattern of encounter and invitation mirrored in many myths and legends across the world. Niamh's siren call is one of a global repertoire, a paradisal canon. These haunting poems and songs are the 'sales pitch' that sells us this dream – a holiday brochure for the soul. These invitations are often in the most exquisite language, or set to the most beautiful music – this is the art of the bard, to take the listener on a healing magical journey. Arguably it is the words or sounds *in themselves* which transport the listener, albeit for a brief time, to the paradises they speak of. They provide auditory doorways, by enabling the audience to enter a different state of consciousness. Drumming, bells, stringed instruments and singing can all be trance-inducing – and at their root shamanic (the drum is known in some Siberian societies as 'the shaman's horse'). The shaman used various tools and tricks of his trade – a rattle, drum, chanting, dancing, costume, incense, firelight – to shift their own consciousness and that of the patient and onlooking tribe.

An essential part of these performances are the healing songs, with their rhythms, melodies, sounds and symbolism. Their magic provides an acoustic gateway to an altered state, an 'island state of mind'. Perhaps such 'island-inducing lullabies' evoke the soothing tones of the mother to its child – one of the first sounds we hear, a tone of voice which we become programmed to associate with security, comfort, peace and plenty: fed by the mother's milk, we nod off into a land of maternal bliss. Soporific, womb-ambient, such songs say to us: 'Everything will be alright, forget fear, you are safe in your mother's arms'.

Many of these tales of otherwordly abduction begin in a liminal place, often by the sea, as in the classic of its type, the *Voyage of Bran mac Ferbal*, one of the three Irish immramas (wonder voyages) that have been passed down to us:

> Long ago, we are told, before the coming of Christ, Bran was walking along a western sea-shore. Suddenly he heard music of enchanting sweetness, and saw an apple-bough covered with white blossom. He took hold of it and carried it to his hall. Thereupon a strangely-garbed woman appeared, and sang of a realm across the sea which knew no death, nor decay, nor care, only human joys going on everlastingly.

(Ashe 1990)

The sibilant sound of waves on a beach, attributed in Wales to a being known as Llyr Llediaith, 'Sea Half-speech' (Dames 2006: 164–5), is well known for being relaxing, changing the listener's brain waves from the shorter alpha to the longer theta frequency. These make further synaptic connections – lateral leaps – that enable 'the crossing' to occur, across the hemispheres of the brain.

The seashore is only one possible location for such encounters. The liminal space can just as easily be a ford, stream, spring, bridge, cave, forest, hill, mountain, tower, gateway or borderland. Liminality need not be restricted to geography – it can be time-based, (dawn, dusk, midnight, full moon, May Eve, Midsummer's Eve, Hallowe'en) or straddle the boundaries between sexes or between human and divine. Many of these otherworldly odysseys begin with an encounter between a man and a woman of varying degrees of divinity. Often, a male protagonist is being enticed to the 'lost island' by a beautiful woman, as in Oisín and Niamh above, or Thomas the Rhymer and the Queen of Elfland (see below). But there are also inverse scenarios – as when Janet meets the Faerie knight, Tam Lin; or the princess Etain is lured beyond by Midhir, a Danaan prince – all of which will be explored in more detail later.

Why is this so common? Is it because the opposite sex is 'another country'? Michael Ondaatje makes the point in *The English Patient* (1993) that the only real countries are people. In every relationship we have to take a leap out of any solipsism – we encounter the 'other'. From an alchemical point of view, this meeting of man and woman is symbolic of the chymical wedding: the union of the masculine and feminine, Sol and Luna, that creates 'gold' (Clarke 1990; Ramsay, 2004; Gilchrist 2007). If we accept that all characters in a story are aspects of the teller, or listener – then what we have in these instances, when 'boy meets girl' or vice versa, is a chymical wedding within, which leads to transformation and revelation. When we have found equilibrium, the balance of Yin and Yang, we can transcend to a state of bliss.

> Coincidences of opposites and of other irreconcilables give a
> shock to the understanding and transport the spirit to the gateway
> of the Other World.

> (Rees and Rees 1961: 344)

In the traditional ballad *Thomas the Rhymer* there is encoded the fullest account of the ritual pattern of encounter and crossing. Musician and author R.J. Stewart, who has studied the fairy tradition as encoded in the oral tradition of the Scottish Borders, says of such magical ballads:

> It gives us a route map to the otherworld which we can use in
> journeying.

> (Stewart 1990)

In *Thomas the Rhymer* we find Thomas of Ercildoune (who actually existed in thirteenth century Scotland) 'sitting out' on Eildon Hills, as I have done on a wild and windy night – though Thomas had better luck, beneath the Eildon Tree (a World Tree or *axis mundi*). Here he has an otherworldly encounter – yet before we go into that note that this introductory scene is rich in liminality – he sits halfway between earth and sky on a hill, beneath a tree (neither inside or out), in a theta state of mind, as anyone generally is who is enjoying a view in a tranquil place ('and in the distance he did see... '). The location – on the Scottish Borders – emphases this interstitiality.

This is a crossing place, a place of territorial and linguistic struggle, with its own dialect, lalands (Lowland Scots) and frequent violent incursions (for example, the cattle-raiding Border reivers). From his high place Thomas sees a 'lady both bold and bright come a riding down by the Eildon Tree.' A similar vision occurs in *Pwyll, Lord of Dyfed*, in the nineteenth century collection of Welsh tales christened *The Mabinogion* by Lady Charlotte Guest, when Pwyll sits upon the mound of Arbeth at his castle in Narbeth (which you can still visit to this day in Pembrokeshire), where it is said 'whoever sits upon it would receive a wound or a wonder.' There he spotted a comely lady on yet another white steed (*de rigueur* transport for fairy damsels). He sent his men to ask her name, but none could catch her, until he finally takes matters into his own hands, races after her and, before she disappears again, calls out: 'Lady, in the name of the one you love best, stop!' She does and declares *he* is the one she loves and will wed no other (like Niamh with Oisín, these empowered women of the Celtic fringes held the reins of the heart firmly in *their* hands). To Thomas the lady decrees:

> 'Harp and carp, True Thomas,' she said,
> 'Harp and carp, but you must come with,
> and serve me above all, for seven mortal years,
> through weal and woe as luck decree.'

Thomas greets her as the Queen of Heaven – presumably either ritual courtship rhetoric or the typical flattery of a male poet. She denies the title, though claims to be the Queen of Elfland no less. She has come 'far' to visit Thomas, and further, to take him back to her realm. As with Oisín, it does not take much to persuade Thomas – he jumps on the back of the fairy steed and with a flick of her jingly rein, they're off! Only later does Thomas realises there is a price, of course. We will look at the details of their journey in the next part of this chapter.

A companion ballad is the famous *Tam Lin*, also from the Scotland Lowlands. Here it is Janet who is the protagonist. She is forbidden by her father to go to Carterhaugh, and so, a typical rebellious teenager, she hitches up her skirt 'above the knee' and off she goes to do just that. Here she 'pulls a rose' and a faerie knight appears (again, this seems indicative of the alchemical wedding of Sol and Luna). Has she conjured him from her fantasies? He warns her not to pull the roses, yet she 'gets by him with child' and finds herself embroiled in a plot to release him from the servitude to the Queen of Fairy (and here it overlaps with Thomas the Rhymer – suggesting it could it be part of the same story and tradition). She has to go to a crossroad at midnight (two classic liminal zones) to wait for the Faerie Rade – a fairy-procession led by the jealous queen – and then she must pull him down from a 'milk-white horse', and hold on for dear life as he goes through various dramatic transformations (adder, bear, lion, red hot iron and burning ember). Janet must plunge him into a well to break the spell, and then wrap the naked knight in her green mantle. This all might be a metaphor for a pregnancy and the labour of child birth, as the embryo conceived at Carterhaugh develops into a foetus 'turning in her arms' and giving her labour pains. Then her 'waters break' and the man-child emerges, nakedly vulnerable, whom she wraps in her green mantle like a babe in swaddling. This is another kind of 'arrival'.

By breaking a taboo, Janet has broken through convention to the 'other side' – an amoral topsy-turvy land where nothing is what it seems. She has entered the Realm of Faerie. She is now, well and truly, in the story:

> Gloomy, gloomy, was the night,
> And eiry was the way,
> As fair Janet in her green mantle,
> To Miles Cross she did gae.

In contrast to the common luring of men to otherworldly paradises by fairy women the reverse occurs not only in *Tam Lin* but also in the Irish tale of Midhir and Etain. Etain, the 'fairest maid in Ireland' receives a 'lost island' invitation from Midhir the Proud, a lord of the Tuatha de Dannan – one of the chthonic inhabitants of Ireland, who were forced into exile by subsequent invasions, becoming the Lordly Ones who still ruled on Tir nan Og, the Irish Eden. Here is an extract:

Fair woman, will you go with me to a wonderful land where
music is? The hair is like the primrose tip there, and the whole
body is the colour of snow.

There, there is neither 'mine' nor 'thine'; white are the teeth there,
black the eyebrows; a delight to the eye is the full number of our
hosts; every cheek there is of the colour of the foxglove.

The ridge of every moor is purple, a delight to the eye are
blackbird's eggs; though the plain of Ireland is fair to see it is like
a desert once you know the Great Plain.

Fine though you think the ale of Ireland, the ale of the Great Land
is more heady; a wonderful land is the land I tell of, the young do
not die there before the old.

Sweet mild streams flow through the land, choice mead and wine;
matchless people without blemish, conception without sin,
without guilt.

We see everyone on all sides, and no one sees us; it is the
darkness of Adam's trespass that screens us from being counted.

Woman, if you come to my mighty people a crown of gold shall
be on your head; honey, wine, ale, fresh milk, and beer you shall
have there with me, fair woman.'

(Irish, author unknown, ninth century; translation T.W. Rolleston
1911)

This is a utopian paradise where there is neither 'mine' nor 'thine', judgement nor
guilt, but – in keeping with ancient Irish and Welsh eschatology – it is a decidedly
earthly paradise, with fine drink and food – a dream born perhaps of hardship.

Etain is wooed, and off she goes to the Otherworld, yet the twist here is that she was
from there originally over a thousand years before – but due to a complicated
sequence of events as told in the convoluted romance, she ended up being reborn an
earthly maiden, until Midhir reminds her of her otherworldly lineage, of the 'crown
of gold' that awaits her like the 'crown of sovranty' Niamh lures Oisín with. It seems
these Otherworlds promise a restoration of our own innate nobility – the divine spark
that gives us all the Divine Right?

Another echo in this tale occurs with 'Thomas the Rhymer': when Etain was cast out
of Tir nan Og through an act of jealousy, she was transformed by her love rival into
a butterfly and was cast about by the winds for seven years – the same length of time
Thomas the Rhymer served in Elfland. Seven is a common number in such stories,
thought to have mystical significance – yet also the length of time it takes for all the
cells in the human body to regenerate – a biological cycle and a form of 'rebirth'.

Here, Etain is not just falling for Midhir's honeyed words, but by accompanying him,
actually returning to her original state. And perhaps the allure of these lost islands is

just that: the possibility of returning to an original state of bliss, innocence, harmony with nature or even godhead. I will explore further in the chapter 'Exiles from Eden'.

For now, let us accompany Oisín and Etain, and all the heroes and heroines, seekers and explorers who have accepted the invitation and embarked.

The crossing

Niamh's fairy steed galloped into the west at breakneck speed, until the green hills of Erin ran out – and kept on going, over the glittering sea on magical hooves, to where the sun set – and beyond, to Tir nan Og, the Land of the Ever Young. In a similar manner Thomas of Ercildoune was transported to the Otherworld – in the eponymous Scottish Border ballad he is whisked off to Elfland on its queen's 'milk-white steed'. Like Oisín, Thomas would be irrevocably changed by his experiences – he would gain the 'tongue that cannot lie' (the gift of prophecy) at the expense of his own. 'My tongue is my ain,' he protests, 'A gudely gift ye wad gie to me!' Yet every ferryman needs to be paid – this is Thomas' price. For seven years he must hold his tongue or he'll never get back home – so the poet must take a vow of silence to win the right to use his gift.

Thomas the Rhymer provides us with a clear geography of this otherworld transition:

> O they rade on, and farther on,
> The steed gaed swifter than the wind;
> Until they reach'd a desert wide,
> And living land was left behind.

Then they rest, and the Queen of Elfland shows True Thomas three roads, of righteousness, wickedness and fairy (which we will look at in more detail soon). Taking the middle path, on they carry:

> O they rade on, and farther on,
> And they waded rivers abune the knee;
> And they saw neither sun nor moon,
> But they heard the roaring of the sea.
> It was mirk, mirk night, there was nae starlight,
> They waded thro' red blude to the knee;
> For a' the blude that's shed on the earth
> Rins through the springs o' that countrie.

The roaring of this benighted sea of blood, akin to Coleridge's 'sunless sea' in his otherworldy poem *Kubla Kahn*, could be an echo of that first amniotic ocean we all experience in the womb – suggesting this is not a journey into the afterlife, but into the state of bliss *before* life. Maybe, ultimately, they are the same place.

The 'fifty silver bells and nine' of the Queen of Elfland's reign provide a trance-inducing sound and rhythm identical to the rattle, drum or reindeer bells of a Siberian shaman. They create an altered state of consciousness, conducive for crossing liminal zones, the no man's land between the known and unknown, between here and there, now and then, reality and the imaginary, the mundane and the sacred.

In the ancient Welsh poem attributed to Taliesin himself, *Preiddu Annwn* ('The Spoils of Annwn') King Arthur Pendragon and a company of his knights set sail in three ships on an Underworld raid, to bring back the fabled Cauldron of Plenty, which would supply the 'hero's portion' to all but the cowardly. Similarly, in the *Voyage of Bran*, the Irish prince Bran mac Ferbal, tempted by the otherworldy princess wielding her silvery apple branch, embarks with an almost identical entourage:

> Resolving to go the way she had pointed, he launched three
> boats, each with a crew of nine. The company rowed out west for
> two days and nights.

In both cases, not many of them make it back. In the *Preiddu Annwn*, 'of the three shipfuls set sail for Annwn, only seven men returned'. Paradise always comes at a price.

Crossings are always hazardous, as the many pilgrims, past and present, to Ynys Enlli (Bardsey Island, off the Llyn peninsula, north-west Wales) would attest. That remote, austere and enchanting Isle of Currents, as its native name signifies, has taken the lives of many who have tried to reach it, those who have tried to cross its strong tidal race – a deadly bottleneck between Cardigan Bay and the Irish Sea.

The Otherworld we seek often becomes Death itself: 'It is the undiscover'd country from whose bourn/No traveller returns…' wrote Shakespeare (*Hamlet* III: 1). Death is the ultimate lost island – not surprising when you consider virtual all otherworldly islands offer a paradisal afterlife – the Irish immrama an eschatology, a road map of the soul at death, as Caitlín Matthews explores in *The Celtic Book of the Dead* (2001), where she suggests the immrama of Bran, Maeldûn and Brendan provide a psychopompic map, akin to the Egyptian and Tibetan Books of the Dead (the Bardo). In Egyptian mythology Osiris, the Lord of the Dead, is said to pass through twelve gates on his night journey (literally through the body of Nut, the goddess of the night sky) in his Boat of a Million Years. This crossing to death by boat seems to be universal. The mortally wounded King Arthur is taken to Avalon by Morgana/Morgen and her dark-robed priestesses in a ship of the dead in one of the most famous scenes in English literature. Yet it is not solely the Matter of Britain, as will be explored in the chapter entitled 'Stick in the Mud'.

A cluster of traditional ballads, often old, anonymous and obscure in origin and symbolism, provide a similar guide – some acting as psychopompic devices themselves, to sing the dying soul into the beyond. Dirges are designed precisely for this. These laments for the dead derive their name from the Latin *Dirige*! ('direct'), the first word of an antiphon used in the Latin Book of the Dead, thus unequivocally spelling out that they were used to direct the newly dead (and often disorientated) soul into the afterlife. The deep notes of the dirge form harmonic signposts for the absconding spirit, theta waves for consciousness to make its final leap, intentionally chilling because they operate on the frequency of death. These songs of passing perform catabolic functions, stripping down the personality of the deceased, testing and winnowing – as the Babylonian goddess Ishtar/Inaana experienced in her descent, forced to shed a layer of 'clothing' at each of the seven gates of hell to win back her Tam Lin/Thomas – Tammuz (Mackenzie 1915: 81–108). This ultimate catharsis is symbolised in British folklore by the haunting figure of the Washer at the Ford, a harbinger of death spotted by the unfortunate soul not long for this world, usually around the witching hour at a ford – washing his or her blood-stained winding shroud. This is the Cailleach, the Scottish Kali, who performs a necessary cathartic function: Midwife Death, bringing us through into the next world. A fine example of this is in the thirteenth century English ballad 'How Death Comes', translated by B.T. Davies and performed with spine-tingling vigour by the Mediaeval Baebes.

Gaelic harper and Culdee priestess Fiona Davidson uses *foanns*: psychopompic chants evoking coastal zones and death-birds. Many cultures have these 'crossing songs'. From the Mississippi Delta comes the spine-tingling blues song, *Lonely Valley* – an echo of 'the valley of the shadow of death' perhaps. The most famous British one is *The Lyke Wake Dirge*, from the north country, the geo-linguistics of which you can hear in every line:

> This ae nighte, this ae nighte,
> Every nighte and alle,
> Fire and sleet and candle-lighte,
> And Christe receive thy saule.
> When from here thou art past,
> Every nighte and alle,
> To Whinny-muir thou comest at last,
> And Christe receive thy saule.
> If ever thou gavest hosen and shoon,
> Sit thee doun and put them on.
> If hosen and shoon thou gavest nane,
> The whinnes shall pricke thee to the bare bane.
> From Whinny-muir when thou art past
> To Brigg o' Dread thou comest at last.
> From Brigg o' Dread when thou art past,
> To Purgatory fire thou comest at last.
> If ever thou gavest meat or drinke
> The fires shall never make thee shrink.
> If meat or drink thou gavest nane
> The fire shall burn thee to the bare bane.
> And Christ receive thy saule,
> And Christ receive thy saule.

The Lyke Wake Dirge provides a chilling account of the afterlife, with karmic consequences every step of the way. The geography is fascinating and possibly useful. 'Whinny-muirs' are common features in the geography of the afterlife, according to many world cultures. It seems the recently deceased soul has to cross an 'endless plain', before reaching a river or body of water bridged by the Brigg o'

Dread. The journey across the desert-like plain makes the weary soul thirsty, and many are tempted to drink – but this is the River of Forgetfulness, with its lethal contents. The 'twice-born' initiate knows not to drink – at least not too much. Next, comes the Purgatory fire, the karma burner – the hell of our own making perhaps, where we are confronted with our transgressions. Yet there is a way out: 'If ever thou gavest meat or drinke/the fires shall never make thee shrink.'

This dirge, though undoubtedly psychopompic, seems to be a paean for Christian charity. However many world religions hold that the way we behave in this life effects what we experience in the next, thereby providing effective salutary warnings and a good guide for life in general, though also providing an effective form of social control. Yet the fundamental law encoded here is 'do as you would be done by.' This is a causal reciprocity none of us can escape, whatever our belief system.

This moral signposting is flagged up best of all in *Thomas the Rhymer*, when the Queen of Elfland shows True Thomas 'visions three':

> 'See you not that broad, broad road,
> that lies by the lily pleasing?
> That is the road to wickedness,
> Though some call it the road to heaven.
> 'See you not that narrow, narrow road,
> all beset by thorns and briers,
> that is the road to righteousness,
> though after it but few enquire.
> 'but see you not that bonny, bonny road,
> that winds about the fernie brae –
> that is the road to fair Elfland,
> where you and I this not must gae.'

The traditional ballad of *The Two Brothers* has some similar moral geography, telling the story of fratricide: An elder questions a young man, who has blood upon his blade. At first, the suspect is evasive, giving various spurious explanations: it is the blood of a bird, or a greyhound or a grey mare, until finally confessing to the murder of his brother. When the priest-like figure asks him: 'What did you two fall out about, my son come tell to me?' The Cain-like son replies:

> Oh it was that he plucked up a hazel bush
> That should have grown to a tree tree tree
> That should have grown to a tree.

This echoes the 'pulling of the rose' in *Tam Lin*, for which the faerie knight chastises Janet – although her transgression leads to new life, not death – and one wonders whether the 'hazel bush' is a euphemism for something, a dryad or young maiden perhaps? Was it a case of sibling rivalry over a woman? The conclusion of this ballad is the most fascinating part. It alludes to the otherworldly voyage, which is the heart of what we are considering here. The elder asks: 'And what will you do when your father comes to know/ My son come tell to me?' The penitent son replies:

> Oh I'll set foot in a bottomless boat
> And sail across the sea
> And sail across the sea.
> And when will you be coming back again,
> My son come and tell to me?
> When Moon and Sun dance in yonder hill
> And that will never be be be
> And that will never be.

A 'bottomless boat' could refer to suicide – and that this journey will be taken after death. There is certainly a sense that the self-doomed brother will never return – and that perhaps he will be cursed to wander forever, like Cain who murdered his brother Abel.

The penultimate verse of *The Two Brothers* echoes the famous ballad of Carrick Fergus, which has a similar sense of a night journey, as in this lost verse rediscovered by Irish-ballad singer Marko Gallaidhe:

> ... O the night was dark and the sky uneasy,
> the mighty ocean was tossed and wild,
> when my own true love, sweet Bridget Macy,
> she crossed the ocean, left me behind,
> left me behind to count my losses,
> and now I see her face in every glass.
> How sweet is life,
> ah, but I am dying.
> How long the dark night she takes to pass...

Echoing the search of Yeats' *Song of Wandering Aengus*, *The Two Brothers* is a lament for the lost muse, as embodied by Bridget (the goddess Brigdhe incarnate). It is a prophecy, as the balladeer foresees his own death; and a psychopompic dirge, as in the *Lyke Wake Dirge*, navigating the borders between life and death, as the dark geography of the poem depicts:

> The sea is wide – I cannot cross over.
> ... I wish I had now a handsome boatmen
> To ferry me over – to my love and I.
> Now in Kilkenny it is reported
> on marble stones there as black as ink.
> With gold and silver I would transport her...

This mirrors the cosmic duality of the 'silver apples of the moon, the golden apples of the sun' of Yeats' immortal *Song of Wandering Aengus*, but is probably older – perhaps even inspiring Yeats. The chiming together of these opposites, like yin and yang, create an elliptical paradox, like a Buddhist *koan*, which flips the mind out of the binary logic into a third space, the space between – a gateway to the otherworld.

> All things are possible in this sacred state between being and non-
> being. The individual who dares to enter it in defiance of the spirit

of reason places himself within reach of salvation, but he also exposes himself to the dangers of annihilation in the river of death that lies under the sword-edge bridge.

(Rees and Rees 1961: 346)

Lancelot must cross one to rescue Queen Guinevere from Meleagraunt. Cuchullain must traverse the Bridge of Leaps to get to Scathach's palace for sword-training. But sometimes the threshold seems insurmountable – what mortal could negotiate Bifrost, the Rainbow Bridge to Valhalla? This is why we need threshold guardians and guides, like Heimdall. Yet some hinder more than help – St Paul at the gates of Heaven or Cerebus at the gates of Hades – but all are there for a specific purpose.

The mention of the 'handsome boatman' is intriguing. The ferryman is a familiar figure throughout world myths. Even Buddha himself, as Siddhartha, plays the part at one point, but in the Western imagination the most famous ferryman of all is Charon, the boatman of the Styx. In the Greek Orthodox tradition corpses have two coins placed upon their eyes – one coin to pay for the outward passage, the other for the return of the soul – presumably when they have healed of their 'wounds' in the Otherworld, Hellenic Arthurs returning to the world.

The tutelary deity of the Isle of Man, Manannan Mac Lir – who commanded the sea with his boat, Wave Sweeper, and a cloak of sea mist – seemed to serve this purpose for Manx fishermen who to recent times would put out with this prayer:

> Manannan beg Mac y Lir,
> Little Manannan, son of the sea,
> Who blessed our island,
> Bless us and our boat, going out well,
> Coming back better with both living and dead aboard.

Here the dead refer to the fish they hope to harvest from the depths, but there is a sense of the fishermen's fates in the hands of this magical boatman.

Breton fishermen would offer a similar service to the dead, putting out to the coast of a misty island where the names of the dead would be called out and the souls summoned.

In the Merlin tradition of the Scottish Borders, as examined by R.J. Stewart, there is an equally powerful soul-mariner to Manannan Mac Lir, called Barinthus, 'to whom the waters and the stars of heaven were well known.' He appears in Geoffrey of Monmouth's *Vita Merlini*, and is the one, not Morgen (Morgan le Fay as she appears later), who ferries the fatally wounded King Arthur to Avalon, accompanied by Merlin and the royal bard, Taliesin. There is a curious resonance here in the word 'ferry' – no more than a coincidence perhaps, but one of those interesting echoes – because ferryman could easily be misheard 'fairy man', and perhaps these walkers between the worlds are just that – not of human blood or values. Yet they are powerful threshold guardians nonetheless, perhaps the ultimate. You only have to think of the fiercesome three-headed Cerebus, Hades' guard dog.

Threshold guardians do not commonly have a sense of humour – it does not feature in the job description. The exception that proves the rule is found in Shakespeare's 'Scottish Play', *Macbeth* – after the gruesome death of Banquo there is the infamous drunken porter scene with its dour gallow's humour. The drunken porter or steward pops up in Welsh legend, in Taliesin's poem, *Cantre'r Gwaelod*, which describes the inundation of the Lowest Hundred, the Bottom Cantre'r of Cardigan Bay – caused by the drunken steward Seithennin, who in his stupor forgot to close the sluice gates.

In the Breton story of Kêr-Ys, the fullest of all lost island flood myths (more of which we will look at in the chapter 'When the Levee Breaks'), the bronze door in the seawall is opened on purpose by the king's daughter, Darhut-Ahes, who is tricked into stealing the key around her father's neck by a daemon lover – to prove her love for him she has to open the gates. His bogus promise to hold back the waters she discovers too late – to the wrack and ruin of the lost city of Kêr-Ys, the aptly-named Fortress of the Deep. To this day the statue of its only survivor, King Gradlon, looks out from Quimper over the Bay of the Dead, Pointe du Raz, off the western tip of Brittany.

Yet not all threshold guardians are so slovenly in their duties. In *The Mabinogion*, Bran the Blessed first wades across the Irish Sea and then uses himself as bridge across the Liffey, when he raises a warhost to rescue his sister, Branwen, saying as he does so: 'let him who is chief be a bridge'.

Threshold guardians whose names identify a place become its tutelary spirit, as in *Aquae Sulis*, with its pre-Roman goddess of the springs, Sul. Connected, if not one and the same, Sillina gave her name to the Isles of Scilly. Manannan mac Lir gave his name to the Isle of Man (Ellen Vannin). He is spotted by the Irish Bran and his crew while they cross the wide ocean:

> Then the sea-god Manannan approached them over the waves in his chariot… He foretold certain future events including the advent of Christ, but not the voyagers' own destiny, though he encouraged them to press on and assured them that marvellous islands lay close ahead, including Emain Ablach, which was his own favourite home.

(Ashe 1990: 263)

Manannan's magic cloak could be shaken to release a mist that would veil his kingdom from invaders or unwelcome guests – creating an island lost to all but the chosen.

Towards such a lost island we wend our way now in the hope of making landfall. But first we must experience the 'Sea of Mist', like Maeldun on his *immram*. This is the symbolic Cloud of Unknowing. Pilgrims to lost islands must be prepared to endure dark nights of the soul. Sometimes it seems unlikely that the destination will ever be reached. The ardent traveller is worn down to the point of despair, to surrender. Only be letting themselves be 'devoured' – 'entering the belly of the whale' – can the Jonah in us achieve rebirth. Any hubris must be stripped away like layers of the personality – the veils of Inaana – before enlightenment. A lost island cannot be reached by the rational mind alone, but by a combination of dead reckoning, intuition and gnosis.

The longed-for destination cannot be arrived at in a straight line – but only by the spiral windings of spirit and serendipity. A 'thousand slimy things' must be encountered, like Coleridge's ancient mariner, on this serpent path. As modern antiquarian and musician Julian Cope says:

> If you live in a straight line you're waiting for the result, you never
> have a journey. If you have a serpentine attitude to life the
> journey is interesting. (Cope 1998)

As in all walks of life, so with lost islands: the mission *is* the journey, not just the destination. The traveller has to accept the process, they have to reach a state of surrender, of passivity, before they are able to 'receive', before the destination they yearn for (often a state of mind or being) can 'enter' them:

> … it is when the voyagers have lost their course and shipped their
> oars – when they are not going anywhere – that they arrive at the
> wondrous isles.

> (Rees and Rees 1961: 346)

The traveller enters the Doldrums, becalmed and helpless, but it is only when they reach this state that the way is revealed to them. As in meditation – try too hard and it does not happen. It is a state of no-mind that must be achieved. Of stillness, silence and humility. It could be seen as an 'oceanic' feel, a dawning realisation of perspective. You are an infintesimal fish in a depthless pond. The universe and its infinite mystery have defeated you. When this is finally accepted, the mists of Manannan part, and suddenly the lost island of your dreams is before you – you have arrived.

Arrival

All the uncertainty and effort finally pays off and land is spotted: Land Ahoy! A glad sight to wave-weary souls, sick of unreliable horizons.

The crossing of a wide ocean is akin to the crossing of the deathly plain. The ocean is a desert of water where everything is stripped away. You do not master the ocean, the ocean masters you. When we achieve the selflessness of ego-death that we can achieve Avalon. This is the moment in Coleridge's *The Rime of the Ancient Mariner* when the self-cursed sailor, becalmed in the Doldrums, finally realizes the beauty of nature, seabirds and marine life, when 'a spring of love gushed from my heart, And I blessed them unaware.' This unconscious benediction breaks the curse:

> The selfsame moment I could pray;
> And from my neck so free
> The Albatross fell off, and sank
> Like lead into the sea.

Statue of the Ancient Mariner, Watchet, Somerset.

With the ballast of guilt shed, the pilgrim is finally allowed to arrive at the state of grace. The ancient mariner did not make it to paradise, but he was granted 'the gentle sleep from Heaven/That slid into my soul,' and what follows on many voyages has the substance of a dream. Lost islands are often '… such stuff that dreams are made on', like Prospero's island in Shakespeare's *The Tempest* , but, like any who have been at sea for long, making landfall is always a relief – our first impressions influenced by cabin fever, religious fervour, scurvy and hunger. Possibly feverish, disorientated, or in devout awe, we finally arrive at our earthly paradise:

> A fair wind came on the warriors after that, and they raised their
> sail, and the boat shipped less water on them; and a smoothness
> fell upon the ocean, and the sea went down, so that there was a
> bright fair calm; and there came a warbling of unknown birds of
> many kinds around them in every direction. And then they saw
> before them the shape of a pleasing land with lovely shores, and

they rejoiced and were glad at the sight of this land; and they
reached the land, and found a beautiful green-bosomed river-
mouth there, with pure-welling pebbles shining all one silver, and
spotted ever-handsome salmon with splendid colours of dark
purple on them; and lovely purple-crested woods round the
pleasing streams of the land to which they had come.

(Irish, author unknown; translation Hurlstone Jackson 1971)

This vivid and enticing scene written by an unknown Irish author in the fourteenth or
fifteenth century calls to something primal in us – perhaps because it is one that has
been enacted countless times since the dawn of humankind, as the pioneering spirit
drove us ever onwards to find new lands of resource-plenty, or just out of sheer
wanderlust. To tread where no man has trod before, to discover that unspoilt
paradise – this is a rare experience these days, in a world which has been criss-
crossed for millennia, and has been mapped and photographed from space. There is
not a corner of the world we do not know about. We can now all be armchair
explorers with the likes of Google Earth. The last time the frisson of virgin wilderness
was experienced was probably in the early twentieth century, in the embers of the
great Age of Exploration. The loose ends of the world were being tidied up. Now we
can only dream of a place so unspoilt, nature undesecrated by Western human
presence – where the flora and fauna are abundant, unthreatening and unthreatened;
where the pact with Nature is not broken: basically, a pre-Edenic state (to be
explored in the chapter 'Exiles from Eden').

Typical of the Otherworld is an almost hallucinatory vividness, where everything has
a self-effulgence and clarity – suggesting an altered states of consciousness (one
gateway to paradise, although really only a revolving door, which offers a possible
glimpse of other worlds but compared to others practices is short-lived and
ultimately unsustainable). The remarkable paintings of rainforest shamans by
Peruvian artist Pablo Amaringo show the jungle as a firework display of fountains of
light, as the energy 'footprint' of everything is revealed – what William Blake referred
to as the 'inmost form' – as well as the filaments of feuding medicine men, their
ectoplasmic emissions like a Jackson Pollock painting: a field of potential that some
claim to be able to manipulate. Foreground and background merge, as in the art of
the Welsh Blake, artist and poet David Jones. Everything is connected.

In such a tropical 'paradise' both shaman and artist would have used psychotropics,
notably ayahuasca, to open the Blakean doors of perception. This, to some, would
be seen as having eaten of the Forbidden Tree (see 'Exiles from Eden'). Certainly fruit
seems to keep cropping up in these places, especially apples. Geoffrey of
Monmouth, that great thirteenth century syncretistic storyteller calls Avalon *Insula
Pomorum,* the Isle of Apples. In the Welsh, it was referred to as Afallach or Avallach;
the Irish equivalent is *Emain Ablach,* meaning 'rich in apple trees'. Whatever we
think of Glastonbury's claim to be the Isle of Avalon, (explored in 'Inventing Avalon')
it is undeniably 'apple country'. Orchards line its flanks and the Somerset Levels
around about. To sleep out under an orchard on the side of the Tor, as I have done,
is sufficient to make you feel you are in Avalon. Another candidate, Bardsey Island

(*Ynys Enlli*, for some the Welsh Avalon), boasts its own variety of apple, which I have tasted – along with local blackberries and cream. Enough to make anyone want to return!

The Greek Fortunate Isle, which some think a prototype for the British Fortune Isles (the Isles of Scilly, blessed with the Gulf Stream, which gives them a sub-tropical climate and famous gardens), echoes this fecundity, as here described by Ashe in *Mythology of the British Isles*:

> It produces all things of itself. The fields there have no need of
> farmers to plough them, and Nature along provides all cultivation.
> Grain and grapes are produced without tending, and apple trees
> grow in the woods from the close-clipped grass. The earth of its
> own accord brings forth not merely grass but all things in
> superabundance, and people live there a hundred years or more.

(Ashe 1990)

This recurring motif of abundance is taken to its extreme in those dream-stories where the ravenous character ends up in a land where everything is made of food. This is as universal as hunger. There is an American bluegrass ballad of this, born from the lean days of the Depression era, featured in the Coen Brothers film *O Brother, Where Art Thou?* (2000), itself loosely based on *The Odyssey*, which sings of 'a land that's fair and bright…'

> In the Big Rock Candy Mountains
> You never change your socks
> And the little streams of alcohol
> Come trickling down the rocks
> The brakemen have to tip their hats
> And the railway bulls are blind
> There's a lake of stew
> And of whiskey too
> You can paddle all around it
> In a big canoe
> In the Big Rock Candy Mountains…

(lyrics by Harry McClintock)

However whimsical such fantasies are, many were born out of extreme hardship, such as the dustbowl of the Mid-West as depicted in John Steinbeck's *The Grapes of Wrath* (1939). Unsurprisingly, these 'food-paradises' are common in an Ireland blighted by the potato famine. But do they echo something deeper as well? Is this a legacy of the oral phase of our infancy, when everything did revolve around food – a land not of milk and honey, but breasts and rusks at least - a world we explored with our mouths? It is important not to reduce everything to Freudian terms, for these mysteries are profounder than psychological obsessions with sexuality and infancy, but I think our physicality does inform myths in a subconscious way. Think of all those underworld rivers of blood and tears – do they not run through our own bodies? As creatures of eighty percent water, do we not have our own 'sunless seas'?

Certainly, we seem affected by lunar tides, just like the rest of this planet Earth, which really should be called Water (since it makes up seventy percent of it), and from space it appears as a 'blue jewel'. Do we call our planet 'Earth' because we are dominated by a 'masculine' materialist mindset, rather than 'feminine', watery, spiritual one?

Arrival in the Otherworld is aesthetically similar to a space traveller's arrival on a new planet – there is the same sense of disorientation and acclimatisation, of wonder and trespass. Not surprising, when the space odysseys of the twentieth and twenty-first century are the mythopoetic descendants of the Irish *immrama*. Gene Roddenberry, the creator of *Star Trek*, may have had the wonder voyages of Bran, Brendan and Maeldûn at the back of his mind: (it has 'Celtic' heroes, à la Kirk and Scotty, and more than its fair share of 'Isles of Women', much to the joy of the womanizing captain. Of course, there are Classical precedents to *Star Trek* as well, in the Mediterranean *immrama* of Odysseus in *The Odyssey* and Jason in the *Voyage of the Argo*, though we should never assume this is the default influence for everything, and nothing good ever existed unless it came out of Egypt, Greece or Rome, glorious as they may have been.

In the ancient Irish *Cormac's Adventures in the Land of Promise* we have a brilliant description of the hero's arrival and welcome. A stranger in a strange land he may be, but he is treated like a king. This is the Irish custom of hospitality, where a visitor is invited in, given the best seat by the hearth, fed and watered before any word is said or question is asked about their name or business (similar to the Muslim tradition). This inevitably leads to an air of mystery in even the most domestic of scenes, and in this extract, it creates a numinous atmosphere and a spell waiting to be broken, if only the protagonist for find the right words for the question on his lips:

> He entered the fortress and saw the vast palace with its beams of
> bronze, its wattling of silver, and its thatch of the wings of white
> birds. Then he saw in the enclosure a shining fountain, with five
> streams flowing out of it, and the hosts in turn drinking its water…
> He entered the palace. There was one couple inside awaiting him.
> The warrior's figure was distinguished owing to the beauty of his
> shape, the comeliness of his form, and the wonder of his
> countenance. The girl along with him, mature, yellow-haired, with
> a golden head-dress, was the loveliest of the world's women.
> Cormac's feet were washed by invisible hands. There was bathing
> in a pool without the need of attendance. The heated stones
> themselves went into and came out of the water.

(Matthews 2002: 48)

The metallic aesthetic here (wall of bronze, house of white silver, beams of bronze, wattling of silver, shining fountain, golden head-dress) could be that of a spaceship, and the magical phenomenon (a fire that refueled itself, a bath without the need of attendance, heated stones which defied gravity) suggest an advanced technology. With a different pair of cultural spectacles (say science fiction instead of fantasy, a technological paradigm instead of a magical one) one could imagine it being explained away so, but that would be too prosaic and limiting an interpretation. There is something magical going on here, which I doubt has anything to do with 'chariots of the gods'! It suggests a situation where the protagonist, emblematic of his race, is out of his depth and discovers humankind is not the most advance species in the universe, that there are more things in heaven and Earth, and that he is not in control here. Whenever we enter an unfamiliar place we become the fool again, and observe everything with wide-eyed wonder. We do not understand and so see meaning in everything. The story is a riddle waiting to be solved. We hope the answer will be revealed, but perhaps there is none – and that we should be content to dwell in mystery.

Again and again, throughout these stories, the otherworldly islanders and their visitors are depicted as living in harmony with Nature: Edens before their Fall, before Adam had to earn his bread by the sweat of his brow, and before humankind was 'cursed' with mortality, when Cronus still slept on the Blessed Isles, and before time began:

> The Greeks told of an Elysium over the western ocean...It was the
> domain of Cronus, and there departed heroes beloved of the gods
> lived on, without care, exempt from death.

(Ashe 1990: 262)

Time commonly runs differently in the Otherworld. A day there often turns out to be a full year in this world, or vice versa. Perhaps the time zones of these Tir nan Ogs do not go across its surface, but downwards, so with each step one plummets down the Well of Time, into the realm of the ancestors – or to a place outside time, where things are ever-present and continually played out, not in repetition, but simultaneously. Perhaps it more indicative of the Celtic sense of time, as Bob Trubshaw suggests in *Sacred Places: Prehistory and popular imagination*:

> ... the Irish Otherworld also reveals the 'otherness' of
> Otherworldly time, but – more surprisingly perhaps – also reveals
> the 'otherness' of everyday medieval Irish views of time,
> compared to modern day ones.

(Trubshaw 2005: 32)

A visual equivalent might be the medieval paintings of royal banquets, where the 'common folk', the servants and hangers on, are depicted as tiny compared to the nobility, the Very Important People. Everything is relative. So in the Otherworld, days take on a larger than life feel, beyond the small everyday concerns. As the brief life of the butterfly to us, so human time to an oak tree, a yew or a redwood: to those who dwell in non-human time, our lives seem fleeting indeed – as though we are stuck in fast forward.

Interestingly the Faerie princess adds the caveat: 'My words are not for all of you... ' This is, if not secret knowledge only for the initiate, then of only specific interest to those willing to forsake the world. Not everyone is willing, prepared or able. Some are prevented by their own 'albatrosses' – addictions and vices: 'Do not sink upon a bed of sloth, do not let your bewilderment overwhelm you' the immram of Bran chides. There are many obstacles that we encounter just as we are about to embark. They are the ten thousand things which trap us within samsara, and they are there to test your resolve. But the apple-princess's instructions are as clear as a hypnotist's breaking of a trance, the snapping of fingers: 'Begin a voyage across the clear sea, to find if you may reach the Land of Women.' It is time to awaken from the dream of life.

The 'call to adventure' is a common motif in the hero's journey (as first recorded by Joseph Campbell in 1949, and canonised by Christopher Vogler in 1992). Often it is the reluctant hero who most needs to undertake the journey, who most needs to change. Further, the 'reluctant messiah' trope is a good sign that the candidate is supposed not to be on a power trip – they haven't chosen this path, it has been forced upon them by circumstances, so they can claim to have had greatness thrust upon them. This occurs again and again in films: Luke Skywalker in *Star Wars* (1977), Neo in *The Matrix* (1999) and Harry Potter in *The Philosopher's Stone* (2001).

This is not surprising now that Vogler's book, *The Writer's Journey* (1992), has become 'the screenwriter's bible', but before his influential book the reluctant messiah was a recurring motif because it is a universal theme and key element of what Campbell calls the 'monomyth'. For us to awaken, we all have to accept this call to adventure. As Morpheus asks Mr Anderson in *The Matrix*: 'How far down the rabbit hole do you want to go?' Unfortunately in the subsequent films, it was only as far as the Wachowski brothers' imagination stretched, which turned out to be not far. However, in the realm of myths, this is far indeed. The 'rabbit hole' goes on forever – it is a gateway to eternity.

The fairy princess normally appears bearing a branch of this otherworldly apple tree – the antithesis of the olive branch, which brought Noah and the flood survivors *back* into this world, the all-clear after God's deluge (which is considered further in 'When the Levee Breaks'). The silver branch is a sign from the Otherworld, a summons into the realm of spirit – a mnemonic of a time when we were at one with the godhead.

> Here is a branch from the apple-tree of Emhain, like those that are familiar; twigs of white silver on it, and crystal fringes with flowers…

> (Irish; anon; seventh-eighth century original, translator unknown)

This recurrent sequence (boy-girl-branch-fruit-beyond) is summed up succinctly and beautifully in W.B. Yeats' *The Song of Wandering Aengus*, when Aengus catches a fish which turns into a woman 'with apple blossom in her hair, who called me by my name and ran, and faded in the brightening air.' Aengus spends the rest of his life looking for her:

> Though I am old with wandering,
> through hilly lands and hollow lands,
> I will find out where she has gone
> And kiss her lips and take her hands
> And walk among long dappled grass,
> And pluck til time and times are done,
> The silver apples of the moon,
> The golden apples of the sun.

It is this faerie maiden who first enticed us to the Otherworld at the beginning of this chapter and, elusive as her calling demands, she has slipped from our grasp. Yet she has given us a sign of the paradise, a covenant of grace, of bliss. And to it we set our course, nailing our colours to the mast – the flag of Imagination. But when we arrive, what do we find?

A hidden place of peace, plenty, good weather, no property, no guilt, no disease, age or death… This lost island grows increasingly more vivid in its utopian quality – this is a place we find easy to imagine, if hard to reach, because it is somewhere many of us desire with all our hearts. We have built it with our imagination and dreams, and visited it often in our longing:

> The Celts of Erin had ideas of the paradisal west going far beyond
> anything Greece could offer. Their imagination was far more
> active in bestowing substance and location. Their western
> Otherworld was multiple and diverse and indeed, by no means
> paradisal. It was a varied archipelago in the realms of the sunset
> with no known limit.

(Ashe 1990)

It is this archipelago of the imagination we will explore throughout the rest of the book, through the spyglasses of literature, religion, archaeology, anthropology, geography, environment and politics – because some of these lost islands are as actual as others are imaginary. Ashe says: 'Before Taliesin describes Avalon he describes a series of other islands, some of them real,' (Ashe 1990: 266) although where one ends and the other begins, it is treacherously difficult to say. All we can do is sit back and enjoy the journey for now. We have been lured into the west, accepted the invitation, made the crossing and arrived – now let us explore the lost islands of literature.

Chapter two

Atlantis to Oz

Silver hooves struck the golden scales of the sun's glittering road as it sank into the west. The milk-white horse galloped over the westering waves, the caverns of the ocean deep were dimly distant below, a glass world shattered with each hoof-beat. Oisín, poet of the Fianna held on for dear life, not too reluctantly to the lissom waist of his fairy princess. He could hardly believe his luck – but what was he letting himself in for? He had often been accused of letting his imagination get away with him. Well, now he was getting away with his imagination! This was an all too real flight of fancy. He thought he was going to be sea-sick… horse-sick… sea-horse sick even. That would not do, not on the shoulder of a fairy princess. He gulped down lungfuls of air and held on as best he could.

Niamh sensed her passenger's discomfort. 'You're encountering reality-nausea,' she called back. 'This will happen as we cross over. Try to enjoy the view.'

Enjoy the view. Right. Oisín gritted his teeth. If only his eyes could stop streaming or focus… He blinked. Out of the dazzling seascape loomed tall shadowy shapes, towers and palaces suspended in the uncertainty between horizon and sky.

'And to your right you will see some castles in the air…' his winsome pilot smiled. The insubstantial towers flickered out as they drew near.

'No one ever reaches them.'

The sun slipped beyond the horizon, setting the sky on fire.

For a while they rode on, gazing dreamily at the afterglow, the rhythm of the horse between them soothing, but strangely stirring.

As the sky gave up the ghost of day, out of deepening twilight a horn-less doe bounded, similarly untroubled by the unstable sward. It was chased by a salt-white hound with one blood-red ear.

'What do these visions mean?' Oisín wondered into the delightful pink shell of Niamh's ear.

'Don't talk about them – it only encourages them, and distracts me! Do you want to fall off?'

Oisín silently watched the pursuit diminish into the twilight.

They rode further on into the gloaming, from where next came a fair maiden on a nut-brown steed, holding a golden apple. She was being pursued by a lusty young man on a white stallion, purple cloak about his shoulders, a gold-hilted sword in his hand. He looked strangely familiar…

'Hail!' Oisín shouts.

'Shhh!' hissed Niamh.

The rider stopped and turned his steed. His fair quarry also stops and wonders impatiently what could be more important.

'Oh, now you've done it!' whispered Niamh. 'Don't say I didn't warn you…'

The two men greeted each other warily.

'I am Oisín, son of Fionn, poet of the Fianna of Erin.'

The other rider's eyes widened. 'And… I am Ossian!'

Their words hung in the air.

The men cast a cool glance over each other, dismissive of each other's taste in clothes. To Oisín, Ossian seemed like a garish stereotype of himself. He wasn't impressed.

'Macpherson has just invented me and I am off to be his literary alter-ego. I have acres of cod-archiac verse to compose. Must fly!'

'No, wait!' implored Oisín, his poetic curiosity piqued. 'This is an interesting philosophical paradox we are confronted with here. Which one of us is the real one?'

The two bards stared at each other in narcissistic fascination, the horses and the faery princesses eyeing each other suspiciously.

'Which one is more real?' the restless waves seemed to taunt.

'Not hard to answer: I am,' replied Oisín to his own question. 'Although I am pure myth, I have come from an authentic tradition, the Gaelic Irish tradition.'

'Well, so do I,' riposted Ossian, 'they are ultimately of the same route. The Scoti originated in Erin after all. The language migrated, and with it, the tales and songs – that isn't so surprising.

'But Macpherson invented his own pseudo-heritage, whileas Erin's is genuine.'

'Is it? You're not telling me you believe in all that Book of Invasions stuff? Somebody must have made it up at some point. Even you.'

'I'm real!' protested Oisín.

'No, I am,' quoth Ossian, 'for although I am invented, I have been invented by a historical personage, drawing on Gaelic ballads and adding his own spin'.

Oisin was feeling queasy. He looked between the horse's hooves at the watery abyss beneath. That didn't help. He needed some firm footing.

'You're entering the Realm of Story,' explained Niamh.

'Haven't we just come from there?'

'Not quite…That was the borderlands. We head towards the source, undiluted by reality. It's heady stuff... '

Oisín watched his opposite turn away in a flamboyant manner, grinning wildly. 'See you in the legends!'

Ossian kicked his horse into a gallop over the waves, after his absconded quarry, who, bored with self-obsessed bards, had wandered off.

'You met your fictional self,' Niamh explained. 'Happens all the time. It threw me the first time too. The first version of myself I bumped into had huge breasts – obviously a male fantasy, that one. The next one had a huge bum. I was furious!'

Bidding farewell to their fictional alter egos, Oisín and Niamh rode on.

~~~~~~~~~~~~~~~~~~~~~~~~

Literature is not only alive with invented – and re-invented – individuals but the environs they dwell within are also imagined – and re-imagined. Authors have been imagining lost islands for a long time. Indeed, arguably all works of fiction are kinds of lost islands, for the writer creates something that does not exist in the real world. It may be a fictionalised amalgamation of personal experience and research, but the unique configuration on the page – the author's particular depiction of reality – exists nowhere else. It is an island confined by the binding of the book, although one with semi-permeable borders, as it bleeds into the reader's mind and even invades reality, if influential enough.

Countless authors have created imaginary islands of one kind or another, and we can but visit only a few here – a whistle stop tour of literature's archipelago of dreams.

One could argue that the literature of lost islands began when the world's myths and legends were first written down (for instance, with the Babylonian epic of Gilgamesh, the world's first 'book'). Further, the sceptic could point out that the literature of lost islands can be found in the sacred text of the world's great religions: the most widely read and accepted 'stories' of all – many of are nigh on inseparable from the preliterate world's treasure house of myths (what ancient Greek scholars termed the 'mythos'). The Judaeo-Christian tradition is no exception: Eden is the ultimate lost island in many ways, and John Milton's *Paradise Lost* the ultimate lost island literature (but that is dealt with elsewhere – see the 'Exiles from Eden' chapter). For now let us focus on secular works and attempt to discern fact from fiction.

Missing continents

The greatest of all literature's lost islands outside of religion is Plato's Atlantis – often confused as a description of a real place. Countless books have been written about the bottomless subject and I do not want to be scuppered in the murky waters of Atlantology – surely one of the world's great time-wasting activities, though such speculative idling is not without its appeal – for, as Jorge Luis Borges observes in his preface to *The Book of Imaginary Beasts*, 'There is a kind of lazy pleasure in useless and out-of-the-way erudition.'

And yet Atlantology is not just the pursuit of the obscure – a worthy scholarly activity – but of the implausible, which verges on insanity, a wilful belief in the unbelievable, and a conviction that everyone else has got the history of the world wrong and you have got it right, somehow spotting the clues that everyone else has missed (a 'missing' continent). Further, Atlantologists attempt to make a 'science' out of a non-science, to attempt to rationalise the irrational, forge knowledge out of pseudo-knowledge. Atlantalogy has become the ultimate past-time for the lonely autodidact, though it has drawn in its fair share of academics and scientists, archaeologists, geologists, even an American president – although perhaps that isn't so unbelievable.

> Perhaps the very impracticality of Atlantism constitutes part of its charm. It is a form of escapism that lets people play with eras and continents as a child plays with blocks.
>
> (De Camp 1970: 3)

However my concern here is not to prove or disprove. I can see the allure of Atlantis and her sister islands – what I call the archipelago of the imagination. That is why I have chosen to write a book about it and run the risk of being sucked into the perilous whirlpools that flow around them – but is the *idea* of such places that I deal with here, not the actuality. I am not looking for evidence of their existence, for that seems to be taking the myths too literally – just attempting a survey of the various manifestations of this universally and perennially popular phenomenon. Island-inventing seems to be something humans have been doing for a long time:

> In all ages there have been men who, disappointed in the world
> as it was, consoled themselves by composing imaginary Edens.
> Utopias, and Golden Ages. Of these builders of Cloud-Cuckoo
> Lands, Plato was the most successful.
>
> (De Camp 1972: 3)

Plato's Atlantis seems to have been intended as a 'sequel' to his *Republic* – the framing narrative is set in the same place, with the same people, sitting around sharing stories, like some bourgeois dinner party, or TV arts show. In essence: storytelling after the feast, an activity as old as humanity. Plato's cast could be cave dwellers, sitting around a fire, shaping the shadows, but these are somewhat sophisticated trogolydytes, fabulating on Plato's patio (via the Socratic conceit) for these are philosophers and VIPs of Greece and so in Western culture we take what they say seriously and sometimes perhaps too literally. Atlantis seems to have been a political fiction, crafted by Plato and expressed by his guests (the novelist's mouthpieces) to make a number of points: a lie that tells a greater truth. Let us look at it in more detail.

Plato's Atlantis is described in two Socratic dialogues, *Timaios* and *Critias*, written in the year 355 BCE or thereabouts. Enjoying the equivalent of 'port and cigars' with Socrates, as Plato relates, Critias offers a 'strange tale' to the gathered guests, which is however certainly true,' claiming to have heard it from Solon, 'the wisest of seven sages,' who was 'relative and great friend of my great grandfather.' These are all classic storytelling devices to create an air of verisimilitude and immediacy, Plato's equivalent of 'I met a bloke the other day down the pub,' or 'Yesterday, as I was walking down the street you wouldn't believe what I saw.' Plato, through his alter ego, Critias, makes no qualms about this:

> I will tell an old-world story which I heard from an aged man.
>
> (translations from Hope 1991)

Relying on the recall of a ten year old boy (Critias) listening to the memory of a ninety year old man (Solon), Plato spins his yarn, and thus begins the greatest load of codswallop ever taken seriously in the west.

> Now, in the island of Atlantis there was a great and wonderful empire…

Alas, this mighty empire meets its end after being defeated by even mightier Athenians. It is destroyed in the famous cataclysm:

> … afterward there occurred violent earthquakes and floods, and in a single day and night of rain all your warlike men in a body sank into the earth, and the island of Atlantis in like manner disappeared, and was sunk beneath the sea. And that is the reason why the sea in those parts is impassable and impenetrable, because there is such a quantity of shallow mud in the way; and this was caused by the subsidence of the island.

This seems to be, on the surface, a classic folkloric explanation for a natural phenomenon, equivalent to the giants slinging mud and rock around to form the landscape of Britain (as with the Giant's Causeway, Cornish Giants and the South Downs). On another level it could simply be a case of creating an imaginary enemy to be defeated, thus proving the prowess of the local boys (Athenians); a victory that the patriotic Plato describes as:

> … the greatest action which the Athenians ever did, and which ought to have been most famous, but which, through lapse of time and the destruction of the actors, has not come down to us.

Although perhaps nothing more than a slice of nationalistic self-aggrandizement, what makes Plato's Atlantis more interesting – and what concerns us here – is the vivid and detailed description of the island, its people, its systems of governance and sustenance, its customs and technology. As in fairyland, the landscape is super-abundant, the people fair, the climate kind, the quality of life high. But most fascinating of all is the description of the special stone, called oricalchon, and the chief power source, which most deem to have been sonic in nature. This is an advanced civilisation, perhaps *too* advanced:

> Such was the vast power which the god settled in the lost island of Atlantis; and this he afterward directed against our land…

Filled with 'unrighteous avarice and power', they basically 'had it coming' and were duly punished, by an act of god – a tsunami, it seems, ordered by Zeus and his special executive; although we miss out on the minutes of the meeting, as Critias' narrative cuts off at that point. A victim of the Athenian Official Secrets Act, or a cunning narrative device – the ultimate cliffhanger, and mystery-enhancer?

So, it seems Plato share with us an entertaining load of old hokum – a parable at best, a 'shaggy god tale' at worst. Nevertheless, many have claimed to have found it, in places ranging from Crete to the Azores, Iceland, Americas, even in the Irish Sea

(Dunbavin 2003). Seemingly people find their Atlantis where they want it to be. The existence of Atlantis is almost a 'given' in New Age circles. There are many in this media-defined movement (as diverse as any cross-section of humanity) who claim Atlantean heritage – the received wisdom is that this is 'where it all began' and was disseminated from, after its fall, usually via Egypt. Instead of an 'out of Africa' scenario for human evolution, it is 'out of Atlantis' instead (and possibly Mu or Lemuria before that – and even Von Daniken-type alien genesis theory preceding that). What may be called the 'Atlantis fallacy' is a consoling fiction to those 'old souls' who claim Atlantean descent – a lineage as bogus as any put forward by that arch-fabulist, Geoffrey of Monmouth (who created a blood line for British kings back to Troy in his pseudo-history). The Altantis fallacy has been purported in countless books, many claiming to be factual. Yet the 'curse of Critias' makes fiction fair no better. This Atlantean fallacy seems to create a failure of critical faculty and of quality in writers who dare use Avalon as their foundation myth. These include Stephen Lawhead, whose 1988 *Taliesin* casts the sixth century Welsh bard, rather spuriously, as an Atlantean prince. Likewise many take as the literal truth – 'this is the way it happened' – the novels by Marion Zimmer Bradley and Diane L Paxson, influential *Mists of Avalon* (1987) and its various sequels and prequels, such as *Ancestors of Avalon* (2004).

Many hold Atlantis up as an ideal – the prototype of civilisation – whereas the myth tells us it doomed itself by its own decadence. Hardly a sign of wisdom! The equivalent is people today being inspired by the 'shining example' of the Roman Empire, or its twentieth century equivalent, the Third Reich. These were corrupt civilisations based on exploitation, extreme cruelty, religious persecution and genocide – hardly role models. Shelley's Ozymandias expresses the folly of such empire-building and worshipping: 'Look on my works, ye mighty and despair!' Everything comes to dust in the end. Atlantis is the prime fictional example of this – it is destined to destroy itself every time its myth is played out – this is its core teaching, in my mind at least.

So, what has attracted people to Atlantis for so long? Could it be:

- The romantic allure of a lost civilisation?
- Confirmation of the fallen nature of humanity, from the Golden to Iron Age?
- A salutary lesson about man's hubris – the impermanency of civilisation?
- A pseudo-lineage for occultists?
- Von Daniken-esque lost technology with Promethean consequences?
- An excuse for left-field research and wilfully eccentric theories that offer alternative narratives to the mainstream history of the world?
- A rattling yarn?

If nothing else, Atlantis provides a powerful parable for all civilisations. In *Critias* Plato observed:

> ... there have been, and there will be again, many destructions of mankind arising out of many causes.

Plato, through Critias, lists the myth of Phaethon, who stole his father's chariot, and burnt up the Earth, and cites the flooding of the Nile. In a post-9/11 world of conflict and climate chaos we have our counterparts of floods, resource-wars and 'peak oil'. Our civilisations, built upon certainties and consistent weather patterns, feel more vulnerable than ever. Is this why the lost island of Atlantis speaks to us more than ever?

More's Utopia

Thomas More's *Utopia* of 1516 first gave a name to the notion of an idealised society in an imaginary location. Like Plato, More wrote a political satire, creating a place that was all that the 'real world' was *not* – a social paradise where there was religious and political tolerance, and no want of food, shelter, security, edification or company.

More initially describes Utopia as an island about fifteen miles from the coast of Latin America, formerly known as Sansculottia. Interestingly, before becoming an island Utopia was originally connected to the mainland by an isthmus. But like a metaphorical Madagascar it became separated and its 'ecosystem' evolved in unique and bizarre ways. Yet this was no paradise to begin with. The industrious inhabitants had transformed a naturally barren island into a rich and fertile one. To modern minds there are many elements to More's vision of the perfect society which seem far from perfect: there is slavery, a Puritan work ethic, military service, capitalism, espionage – and no beer!

Each household has two slaves, consisting of either outside criminals (who are treated 'reasonably well') or local ones (who are treated badly). Suicides are thrown into a pond. 'Work is the whole basis of Utopian society', 'Wives are subordinate to their husbands', there is no private property or money, but also no fashion, no individualism ('everyone wears the same style of clothes'). Makeup is frowned upon, as is any excess decoration – it is a most austere paradise, a Puritan Communism which starts to sound like some awful 'Year Zero' regime.

Utopianism is a dangerous philosophy: one person's utopia can be another person's dystopia. The most extreme example of this is Hitler's Germany, which was meant to be a kind of heaven for Aryans, but most certainly was hell-on-Earth for Jews, gypsies, homosexuals, the handicapped, artists, intellectuals and anyone else who the Nazis did not like the look of. The same happened in Stalin's Russia, Mao's China, Phol Pot's Cambodia, Pinochet's Chile, and persists in too many places in the contemporary world.

The notion of a Year Zero, where everything from the past is rubbed out – people, libraries, cultural heritage (as in the Chinese invasion of Tibet, the Taliban blowing up Buddhas in Afghanistan, or American troops building their base on top of the key Babylonian temple in Baghdad) – is chilling. But one can see the general appeal of starting over, starting afresh, making a go of it somewhere else – a *tabula rasa* – although of course it never is, as we bring our demons with us (as with the New World, see below). On a simple, human level, this 'back to basics' approach can be positive, for instance, Henry David Thoreau's healthy self-reliant downsizing in his 1854 book *Walden*. However there will always be those who would find such ascetic rigours hellish, in the same way that even in a 'new world', where laws and systems are created supposedly for the benefit of all there, there will inevitably be some who feel real reasons for resentment, as when a country is founded on genocide and slavery. A prime example is North America, where the 'American dream' has turned incredibly sour; this is explored further in the chapter on 'How the West was Lost'.

The history of utopias is a history of failures, although that does not necessarily make them futile exercises, as Charles Maclean observes in his reflections on the lost idyll of St Kilda:

> Utopianism which emphasises the ideal and the unobtainable
> serves a useful but restricted purpose in as much as it contributes
> to the process of criticising and attempting to improve upon the
> existing conditions of society.

> (Maclean 1972: 166)

In 1819 Dr John Macculloch said of Kilda: 'If this island is not Utopia so long sought, where will it be found?' The Victorians over-enthusiastic and consequently destructive reaction to the 'unspoilt simplicity' (as it was reported and packaged) of St Kilda echoed that of More's literary lost island, taking it *too* literally – as when a priest asked where Utopia was because its inhabitants plainly needed Christianising! This is the same as when a soap opera character dies and viewers send in flowers: something that could be called a reality-perception malfunction, or just plain dumb.

More's Utopia inspired many imitators, who took his idea and ran with it. Jonathan Swift was one of the first, with his anti-utopian wonder tale of 1727 *Gulliver's Travels into Several Remote Nations of the World*, which Swift – through the persona of Captain Gulliver – admits to be: 'a very loose and incorrect account of my travels.' Just as in Plato's *Critias*, with its claim of veracity, the publisher pretends to have heard the story from the man himself, albeit with a nod and a wink to the reader:

> The author of these Travels, Mr Lemuel Gulliver, is my most
> ancient and intimate friend: there is likewise some relation
> between us on our mother's side.

There follows the most entertaining tale of extreme contrasts, size displacement being only one of them – foreshadowing the topsy-turvy inversions of Lewis Carroll's *Alice's Adventures in Wonderland* (1865) – with Gulliver finding himself a giant in Lilliput, the tiny source of curiosity in Brobdingnag, and a fish out of water in other lands of the absurd. A satire of the absurdist values of the day, especially as found in the court of King George I, the Royal Society with their experiments and inventions, and in Europe at large with its multiple sects and political systems. *Gulliver's Travels* has remained a comic classic, although less appreciated as a work of the imagination and even proto-science fiction, with its flying island (Laputa), aerial bombardments, an early kind of computer (the Engine) and a myriad of strange beings – what would be called Steam Punk these days, that is low-fi sci-fi (as in *Howl's Moving Castle* by Diane Wynne Jones, 1986).

In 1872 Samuel Butler wrote *Erewhon* (an anagram for 'nowhere'), a witty story of a distant land in the vein of *Gulliver's Travels*, where machinery is forbidden, sickness is a punishable crime, and criminals receive compassionate medical treatment. Butler's utopian novel lampoons such hallowed institutions as family, church and mechanical progress in a satirical way, like the Georgian cartoons of Gilray, Cruickshank and Hogarth. In 1891 William Morris published *News from Nowhere, or, An Epoch of Rest: Being Some Chapters from a Utopian Romance,* in which a man awakes in the distant future to find himself in a world without capitalism, industrialization or alienation – presenting an extended allegory of Morris' socialist ideas.

Yet side by side to these political allegories was the English 'visionary tradition', as charted in Peter Ackroyd's history of English cultural history *Albion: The origins of the English imagination* (2002), which saw these otherworlds not as metaphors, but as living realities. Ackroyd listed several 'Cockney visionaries': William Langland (*Piers the Plowman*), William Hogarth (the painter and engraver), John Bunyan (*Pilgrim's Progress*) and William Blake (who raised his City of the Imagination, Golgonooza, in London itself).

> To hear the music of the stones, to glimpse the spiritual in the
> local and actual, to render tangible things the material of
> intangible allegory, all these are at the centre of the London
> vision.

> (Ackroyd 2002: 307)

Blake and his spiritual peers performed a major act of the imagination: they turned the British Isles itself into a lost island paradise, rendered unfamiliar through the lens of mythos. They had brought utopia home.

Building Jerusalem

For Blake, his lost island was not elsewhere, it was beneath our feet: Albion, the 'inmost form' of England, an immanent kingdom waiting to be re-awakened, to be called forth by ritual outpourings of poetry, art, music and the power of the imagination. It was there for those with eyes to see it – a dormant giant in the land itself, alluding to the Classical myth of the chained Titan, Cronus, shackled for his god-crimes beneath this Land Beyond the North Wind, chilly and damp Hyperborea.

For Blake, who as a child saw angels in the trees and God at the window, the divine was always close. He imagined the Lamb of God amongst England's pastoral idyll –

perpetuating the myth that Joseph of Arimathea brought the twelve-year old Christ here, on a kind of protracted gap year before he accepted his world-changing destiny. So if the Word was brought to these shores, then why not the Holy City itself? Blake sent out the rallying cry to build Jerusalem here, a case of insisting the mountain come to Mohammed. Blake considered 'everything that lives [as] holy' and every clod of earth sacred. His own garden at 13 Hercules Building, Lambeth, became his personal Eden, which he famously enjoyed naked with his wife, Eve to his new Adam. His cottage at Felpham was 'the dwelling place of immortals.' The Holy Land was not in the Middle East, it was on the edge of London; it was everywhere or nowhere. It was just a matter of perception. He refuted empiricism, that the world can be understood through the evidence of the five senses. He argued that we must shed those shackles to be free, the tyranny of the Age of Reason and its ambassadors, Newton, Locke, *et al*, as epitomised in Urizen, against whom his god of imagination, Los, rebels in Miltonian manner. In the *Proverbs of Hell*, Blake famously says: 'When the doors of perception are cleansed, man will see everything as it truly is, infinite.' Then it is possible to 'see a world in a grain of sand, heaven in a wild flower.' The particular becomes universal.

Blake himself was a kind of lost island – a prophet not honoured in his own country, certainly not in his own lifetime, except for a handful of followers. All his life he struggled against poverty and petty-mindedness, as recorded heartbreakingly in 'Another Sun', written in a letter to Thomas Butts, 22 November 1802:

> My hands are labour'd day & night,
> And Ease comes never in my sight.
> My Wife has no indulgence given
> Except what comes to her from heaven.
> We eat little, we drink less;
> This Earth breeds not our happiness.
> Another Sun feeds our life's streams,
> We are not warmed with thy beams;
> Thou measurest not the Time to me,
> Nor yet the Space that I do see;
> My mind is not with thy light array'd.
> Thy terrors shall not make me afraid.

Most touching of all was to be his fate: buried in an unmarked grave. Not the grandeur of Westminster Abbey for him. Blake is buried in the Dissenters' Graveyard in Bunhill Fields, East London – although a commemorative stone celebrates his presence, it is in the wrong place. It was not until 2006 that his actual grave was discovered by two researchers who used the grid system of the churchyard and old records to locate it. On his deathday, 12 August, that year, Blakeans turned up without anyone organising anything for a Blake picnic and poetry recital, an impromptu happening – members of The Blake Society, Blakespeare and Mental Fight were present, along independent poets and general public. Poignantly Britain's greatest poet and unwitting composer of the country's unofficial national anthem, Tory hymn and excuse for wag-flaving, *Jerusalem* (all of which would make Blake turn in his grave) is buried in an unmarked grave and honoured, it seems, only by outsiders, misfits and eccentrics, indeed like Blake himself. Blake's grave, a 'lost island' of visionary radicalism in the heart of London may one day be officially marked – until then it remains a lost island, albeit for 'offerings': a makeshift shrine. It is a resonant spot, as Iain Sinclair, points out:

> We were in the enclosure between the graves of John Bunyan,
> Daniel Defoe and William Blake: the energy lines of England run
> out from this spot.

(Sinclair 2005 (2006: 294))

Blake used his engraver's stylus to demarcate his own territory – in ironic counterpart to Newton and his compass – on the postcard-sized copper plates he worked on: surprisingly tiny and frail compared to the mighty words written upon them (in exquisite copperhand mirror writing), words engraved into the English language. The technology of the time was not sufficient for Blake's vision and so he created his own method of printing which allowed text and image to be printed together on the same plate for the first time: the 'infernal method' he called it. Instead of the required line being engraved *into* the copper plate, it was protected by a wax-resistant wash and the surrounding area bitten away by the acid, creating 'islands' of raised text and graphic to be inked. Blake had thought outside of the box and come up with a successful technological solution that allowed him to create the equivalent of medieval stained glass windows on the page – printed by Blake, and hand-coloured by his wife, Catherine. As a jobbing engraver he sustained himself, along with the patronage of Butts and Johnson. This gave him the freedom to follow his muse. He self-published his own chapbooks and limited edition prints, and over a lifetime forged a vast cosmic vision through his epic illustrated poems.

In his poem *London* Blake uses the phrase 'mind forg'd manacles' – all of his life he railed against enslavement of any kind, and believed in the emancipation of the imagination. His imaginative vision of Albion, the utopia which *might* exist here-and-now rather than elsewehre, is Blake's enduring contribution to the mythos of lost islands.

Lost England, or before Mordor

Loss has prompted some of the greatest literature in the English language. Loss of a friend inspired *Adonais*, Shelley's elegy to Keats. Loss of a monarch moved Tennyson thrice: *In Memoriam; Idylls of the King* and *Le Morte d'Arthur*). Loss of nature is invoked in Gerard Manley Hopkins' *Binsey Poplars*), while loss of the past is the basis of William Wordsworth's *The Prelude* among much else.

Sometimes loss can be a positive thing, a wilful rejection of what is present, a hearkening back to some Golden Age, or, as in our next writer's case, an apocastasis set in the future. Richard Jeffries (1848–87), a Wiltshire-born nature writer par excellence, worked in London as a journalist for a number of years before returning to the West Country. Here he penned his prophetic apocalyptic classic, *After London* (1885), in which he describes a Britain of the future returned to a wild state and largely flooded: an eerie vision of Britain as a 'lost island' – the victim of climate change and sea levels rising. (This, and other flood fiction, is looked at in more detail in the chapter on 'When the Levee Breaks'.)

Jeffries' earlier writings (*Wood Magic*, 1881; *Bevis*, 1882) harked back to the lost islands of childhood, to Edens of makebelieve, but it is with *After London* that the Biblical imagery of the late Romantics became manifest – thus following in a long tradition of disillusioned or malcontent doom-mongerers.

The Apocalyptic Sublime, as it became known, was popular in the early nineteenth century against the backdrop of the Hundred Years War; a time of revolutions, twitchy heads of state, fearful citizens, political and economic uncertainty – the premillennial tension of its day. The equivalent of the Millennium Bug, or Y2K as the media branded it, was the French Terror, a similar product of the popular press. As an indication of the paranoia of the French Terorr era Wordsworth, later to be thought of as a quintessential bastion of Englishness, was put under surveillance, along with Coleridge, as possible 'spies', or French sympathisers as were a number of other intellectuals. A similar incident happened in the 1950s to Dylan Thomas who was out drinking in Marshfield, a village near Bath and near Colerne airfield, with some Irish literary friends, when locals reported them as 'spies' because they spoke in odd accents. Thomas was duly banged up for the night in the village clink – no stranger to the drunk tank, but this time an innocent victim of Cold War paranoia.

The Romantics saw the sublime in nature and in lost islands all around – childhood being a main one for Wordsworth; whileas Coleridge discovered inner lost islands, most famously Xanadu in *Kubla Khan*, which in itself is a kind of lost island – the composition of which being famously interrupted by a man from Porlock, who prevented Coleridge from writing down the hundreds of lines he had crafted in his head while in his laudanum dream. Coleridge had been reading Samuel Purchas' *The Pilgrimage* (1614) – 'In Xanada did Cublai Can build a stately Pallace' – but it was through his own laudanum-fueled imagination that he was to explore his own Xanadu.

Some of the Romantics took the trouble to actually physically travel, like Shelley and Keats. The Grand Tour of Europe became *de rigeur* for the upper classes, but some went beyond this well-heeled comfort zone. Lord Byron, disdaining the 'tight little island' of Britain where he had become a notorious celebrity, took part in the fight for Greek independence, dying of fever in Missolonghi. He was duly honoured by the Greeks – his statue looks out over the harbour there to this day – and established a pattern of travel for literary men of action followed by Rimbaud, Melville, London, Conrad and Hemingway.

Robert Louis Stevenson's travel bug was instigated by his severe bronchial condition, which drove him initially in search of an agreeable climate that he found eventually in the South Pacific; yet even paradise could not postpone his fate for long – he was to die of a brain haemorrhage there, buried on a Samoan mountaintop above his adopted home. His colourful travels influenced and inspired his prolific writing – *Travels with a Donkey in the Cévennes* (1879) was one of many travel books he wrote. Yet the alembic of the imagination produced his most resounding successes. On his return to England in 1883 his 'lost island' novel was published, *Treasure Island*, and with it he struck gold.

Other novels from Stevenson followed on the wave of its success: *Kidnapped*, *The Black Arrow* and *The Strange Case of Dr Jekyll and Mr Hyde* – the latter inspired by his knowledge of the Edinburgh Underworld. These, like fellow countryman's Walter Scott's prolific outpourings before him, proved popular escapist fictions in the age when the Industrial Revolution was going full steam ahead, and many were being driven from the land to the cities to live in squalid conditions where poverty, disease, violence and crime prevailed.

Coleridge and Poet Laureate-to-be Southey dreamed of an idealised society where everyone was equal and they could idle away their days in poetic reverie, only working when they needed to, to feed, clothe and shelter themselves, for a maximum of two hours a day, the rest of their time spent in leisure and creative pursuits. Their idler's utopia would be established on the banks of the Susquehanna river, as inspired by Longfellow's *Song of Hiawatha* (1855) – itself a noble savage utopian myth.

There is perhaps a hint of this in the rustic quaintness portrayed in the urbane wordsmiths Boswell and Johnson's accounts of their 1773 journey through the Highlands and Western Isles of Scotland, like a tour of an asylum by 'sane' and socially-concerned gentle folk. Johnson published his great account, the *Journey to the Western Isles of Scotland* in 1775, and it became one of the most acute and widely-read social commentaries of its age. After his travelling companion's death Boswell composed his more anecdotal and high-spirited, *A Journal of a Tour to the Hebrides* in 1785.

Boswell and Johnson, although they did not know it, provided one of the rare accounts of a dying way of life, threatened by the Industrial Revolution on the horizon. Other accounts, such as William Cobbett's *Rural Rides* (1830) and George Borrow's *Wild Wales* (1862), also captured this fleeting glimpse of a rural world soon to be irrevocably changed by the advent of the Machine Age.

The Celtic twilight

We need to use the term Celtic as a literary conceit here, not as any demarcation of race or culture. 'Celtic' is best thought of as a nationalist mark of independence, freedom from the English yoke.

The term 'Celtic twilight' carries elements of nostalgia, melancholy and world-weariness, as epitomised in W.B. Yeats' poem of the same name:

> Outworn heart in a time outworn,
> come clear of the nets of wrong and right.
> Laugh heart again, in the dew morn,
> Sigh heart again, in the grey twilight.

Yeats called his collection of Irish folk tales *The Celtic Twilight* (1893). It was the imagined dying embers of an ancient culture, with the oldest literature in Europe, a swan-song like that of the Children of Lir, who had journeyed for nine hundred years trapped in their form by the enchantress Aoife, finally to be released from their spell when a 'woman of the south wedded a man of the north' (a prophetic symbol of the union of Ireland that still needs to take place, but is at least closer with the end of hostilities in Northern Ireland). As with Oisín's tale, apocryphally recorded by St Patrick, there is a sense of the last vestiges of a lost culture being recorded before fading out completely:

> When white moths are on the wing,
> And moth like stars are flickering out...

> (Yeats, *Song of Wandering Aengus*)

This trope of recording the 'twilight' of an almost-lost tradition was much in vogue at the time – a particular Victorian obsession to pin down and catalogue (in doing so ironically accelerating extinction, as the stuffed heads and preserved carcases of evolution's dodos and deadends in the numerous museums testify). Alexander Carmichael''s *Carmina Gadelica* (6 vols, 1928–71); Sir James G. Frazer's *Golden Bough (13 vols, 1890–1915)*; Francis James Child's *The English and Scottish Popular Ballads* (5 vols, 1882–8); Cecil Sharp collected many recordings and transcripts for the English Folklore Society from 1903 to his death in 1924. If not for these people much of this material would have been lost; as the cycle of the oral tradition was largely broken by populations displaced by the Industrial Revolution, Highland Clearances, the Irish Famine and transportation to the colonies – a process compounded by two World Wars, which irreparably sundered generations.

Perhaps prescient of this forthcoming doom, the writers of the Celtic Twilight – Yeats; Lady Gregory; 'A.E.'; Fiona Macleod; George Macdonald – turned against the tide of progress and wilfully plunged into the chthonic depths of native mythos. Finding little satisfaction in the world they found themselves in, they evoked their own hidden kingdoms.

Ironically, like Dylan Thomas who could not speak Welsh, Yeats was a non-Gaelic speaker but drew upon Gaelic mythology and cadence in his work. Perhaps as an Anglo-Irish poet caught between worlds, he yearned for identity and a sense of belonging more than most: something that might explain the many personas, or masks, he adopted in his lifetime.

As well as being between the worlds of two real nations, Yeats expressed a melancholic yearning for the otherworld again and again in poems. This is captured most memorably in *The Lake Isle of Innisfree*:

> I will arise and go now, and go to Innisfree,
> And a small cabin build there, of clay and wattles made:
> Nine bean-rows will I have there, a hive for the honey-bee,
> And live alone in the bee-loud glade.

> And I shall have some peace there, for peace comes dropping
> > slow,
> Dropping from the veils of the mourning to where the cricket
> > sings;
> There midnight's all a glimmer, and noon a purple glow,
> And evening full of the linnet's wings.
>
> I will arise and go now, for always night and day
> I hear lake water lapping with low sounds by the shore;
> While I stand on the roadway, or on the pavements grey,
> I hear it in the deep heart's core.

This lost island longing 'in the deep heart's core' is echoed in *The Stolen Child*, where the child/reader is lured, like Oisin by the fairy song:

> Where the wave of moonlight glosses
> The dim gray sands with light,
> Far off by furthest Rosses
> We foot it all the night,
> Weaving olden dances
> Mingling hands and mingling glances
> Till the moon has taken flight;
> To and fro we leap
> And chase the frothy bubbles,
> While the world is full of troubles
> And anxious in its sleep.
> Come away, O human child!
> To the waters and the wild
> With a faery, hand in hand,
> For the world's more full of weeping than you can understand.

Here is a consoling fiction, imbued with the enchantments of soporific language – spell-binding sibilance and soothing word-music – enticing the world-weary away from the mournful adult world. While the world is 'anxious in its sleep', the child is enticed to a land of dreams.

English Shangri Las

Such 'Twilightism' was not a purely 'Celtic' phenomenon. Victorian England had gone misty-eyed over the mediaeval period, which was perceived to be a 'lost England', a golden age. The Pre-Raphaelites, by their very name, yearned for a pre-Renaissance period when life, it seemed, was simpler, more honourable, or at least more *aesthetic* – as opposed to the uglification of the Industrial Revolution. The Matter of Britain – the story of King Arthur – was resurrected again, as it had been in Tudor times by Malory. The dream of Camelot symbolised an apogee in English culture, a Platonic Ideal if not a reality – a blueprint for the future, a place to find in the present. An Englishman's home became his castle at this time of popular gothic pastiches.

Yet this was not a new thing even then. From the medieval to the Victorian era there had been the concept of the 'Norman Yoke' under which the good honest yeoman struggled, 'free-born' Saxons robbed of their rights by since 1066, creating a desire for a Free Saxonia. J.R.R. Tolkien lamented the Norman Conquest as the worst thing to ever happen to England, and created his own version of his beloved land without its linguistic influence – his own literary refugium to resist the tides of cultural evolution.

Thomas Hardy's own 'lost island' was his semi-fictional Wessex, though in later years it became his deceased wife – who inspired his most haunting poetry in her absence, which he mourned bitterly, having failed to love her properly whilst she lived. She represented everything he had lost. Hardy captured a more literal feeling of the otherworld in his poem *When I Set Out for Lyonesse*:

> When I set out for Lyonnesse,
> A hundred miles away,
>   The rime was on the spray,
> And starlight lit my lonesomeness
> When I set out for Lyonnesse
> A hundred miles away.

As the map of the world turned Empire-pink there was little left to conquer or explore. Writers were forced to look to the edges of the map, or to neglected corners for the location of their lost worlds.

The genteel author of Sherlock Holmes, Arthur Conan Doyle, took something of a departure from his whodunits with *The Lost World* (1912), with a distant and inaccessible plateau in South America (Tepuyes in Venezuala) serving as Doyle's lost island where dinosaurs still roamed, surviving in a *refugium* from evolution and the savagery of man – almost. Professor Challenger mounts a perilous expedition there to prove its existence. There follows a series of thrilling encounters.

The tale of *King Kong* first appeared as a novel in 1931, with the film following the next year, and features one of the most famous lost islands in popular culture, Skull Island, brought to life in Peter Jackson's cinematic version. Skull Island is decidedly an anti-utopia, with hostile natives and deadly megafauna. This was the prototype for Crichton and Speilberg's *Jurassic Park* (1993). Despite this later treatment Skull Island is not the kind of place most people would want to visit on vacation. For some unexplained reason, dinosaurs still dwelt in Skull Island. Like Doyle's Jurassic plateau, it is another place that evolution forgot – although Kong's world was also influenced by Edgar Rice Burroughs' 1918 humans-meet-dinosaurs novel, *The Land That Time Forgot*. Inevitably, the arrival of twentieth century humans tips the fragile 'balance' of these worlds-within-worlds, and lead to their destruction or desecration – an inevitable repercussion that Ray Bradbury was to capture in his influential 1953 science-fiction paradox parable, 'A Sound of Thunder', where trigger happy time-travellers to the Jurassic period inadvertently bring about the end of human history.

This 'fly in the ointment' trope was to surface again and again, most notably in *Lost Horizons* by James Hilton. Published in 1922, this describes the discovery of a lost civilisation of ancient wisdom, Shangri-La, in the remote Himalayas by survivors of a crashed plane bringing all of their modernist baggage with them – and leading to its eventual loss. Hilton coined the term Shangri-La from the combination of an exotic neologism, 'shangri', and the Tibetan for mountain pass, 'la'. It has come to mean any imaginary earthly paradise.

Lost Horizon's success, as a novel and in 1937 as a Frank Capra film, was due in no small part in tapping into the zeitgeist. Its protagonists were representational of what is now known as the Lost Generation – the victims of the First World War; the survivors and the bereaved, shell-shocked, traumatised, disillusioned, faithless – in search of consoling fictions of hedonism and spiritualism, as also explored in my 1920s novel *The Long Woman* (2004).

After the carnage and breakdown exacted by the First World War on Europe, the West was adrift – God was famously dead, according to Neitzche and his disciples. Dadaism and Surrealism reflected the randomness and craziness of modern life. Novels by Joyce, Woolf, Miller, Hemingway and Huxley mirrored its bleakness, fetishes and neuroses, as did Brecht's plays. The poetry of T.S. Eliot, the cubism of Picasso and Braque, the broken notes and rhythms of jazz – all of these suggested a breakdown of classical harmony, of the status quo that had brought about devastating mechanised war.

John Cowper Powys epitomised and explored the complexity of this age in his quartet of singular novels – *Wolf Solent* (1929), *A Glastonbury Romance* (1932), *Weymouth Sands* (1934) and *Maiden Castle* (1936) – which explored the lost islands of Wessex with their lost lives, dialects, landscapes, customs, quirkiness, and customs. After he returned from his North American lecture tours, where he had written many of these novels with the 'ink blood of home', he carried on his deep psychogeographic journeying in Wales, where he became naturalised, claimed Welsh descent, penning obscure Celtic novels: *Owen Glendower* (1940), *Porius* (1951) and *Atlantis* (1954). The last is perhaps the oddest addition to the oddest of canons, Atlantology, and spun with his own particular brand of uncompromising weirdness. He is, nonetheless, a writer of considerable weight, attracting followers like Henry Miller, George Steiner, Iris Murdoch, Angus Wilson, Jeremy Hooker and recently Margaret Drabble. Drabble describes the 'dangerous' realm of Powys:

> Like Tolkien, Powys has invented another country, densely
> peopled, thickly forested, mountainous, erudite, strangely self-
> sufficient. This country is less visited than Tolkien's, but it is as
> compelling, and it has more air.

> (Drabble 2006)

Drabble praises his liminal status as an untouchable of the mainstream critics: 'He is so far outside the canon that he defies the concept of canon.' In a description of the eccentric visionary Sylvanus Cobbold in *Weymouth Sands*, Powys could be describing himself: 'Always a rebel, always dwelling in a mystical borderland of his own.' (Powys 1934: (2000: 269)) Powys seems to float off on his own island, barely attached to the mainstream. In a similar way he describes the penitential quarry, the Isle of Portland, Dorset, in *Weymouth Sands*:

> … Portland, as it lay before them, rising tier by tier over its
> terraces of old walls and grey roofs, seemed to be tugging at its
> tether in that luminous and liquid haze, seemed to be straining at
> this gigantic rope of transparent stones, agates and carnelians,
> which bound it to the mainland. The huge limestone rock seemed
> to have no roots, under this enchanted light, in any solid earth. It
> seemed to be riding, just as the battleships in the harbour seemed
> to be riding, upon a liquid abyss of opalescent water that sank
> down to the antipodes. And the Jobber got the impression that this
> stupendous mass of oolite was really afloat today in this
> translucent calm; not only afloat, but longing to drift off, to sail
> out and away, over the surface of that halcyon sea.

> (Powys 1934)

The trope of floating islands crops up infrequently throughout literature, although it could be seen as a metaphor for the more frequent ethereal Shangri-Las, barely anchored to reality, and is a subspecies of the greater lost island trope and the close siblings of island-like utopias and Edens. During the twentieth century English Edens continued to be created in many diverse forms. To name some of the classics: *Winds in the Willows* (Grahame 1908), *The Secret Garden* (Frances Hodgson Burnett 1909); *Lud-in-the-Mist* (Mirrless 1926), *Swallows and Amazons* (Ransome 1930); *The Lord of the Rings* (Tolkien 1954–5); the *Narnia* books (Lewis 1950–6); *Tom's Midnight Garden* (Pearce 1958) and *Stardust* (Gaiman 1998). For some modern tastes, they have little substance, no shadow, and the twentieth century was undoubtedly a journey less to Edens than into the heart of darkness.

Hearts of darkness

What could be called a process of endarkenment took place parallel to the rise and fall of the British Empire. Slave trade, genocide, the Clearances, the Potato Famine perhaps all contributed to this as the world was 'tidied up'. If you did not toe the line, you were transported to lost islands like Van Diemens Land and Tasmania – or the Americas. The 'noble savage' was invented to assuage the 'white man's guilt' of empire building. This ideal was yearned for in the eighteenth and nineteenth century when the notion of the 'primitive' took hold in art and literature. Western standards and obsessions were transposed onto the 'wildman' from John White's fifteenth century watercolours of First Nations people to Edward S. Curtis' haunting photographs of a doomed race. This is explored more in the chapter 'How the West was Lost'.

The wildman has been a recurring pattern since the birth of civilisation – often cited as being in ancient Babylon in modern-day Iraq. The oldest-surviving book describes how the Babylonian King, Giglamesh, 'civilised' Enkidu the Wildman by arranging for him to be seduced by a prostitute, then felling a sacred tree: literally cutting himself off from his roots, from his own nature. Afterwards, the animals Enkidu once shared a rapport with then shun him, sensing his 'human otherness'. Enkidu eventually dies and Gilgamesh mourns his lost 'wild self', going on a quest to restore him to life. The recalcitrant king fails, but humanity has been on this quest ever since – to restore our lost rapport with nature; perhaps lost from the moment humanity gained self-awareness.

This endarkenment, the idea that man corrupts the very paradise he seeks, manifested in literature negatively, most notably in Joseph Conrad's *Heart of Darkness* (1902); and more positively in W. Somerset Maugham's *The Moon and Sixpence* (1919), about Gauguin's experiences in his adopted Polynesian 'lost island', Tahiti.

Joseph Conrad wrote the *Heart of Darkness* in the twilight of the nineteenth century, the first of three parts serialised from 1899 in *Blackwood's Magazine*, although it was not published complete until 1902. It was based upon his own 'disastrous experiences in the Congo in 1890', and is seen as the first twentieth century novel – Modernist in tone and a key-note for the bloodiest and darkest of centuries.

Conrad seems to have had a 'dark past' involving intense hardship (his Polish parents, exiled to Vologda for conspiring against Russia, died when he was eleven), gun-running and gambling debts. Conrad attempted suicide, shooting himself in the chest and narrowly missing his heart – an experience which must have stayed with him, a physical 'heart of darkness', a hole, a painful absence to be filled.

Perhaps echoing Conrad's own sentiments, Marlow describes his early wanderlust:

> Now when I was a little chap I had a passion for maps. I would
> look for hours at South America, or Africa, or Australia, and lose
> myself in all the glories of exploration. At that time there were
> many blank spaces on the earth, and when I saw one that looked
> particularly inviting on a map (but they all look like that) I would
> put my finger on it and say, When I grow up I will go there…

(Conrad 1902 (2002: 11))

By the time Conrad was old enough to fulfil his dream, to visit the 'biggest, the most blank' – the Congo:

> …it was not a blank space any more. It had got filled since my
> boyhood with rivers and lakes and names. It had ceased to be a
> blank space of delightful mystery – a white patch for a boy to
> dream gloriously over. It had become a place of darkness.

(Conrad 1902 (2002: 12))

Marlow journeys there and is sucked into the vortex that is Kurtz, an ivory dealer gone AWOL, a point of singularity at the centre of this black hole. The river journey is a journey to the Shadow, to the place of primal fear and savagery:

Going up that river was like travelling back to the earliest beginnings of the world...

(Conrad 1902 (2002: 48))

At the heart of the world is: The horror! The horror!' as Kurtz famously says, lines famously improvised by Marlon Brando in Francis Ford Coppola's unforgetable version *Apocalypse Now* (1979). Conrad's mythic heart of darkness has stayed in the Western imagination throughout the twentieth century, in parallel with the horrors of the World Wars, Stalin's Russia, Pol Pot's killing fields, et cetera. It was an endarkenment repeated again and again, as humans continued to plumb the depths of their psyches through countless atrocities.

William Golding explored this same dark path – that of humanity's inherently savage nature easily stripped away by circumstance – in *Lord of the Flies* (1954), changing the crew to schoolboys who find themselves marooned on a tropical island after a nuclear apocalypse who soon revert to atavistic tribalism, echoing Shakespeare's adage from *King Lear*: 'As flies to wanton boys are we to the gods; they kill us for their sport.' (IV, I) For Golding the island serves as a Manichean playground where the forces of light and darkness, as embodied in Ralph and Jack's struggle for supremacy.

Herman Melville, like Robert Louis Stevenson his Scottish contemporary, caught wanderlust and travelled extensively about the South Pacific, first gaining success with *Typee: A peep at Polynesian life* (1846), although he failed to replicate this accomplishment in a South Sea sequel, *Omoo: A narrative adventure in the South Seas* (1847). His most well-known novel is of course *Moby Dick* (1851), its reputation is so vast now it is hard to conceive how it failed to be appreciated in his lifetime, and was only rediscovered in the 1920s – the start of the Melville Revival. Melville has since been called 'America's Shakespeare' by the panel of judges who in *Atlantic Monthly*'s December 2006 list voted him one of 'The 100 Most Influential Americans of All Time'. His monumental book has lived on in various editions and adaptations: its theme of destroying obsession is as relevant today as ever, although its whaling theme is less palatable to some modern readers – even though these were the core experiences of Melville's that shaped the book's genesis. Anecdotes from his whaling days were used to add drama to *The Encantadas, or Enchanted Isles* (1854), Melville's memoir of the Galápagos Islands, where only a few years before Darwin had voyaged on the *Beagle* and made observations that led to the paradigm-shifting origin of the species – explored more in the chapter 'Did the Earth Move?'

The notion that islands are places where Godgames can be played out in the Western imagination. A Godgame is 'a tale in which an actual game (which may incorporate broader implications) is being played without the participants' informed consent' (Clute 1997 414–5). Well-known examples of Godgame islands feature in Shakespeare's *The Tempest* (1623), H.G. Wells' *The Island of Dr Moreau* (1896) – where hideous genetic experiments take place, a parable against animal vivisection, a topic much in debate at the time – and John Fowles' *The Magus* (1965). More recently the TV series *Lost* has resurrected the Godgame island mythos (explored in detail in 'How the West was Lost').

During the same period as Wells was describing *The Island of Dr Moreau* the other grandfather of science fiction, French author Jules Verne, was charting the voyages and adventures of his latter-day Renaissance man and self-proclaimed saviour of the deep, Captain Nemo, (Latin for 'no-one': the perfet cognomen for a utopian hero) who first surfaced in *Twenty Thousand Leagues Under the Sea* (1870). Despite acting aloof at times, Nemo is the antithesis of Robur, Verne's malevolent *Master of the World* (1904) with his invisible all-element vehicle. Time and time again, in contradiction to his coldness and contempt for humankind, Nemo rescues people, wracks himself with guilt over those he loses and wreaks revenge on the oppressors of the weak. He operates from some deep motive of justice from a hidden base explored in *The Mysterious Island* (1875), the fictitious Lincoln Island, with its coast resembling an elephant head. Like all good lost islands, this one explodes in a volcanic eruption and sinks below the waves, taking Nemo and his *Nautilus* – a good captain going down with his ship – and his advanced technology, with it because 'humanity is not ready for it' (in the 1961 film version depicted as atomic power).

Nemo warned against the perils of mechanisation, as *Gulliver's Travels*, *Erewhon*, and *News from Nowhere* had done. This prophecy was to come bitterly true in the battlefields of the First World War, which saw the devastating results of the machine: tanks, machine guns and aerial bombardment – as prophesised in H.G. Wells *The War in the Air* (1908). With the wholesale slaughter of young men things got as dark as they possibly could. Humankind had found its heart of darkness – within itself.

Yet before the lights went out all over Europe, the Edwardian Age gave birth to a brief flowering of fey joy, a breath of golden summer.

Pipers at the Gates of Dawn

Seemingly the innocence of perception, associated rightly or wrongly with childhood, allows access to this other realm. J.M. Barrie's *Peter Pan* (his full novel version was published in 1911, although Peter first appeared in his story, 'The Little White Bird', 1902 and then on stage two years later) is the tale of the boy who never grows up, and the otherworldly lost island of Neverland is only attainable by the young, or at least the young at heart. Barrie starts his description by likening Neverland to 'a map of a child's mind', which is perhaps the most psychologically accurate analogy of a lost island so far:

> Neverland is always more or less an island, with astonishing
> splashes of colour here and there, and coral reefs and rakish-
> looking craft in the offing, and savages and lonely lairs, and
> gnomes who are mostly tailors, and caves through which a river
> runs, and princes with six elder brothers, and a hut fast going to
> decay, and one very small lady with a hooked nose.

(Barrie 1911 (1995: 6))

For a children's classic, Barrie adds many adult interjections, even in his description of Neverland, where he adds a list of everyday mundanities – 'school, religion, fathers, the round pound, needlework, murders, hangings' (Barrie 1911 (1995: 6)) – which stubbornly disturb the idyll:

> … either these are part of the island or they are another map
> showing through, and it is all rather confusing, especially as
> nothing will stand still. (Barrie 1911 (1995: 7))

This second map suggests how everyday reality is the white noise of life against which these tales are read, a different paradigm that can conflict with fantasy, although in fact most children have no problem at all at shutting out this background buzz with their ability to instantaneously make believe, perhaps too successfully:

> When you play at it by day with the chairs and table-cloth, it is
> not in the least alarming, but in the two minutes before you go to
> sleep it becomes very nearly real. That is why there are night
> lights though, and it is all rather confusing, especially as nothing
> will stand still.
>
> (Barrie 1911 (1995: 7))

This adds another level of sophistication to Barrie's tale, a child's world seen through a shrewd adult lens, but ultimately it is an awareness that prevents us from entering with the same ease:

> On these magic shores children at play are for ever beaching their
> coracles. We too have been there; we can still hear the sound of
> the surf, though we shall land no more.
>
> (Barrie 1911 (1995: 7))

This is a mournful admission to maturity and the loss of innocence it brings.

Ironic that although Peter Pan may never grow up, his UK copyright expired at the venerable age of 96 in 2007 (extended by a European Union directive from 1987, 50 years after Barrie's death). Great Ormond Street Hospital which has benefited from the royalties for so long had to commission an official sequel (there had been numerous unofficial ones) from one-time Children's Laureate, Geraldine McCoughrean which appeared as *Peter Pan in Scarlet* (2006). This selfsame copyright has prevented the UK publication of Alan Moore and Melinda Gebbie's notorious *Lost Girls* (2006) 'pornographic' graphic novel, featuring the sexual adventures of Wendy, Dorothy and Alice in their post-Children's Classic life. Some girls are never allowed to grow up either.

Philip Pullman explores this territory of necessary transgression in his boldly Miltonic trilogy *His Dark Materials*, (comprising *Northern Lights,*1995, *The Subtle Knife,* 1997, and *The Amber Spyglass,* 2000), set initially in an alternative Oxford, his first of many multi-dimensional 'lost islands' (Citigazza is another, a Marie Celeste-style Mediterranean port haunted by soul-eating spectres) which are discovered by the adolescent protagonists Will and Lyra. *Lyra's Oxford*, an addition to the trilogy, was presented as a retro guidebook and almanac, complete with foldout map (Pullman 2003). The first book, *Northern Lights*, came alive after attempting the first chapter for the umpteenth time, with what he described as 'the best idea he ever had' (South Bank Show special, ITV 2003) – depicting the shift from prepubescence to adolescence by the 'fixing' of each child's 'daemon': a kind of totem animal that alters shape according to the mood of the child, but becomes fixed when puberty is reached.

Pullman flouts the clichéd advice to actors: 'never work with animals or children' with typical imaginative daring. By using anthropomorphic animals Pullman is following in the footsteps, or pawprints, of many classics of childrens' literature – all of which recreate an Edenic state where humans understood the language of animals, or even before humans were present. Animals step in as human analogues in many of these tales; for instance, the Oxford dons transmogrified until transformed into owls and turtles in Lewis Carroll's *Wonderland*, a conceit Pullman wittily subverts by having dons with pet daemons. Perhaps most memorably of all, Kenneth Grahame captures a lost English idyll in his timeless classic of Mole, Ratty, Badger and Toad – aeons apart from Pullman's quantum re-creation myth, yet drawn from the same spiritual inkling well.

In *Wind in the Willows* (1908), Kenneth Grahame evoked a quintessentially English genius loci, a Home Counties arcadia of 'messing about on the water', the fictional equivalent of the Henley Regatta but no less charming for that. Grahame evokes, with his poetically alliterative title, a sense of the impermanence and inconsequentiality of things. It tells the reader 'all contained therein is stuff and nonsense – enjoy'. The book is intended to be as soothing as the soughing it suggests (worlds apart from Blackwood's sinister willows). But at its heart, there is the most unexpected epiphany in a chapter called 'The Piper at the Gates of Dawn', through which a very different air blows – from Faerie itself, it seems – 'a difference that was tremendous', (Grahame, 1908: 131). Ratty and Mole, searching for their friend, Otter, row into the night, entering a moonlit 'silent, silver kingdom' in the lunar quietus before dawn. After moonset, and just before sunrise, a piping can be heard, ethereal and elusive:

> "It's gone!" sighed the Rat, sinking back in his seat again. "So beautiful and strange and new! Since it was to end so soon, I almost wish I had never heard it. For it has roused in me a pain, and nothing seems worth while but just to hear that sound once more and go on listening to it for ever... "

(Grahame 1908 (2007:133))

Unlike Shakespeare's 'stuff that dreams are made on', it is 'such music never dreamed of, and the call in it is stronger even than the music is sweet.' However, only some can hear it. Mole hears nothing 'but the wind playing in the reeds and rushes and osiers', whileas Ratty is 'rapped, transported, trembling'. Perhaps Grahame is suggesting only a few hear the call to Faerie – the music that summoned

Oisín to Tir nan Og, that calls away the human child in Yeats' poem, that has rung out through the literature of lost islands.

Grahame's lulling idyll comes complete with its own lost island, as though Pan was an endangered species, the victim of cultural islandisation, left marooned in a world that had moved on:

> In midmost of the stream, embraced in the weir's shimmering armspread, a small island lay anchored, fringed close with willow and silver birch and alder. Reserved, shy, but full of significance, it hid whatever it might hold behind a veil, keeping it till the hour should come, and, with the hour, those who were called and chosen.

> (Grahame 1908 (2007: 134))

Passing through 'broken, tumultuous water', Ratty and Mole make landfall on this mysterious island. They find a blossom-bordered grove:

> "This is the place of my song-dream, the place the music played me," whispered the Rat, as if in a trance. "Here, in this holy place, here if anywhere, surely we shall find Him!"

> (Grahame 1908 (2007: 134))

'Him' turns out to be no less than 'the Great God Pan', then in vogue in Edwardian England – as seen in the writings of Arthur Machen and Aleister Crowley – a safe garden god (the '2CV of deities', so Ronald Hutton, giving his inaugural lecture as Professor of History at Bristol University on the subject of the Cult of the Horned God, amusingly designated him). Yet once Pan afforded greater respect, and Grahame's river-dwellers pay due homage:

> The two rivernauts approached and Ratty 'felt a great Awe upon him, an awe that turned his muscles to water, bowed his head, and rooted his feet to the ground.'

> (Grahame 1908 (2007: 134))

Transcending the Divine Terror, finding the call impossible to refuse, Ratty looked up and:

> … looked in the very eyes of the Friend and Helper; saw the backward sweep of the curved horns, gleaming in the growing daylight; saw the stern, hooked nose between the kindly eyes that were looking down on them humorously, while the bearded mouth broke into a half-smile at the corners; saw the rippling muscles on the arm that lay across the broad chest, the long supple hand still holding the pan-pipes only just fallen away from the parted lips; saw the splendid curves of the shaggy limbs disposed in majestic ease on the sward…

> (Grahame 1908 (2007: 135))

Fortunately, like so many visitors to Faerie, they are given the 'gift of forgetfulness':

> Lest the awful remembrance should remain and grow, and
> overshadow mirth and pleasure, and the great haunting memory
> should spoil all the after-lives of little animals helped out of
> difficulties, in order that they should be happy and light-hearted as
> before.

(Grahame 1908 (2007: 136))

Thus Ratty and Mole are spared the fate of many who venture too near the borders of Faerie. Many sicken for the Shining World and literally die to return, or are changed forever in some way – perhaps with a double-edged gift (such as 'the tongue that cannot lie', like Thomas the Rhymer).

This ambivalent boon is captured in Elizabeth Barrett Browning's 'A Musical Instrument', a haunting Victorian poem that could have been at the back of Grahame's mind:

> Yet half a beast is the great god Pan,
> Down in the reeds by the river,
> Making a poet out of a man.
> And the true gods sigh for the cost and the pain
> For the reed which will grow never more again
> As a reed with the reeds by the river…

Pan's island in the river (an eyot) from *Wind in the Willows,* and its music, its spirit of place appears, Brigadoon-like, in surprisingly different locations: Susan Cooper's *The Dark is Rising* (1984), and Algernon Blackwood's short story *The Willows,* (from *Tales of the Uncanny and Supernatural,* collected in 1949) both of which depict 'the island in the river' in a darker way, yet with the same sense of immanent magic amongst the mundane. The closeness of these Shangri-Las is undeniably part of their appeal. They can, in theory, be reached. This was why Francis Spufford in *The Child that Books Built* (2002) preferred the Narnia books with its many creative anachronisms (lamp-posts and Turkish delight) to anything as rarefied as Middle Earth. Here he explains something of their allure:

> Narnia, of course, was not supposed to be Heaven. It was more
> like an imaginary other island, farther out than ours perhaps,
> where longing could be briefly stabilised. What could only be
> longed for in this world would be possible in Narnia.

(Spufford 2002: 99)

For Spufford as a boy, Lewis 'invented objects for my longing, gave forms to my longing' (Spufford 2002: 87). The idea of a place 'where longing could be briefly stabilised' is critical to our understanding of lost islands and their appeal. These places provide a sanctuary for our fantasies and desires. The Welsh have a word for it, *hiraeth,* in essence, 'longing'. So these islands could be called '*hiraeth*-zones'.

Everyone has one: it could be a holiday destination, a cottage, a sports car, a job, a girlfriend, a pair of trainers. We project our happiness onto them.

Like a taste of the forbidden fruit from Eden, or one of the fairy fruit from *Lud-in-the-Mist*, 'Once opened, the door would never entirely shut behind you either.' (Spufford 2002: 85). Lewis once supposed a 'violation of frontier' and from this notion came Narnia. Once the walls of reality were knocked down, it would be difficult to rebuild them. Where once only a handful passed, now the disillusioned flocked in their hordes, in search of their longing.

Pink Floyd quoted from Grahame's title in their Sixties psychedelic hit *A Piper at the Gates of Dawn* – an album and mind-set that couldn't be further from the innocent times spent 'messing about on the river'. Or could it? Weren't the psychedelic visions of the Floyd and the later Beatles (*Lucy in the Sky with Diamonds, Strawberry Fields Forever, Number 9 Dream*) just an acid -pop annexisation of the English Shangri-La? In fiction Moorcock and his followers had squatted the favoured halls of elf-friends and skinned up. Gandalf's Garden was now a head-space to hang out in, a counter culture cafe. This huge shift would come about because of the Second World War and its fallout – the shadow of the A-bomb – which would shatter the walls of reality forever.

Lost islands in the Atomic Age

Tolkien's Ring was seen by some (but not the author himself) as a metaphor for the perils of the atom bomb – 'one ring to rule them all', a poisoned chalice of absolute power. Politics and power mongering aside, the effect on Western consciousness would be devastating. All status quo would be blown apart, giving birth to Cold War angst; Reds-under-the-bed McCarthyism (as encapsulated in Arthur Miller's 1953 play, *The Crucible*); Angry Young Men (quintessentially Jimmy Porter in John Osbourne's seminal Fifties' play *Look Back in Anger)*; the existentialism of the French new-wave philosophers (Sartre and Camus); and the American Beats (Kerouac, Ginsberg, Burroughs). Like Berlin, the world had been divided into a schizophrenic mask, the jagged line of wall demarcating opposing paranoid states, a cracked atlas of Gollums and Smeagols. Carol Reed's *The Third Man* (1949) captured a post-war divided Vienna in the film-noir classic starring Orson Welles as the slippery Harry Lime, who captured the amoral zeitgeist.

Now nowhere was safe, no one was an island – in a world on the brink of destruction. If the missiles did not reach you, the fall-out would.

Aldous Huxley imagined his own utopia in his last novel, *Island* (1960). This visionary novel lucidly describes an island where every strata of human life has been worked out in a wise and tolerant way. Alas, no man is an island – as the peaceful and unprotected inhabitants discover, when their resource-wealthy island paradise is invaded by belligerent and acquisitive neighbours, destroying its precious dream. Huxley once chillingly said: 'Maybe this world is another planet's Hell.' This is dystopian to the extreme, and seems especially bleak but is no more than the Cathars were burnt for. It echoes on a larger scale what Sartre said: 'Hell is other people.'

Huxley's view of humanity was cynical: the nihilist streak comes across clearly in his early novels (*Crome Yellow* 1921, *Antic Hay* 1923, *Point Counter Point* 1928) then flourishes in his nightmarish vision of the future *Brave New World* (1932). This nhilism is a virus that even infects his own vision of paradise on Earth – because he is realistic enough to realise the impossibility of a sustained utopia. Even if we somehow achieve a perfect state, humanity will always be the fly in the ointment.

This trope is used time and time again in J.G. Ballard's many dystopian novels, set in post-apocalyptic zones, where either flood (*The Drowned World 1962*), drought (*The Burning World* 1964), global warming (*The Day of Creation* 1987) or other disasters wreak havoc. In his later novels, (*Super-Cannes* 2000, *Kingdom Come* 2006) the islands become urban, high-tech elitist enclaves, yet they still explore the opulent decay he experienced as a boy in the colonial tropics (as portrated in his semi-autobiographical novel, *The Empire of the Sun*, 1984) and our anxiety about technology and the darker side of human nature. Indeed, the adjective 'Ballardian' has been included in the *Collins English Dictionary* where it is defined as 'resembling or suggestive of the conditions described in J.G. Ballard's novels and stories, especially dystopian modernity, bleak man-made landscapes and the psychological effects of technological, social or environmental developments.' In effect, Ballard is the prime psycho-geographer of manmade lost islands: highrise tower blocks, shopping malls, high-security compounds for the privileged, even the auto-erotic autonomy of automobiles (as in *Crash,* 1973, later a David Croneberg film).

Perhaps since the advent of psychoanalysis the portrayal of lost islands has altered – from an otherworldly paradise unspoilt by man, to one spoilt by man – when the Ideal meets the Shadow, in effect. This first started to be portrayed in popular culture around the time of fragmentation of the British Empire, with Kipling's *The Man Who Would Be King* (1888), which depicts what can happen when English gentlemen play god games with locals, and are duly punished for their hubris – the first inklings of white man's guilt perhaps, after decades of meddling in India? Kipling was the opposite of an apologist for British empire-building though – despite later being accused of jingoism. His children's novel *Puck of Pook's Hill* (1906) somewhat redeemed this, with an imaginative celebration of England's past through place-memory. Two children come across a mischievous guide who introduces them to England's dramatic past. It is a sortie through history which sums up something positive and enchanting about 'Merlin's Isle of Gramarye', as Kipling calls it in 'Puck's Song':

> She is not of any common earth,
> wood, water or air,
> but Merlin's isle of Gramarye
> where you and I shall fare.

This refers to *Clas Myrddin*, Merlin's Enclosure, as Britain was said to be known as, after its tutelary spirit. Merlin was said to live backwards, starting old, indeed wizened, and getting younger. The British sci-fi hero *Dr Who* seems to be a modern Merlin and guardian spirit of 'this small, damp island' – as the Eccleston-incarnation called it – similarly starting old (a frosty William Hartnell) and getting younger and more dynamic (the current incarnation is the youthful and energetic David Tennant). Merlin was said to end his career in a crystal cave, or in a tower made for him by his sister, Ganeida, with seventy-seven windows – which could describe the inside of the Doctor's time machine, the Tardis, akin to a time-travelling island. There is even an echo of the dynamic between Merlin and Nimue or Vivian, with the Doctor taking on a new (usually female) assistant each season or so – someone to download his timelordly wisdom onto, as he saves the world every week from yet another alien invasion or otherworldly villain. Dr Who has been repeatedly voted the most popular science fiction character of all time, and illustrates the British genius for the genre. For many disillusioned with the past, they look to the future for their lost islands.

Golden Age to New Wave

Arguably all science fiction deals with lost islands, with imaginal places that we project our desires and fears onto. The Fifties saw a rise in popularity of the genre, which began a long while previously – the writings of More, Swift and others had elements but it was not until Mary Shelley's *Frankenstein or the Modern Promotheus* (1818) that the genre was given life. Sci-fi provided a mirror in which to explore modern concerns about worrying trends, especially in technology. This accelerated with the race of progress, which reached its zenith in the Industrial Revolution and created its two founding fathers, Verne and Wells, who heralded the twentieth century with a raft of prophetic tomes. Belief in the benefits of technology was shot down in flames in the First World War, and the myth of progress took a severe blow. Maverick David Lindsay's *Voyage to Arcturus* (1920) was a was one of the first literary counterparts to the pioneering explorations of science fiction in the new medium of cinema, such as George Méliès *Le Voyage dans la Lune* (1902) and Fritz Lang's *Metropolis* (1926). Only in the Thirties did sci-fi stoires get off the ground again – this time charted in a darker way by the likes of Huxley and Olaf Stapledon (*Last and First Men* 1930, *Last Men in London* 1932, *The Starmaker* 1937) and in classic Silver Age films like *Things to Come* and *When Worlds Collide* – to be discussed in the final chapter, 'This Island Earth'. The Forties saw book production diminish through paper shortages, and not until the Fifties was the dormant genre was relaunched with gravity-defying velocity, thanks to the rocket scientists of the Second World War: it was the dawn of the Space Age.

Post-Hiroshima, in the shadow of the mushroom cloud that threatened Earth's destruction, lost islands became projected into the virgin utopia of space, from the Moon to Mars (most successfully in Ray Bradbury's 1950 novel *The Martian Chronicles*) and beyond. Many of these were nothing more than immrama in space – the oldest stories transposed to a new setting – Homer's odyssey in space, acknowledged by Arthur C. Clarke in *2001: A Space Odyssey* (1969). For America, this became the new frontier after the West was finally won. Originally called 'Wagon Trek to the Stars', the cult Sixties TV series *Star Trek* was basically an intergalactic immram – with its share of 'Celtic' crew (Scotty, McCoy, Kirk – all larger than life, like Conan, Dermot, Finn and Oisín – womanising and outwitting their way across the cosmos), and Isles of Woman, monsters and other wonders.

Back on Earth, writers were revisiting imaginary islands, or secondary worlds, in the wake of the explosion of interest in *The Lord of the Rings*, which spawned countless pastiches and rip-offs. 'Sword and Sorcery', as it became known, was back in vogue. Le Guin's original 'Earthsea' trilogy (1968–72) was one of the more superior manifestations of this.

Yet other writers explored lost islands in more serious ways, especially Keith Robert's alternate history *Pavane* (1968), which gave birth to the Steam-Punk genre – basically retro sci-fi. *Perdido Street Station* by China Mieville (2000) is a more recent example. Readers and writers were getting nostalgic for old school sci-fi, perhaps having grown up on 'Dan Dare: pilot of the future' in the original *Eagle* comic – itself a throwback to the 'Flash Gordon' and 'Buck Rogers' pulp serials of the Thirties.

More recent lost island fiction has explored the theme in a variety of ways. The Eighties saw a darkening vision and creative minds created their own *refugia* to sit out the bleak decade. Robin Hood burst back on our screens in Richard Carpenter's 'Robin of Sherwood' (a mid-1980s HTV production) – the wildwood being a lost island for outlaws and discontented souls of Thatcher's Britain: the dispossessed, the dissenters, the Poll Tax rioters and New Age travellers, who the Iron Lady famously called 'medieval brigands'.

Gwyneth Jones' *Bold as Love* (2001) and her subsequent novels have explored this counter culture in a near-future setting. A cataclysm has happened, and Britain has reverted to a neo-tribalism. This is a sub-genre called Future Primitive, as illustrated in the anthology of the same name: *Future Primitive: The new ecotopias*, edited by Kim Stanley Robertson (2004). Richard Jeffries' *After London, or Wild England* (1885) is possibly the earliest example of this – a reversion to an earlier state; a lower level of technology, a New Iron Age.

In the Seventies, with worries of a new global winter, either caused by 'global cooling' (at the time it was thought high levels of air-borne pollution would block out the sun's heat) or a nuclear winter this seemed to be the gloomy scenario envisaged by many writers, although some saw it not as a negative thing. TV sci-fi like Terry Nation's *Survivors* and *Doomwatch* had a certain morbid appeal. Fears of a Malthusian overcrowded world (as depicted in the movie *Soylent Green* 1973) triggered a desire for its opposite: a world emptied of queues, traffic jams, rules and the monotony of everyday living, where one had to focus on the basics of food, shelter, warmth, friendship – a primal dream.

Others explored this regression in the other direction – by going far back into the distant past. Robert Holdstock's *Mythago Wood* sequence (starting with the eponymous title of the series in 1984) ingeniously explores the lost island theme from the 'polder' perspective, an Old Dutch word for a tract of low-lying land reclaimed from a body of water and generally surrounded by dykes applied by John Clute and John Grant in their *Encyclopaedia of Fantasy* to describe 'Enclaves of toughened reality, demarcated by boundaries from the surrounding world.' (Clute and Grant 1999: 772) Polders have been used as a device throughout literature, and more recently in cinema, cropping up in Peter Weir's films, *Witness* (1985) and *The*

Truman Show (1998), Tim Burton's *Big Fish* (2003) and M. Night Shylaman's *The Village* (2004). The cinema auditorium itself is a kind polder, keeping reality at bay; as indeed is a book.

In Robert Holdstock's novel *Lavondyss* the fictional Ryhope Wood is a remnant of primal woodland that has somehow survived from the last Ice Age (like Wistman's Wood on Dartmoor) populated by the ghosts of our ancestral past, still contained in our memories and drawn out and given shape by the sentient wood. Holdstock terms these mythic images *mythagos* – a salient (or should that be sentient?) metaphor for how such atmospheric places stir the imagination and often get us 'seeing things', as in the 'mystery big cat' phenomenon. Wild places trigger the wild in us, possibly activating ancient parts of our cerebral cortex: the instinct of flight or fight, what has been termed 'panic' after the god who supposedly causes it, Pan.

Places such as Ryhope Wood are in effect 'enclaves of altered reality' separated from the surrounding world in the same way as the polders of fantasy writers. They harkback to an all-but lost medieval mythos of the 'wild wood' where all-too-real wolves, bears and boars still roamed and any number of elves, gremlins and other supposedly-real entities made life perilous for those who ventured therein. The mythos persisted into late eighteenth century moralistic tales such as 'Little Red Riding Hood'. To this day entering a wood means entering something different from most people's everyday experiences, as if entering an island-like parallel existence.

The New Wave (as the Sixties sci-fi writers were called) expired when it hit the sea wall of the millennium, for now we were living in the future – our imagined utopia or dystopia for so long – and reality was proving far more complex, surprising and tumultuous than anything envisioned. The map of reality was interfering with the map of fantasy too much. It was the end of Neverland.

The end of literature

The Nineties saw Alex Garland's *The Beach* (1996) develop a modern spin on the 'fly in the ointment' scenario, using the contemporary phenomenon of Generation X exiles heading for south-east Asia for consolation, inspiration and partying – to escape the doldrums of a Tory-blighted recession Britain with draconian measures, such as the Criminal Justice Act, outlawing gatherings and effectively killing off the massive rave culture which came out of the 'second summer of love', 1987, when 'acid' returned to the streets of Britain, providing the disaffected with a ticket to the lost islands in their heads, if not the return fare. With airfare going down in price, Generation X-ers fled Britain in droves, in search of acid arcadias; their own Xanadu. Garland's novel postulated a counter culture community on a remote Thai island, infiltrated by an interloper whose presence brings about its ruin. Failing to heed this lesson, some are trying to replicate the lost island ideal in TribeWanted.com (see the chapter 'No Place Like Home').

Booker-prize winner Ben Okri explored his own magical island in the beguiling god game *Astonishing the Gods* (1995). and *In Arcadia* (2002) he deconstructed the myth of the rural idyll, when he recounts how a television crew accompanied him on a train journey to the region in Peloponnesian Greece that gave its name to the 'ideal rustic paradise': Arcady.

At the cusp of the millennium, the Italian fabulist Umberto Eco explored *The Island of the Day Before* (1995), the story of a seventeenth century Italian nobleman who is the only survivor of a shipwreck during a fierce storm. He finds himself washed up on an abandoned ship in a harbour through which, he convinces himself, runs the International Date Line. Although he can see land, his inability to swim leaves him marooned and he begins to reminisce about his life and his love.

Lost island literature in the twenty-first century began with the success of David Mitchell's *Cloud Atlas* (2004) – set on a number of 'islands' in different periods (Chatham Islands in the nineteenth century, Belgium in 1931, California in 1975, present-day Britain, Korea in the near future, and Hawaii in a post-apocalyptic distant future) in a self-consciously erudite manner. And Yann Martel's Booker-winning *Life of Pi* (2001) is effectively a wonder tale, an unlikely journey (a boy and a tiger in a boat) complete with a carnivorous island – told straight, as all travellers' tales should.

Recent additions to the canon of lost island literature include Rupert Thomson's *Divided Kingdom* (2005) which portrays an alternative Britain segregated into four zones according to the medieval physic of the four humours. Andrea Levy's prize-winning *Small Island* (2004) depicts postwar Britain with its island mentality and endemic racism, as experienced by Caribbean immigrants, invited to the country to plug the male labour force gap left by the casualties of the Second Worrld War.

Even Bill Bryson's *Notes from a Small Island* (1995) plays on Britain's endearing and infuriating oddness, as does the cult television comedy show *Little Britain*. Brits like to laugh at themselves, and read about themselves, as do most people. We are all 'islanders' in that way – culturally discreet units. Each paradigm, period and place is a kind of island, indeed every book is.

It seems like the phenomenon of 'lost island' literature is not diminishing. With recent additions like John Connolly's *The Book of Lost Things* (2006) the list is long and still going strong.

Not in Kansas anymore

We have covered a lot of time since Plato's Atlantis – as Dorothy said in *The Wizard of Oz* (1939), 'We're not in Kansas anymore, Toto!' – although we inhabit the same space, in effect, that of a lost island. How Kansas becomes Oz is perhaps just a matter of perception. The writer re-presents reality to us and makes us reconsider our surroundings, our relationships. Novels help us to remember: they dislodge fragments of our own memories, and help us to recover what has been 'lost'. By sitting down and reading a book a theta state of mind is reached, often we become more reflective and things bubble up from the subconscious or long-term memory. In *The Child that Books Built* Francis Spufford comments on how books shaped him in his memoir of childhood and reading:

> My favourite books were the ones that took books' implicit status
> as other worlds, and acted on it literally, making the window of
> writing a window onto imaginary countries.

(Spufford 2002: 82)

All books are lost islands waiting to be found. Each one is a world of words. Reading it we enter the mind of the author, experience their paradigm, suspend disbelief (if it is a novel) or agree/disagree with their argument. Of course, some books are manuals, or full of trivia – it is not those that concern us here, but works of great literature – literary lost islands, which have took hold in the Western imagination, becoming almost real, as many fans of Middle Earth, Narnia and Hogwarts and a thousand and one other analogues for the imaginal would attest. Some would say this has unhealthy, and even some of the creators of these zones of terra incognita chose to destroy their own handiwork, as Rowling has done with the last fatal instalment of her 'magician's apprentice' *bildungsroman* septet, (*Harry Potter and the Deathly Hallows*, 2007) and as Lewis did in the final Narnia book (*The Last Battle*, 1956) where a giant rather implausibly crushes out the sun, like a sullen creator god destroying his toys in a fit of tantrum: an act of creative Ragnarok. Some, like Spufford, did not want to stop playing:

> Lewis might have felt the need to abolish his imaginary island, but
> his reasons were obscure to me; and when he pushed me to
> choose, I found that I didn't want to go through his Door into
> death. In the end, I did not want to be transformed. I wanted to
> linger on the island, not swim out to sea.

(Spufford 2002: 106)

The lost idyll is a theme that has fascinated writers and readers for a long time, and will no doubt continue to do so. Next we shall look at lost islands that exist in this world, when we go 'Walking on Brigadoon'.

Chapter three

Walking on Brigadoon

Exhausted and exhilarated they chased the sunset. Niamh's silver-shoon steed was so swift it seemed able to keep up with the rapidly retreating orb, the night forever at its heels but never quite catching it. And as the sun slipped over the horizon, they went with it on the last beam of sunlight to Tir nan Og.

And suddenly there it was before them, beyond all hope or probability. Floating between worlds, a paradox, a paradise. Its welcoming bays of snow-white sands, delightful plains, deeply-wooded hills, and distant peaks, were bathed in golden light. Niamh's steed made landfall, if you could define it as such. It was hardly terra firma, mused Oisín, as they dismounted, dropping into sand as soft as moss. He felt the warm sun on his face, the gentle sea-breeze on his skin, smelt the sharp tang of salt and seaweed, mixing bittersweet with the intoxicating perfume of Niamh.

And yet nothing felt stable.

It wasn't anything he could his finger on. That was the problem. It was only when he wasn't looking at something – a rock, a tree, an orchid – that it seemed to shift about. Shift colour. Shape. Become mineral. Vegetable. Animal. Things *moved*.

Oisín stared at a tree swaying in the wind. It seemed to be a giant hand, its trunk the wrist, its branches, fingers, from which leaves burst. Its bark was like skin. 'What kind of tree is that?'

'A palm tree,' waved Niamh nonchalantly, guiding her steed to a grove.

Oisín watched birds fly by, the colour of flowers, then he realised they *were* flowers. Flowers picked themselves, and fluttered away on petal-wings.

'Welcome to Tir nan Og,' Niamh smiled, her wind-teased hair snakes of living gold.

~~~~~~~~~~~~~~~~~~~~~~~~~

Arriving on an island is always a chancy business. Actually just *getting there* is never a sure thing, even before you make landfall. The ardours of the journey make us appreciate the fact of our arrival, of simply being there.

It takes a while to attune. An island insists, quietly, that we slow down, sense the stillness, listen to the silence. We have to pay attention because – this is it. A peninsular limits options as it dwindles to nothing, an island even more so. People choose to live in such places to keep the world at bay. But as visitors to an island we carry our own world within us – our personal history, our job, our home, family, partner, preoccupations. What has been the alluring 'otherworld' for so long becomes real, and the 'real world', back on the mainland, now becomes the allusive 'other', which we may or may not get back to – depending on the whims of the weather and the ferryman. These two worlds jostle for importance for the first day or two, as we undertake 'reality detox', until the 'otherworld' back home diminishes in importance and this new world gains precedence, becomes more real. All the concerns of our daily lives seem so petty in such a place: the arguments and anxieties over parking spaces, taking out the trash, doing the washing up. And the texture of its reality so false: the Legoland towns, the fads and fashions, the white noise of the media, the pontificating of the politicians, the posturing of celebrities.

On a small island, especially one with no electricity, flushing toilets, telegraph poles, metalled roads or lamp-posts, the visitor's concerns are reduced to the basics: food, water, shelter, warmth. Boiling up a kettle for hot water to do the washing up, or for a personal wash. Emptying the bucket of the outside loo into the sceptic tank. Carefully monitoring candles used for illumination in the evenings. Making sure you have everything you need because you cannot 'pop to the shops', although it turns out you do not need much at all – certainly not the clutter we fill our lives with back home. Apart from warm, all-weather clothing, a good book is perhaps the only essential for me. And a notebook and plenty of pens. If you are an artist maybe a sketchbook and watercolours, or a camera. Maybe a pair of binoculars if you are into birdspotting, a field guide or two and a flask… Enough for a daysack, but not much else. Perhaps you do not even need these. First and foremost we should be fully present: experience as directly and intimately and sensitively as possible what is around us. The mustard lichen on the low stone walls, a wild orchid among the grasses, the flash of a merlin from the clifftop, the mournful song of the seals by day, the eerie keening of the Manx shearwaters in the night.

But *before* this, we experience the island as an accretion of myth, of history, and perhaps personal experience, as historian Simon Schama points out in *Landscape and Memory* 'Before it can ever be a repose for the senses, landscape is the work of the mind, its scenery is built up as much from strata of memory as from layers of rock.' (Schama 1995: 6–7)

The island is always fluctuating in this way, between the perceived and the projected, between the actual and the imaginary. In his poem, 'Bifocal', William Stafford captures this phenomenon:

So, the world happens twice –
once what we see it as;
second it legends itself
deep, the way it is.

To differentiate between the two is often difficult, but perhaps we do not need to: to pigeonhole the world into the subjective and objective, into artificial mental categories is maybe missing the point. Surely, such places should be experienced holistically, with all their attendant layers and subtleties, undivided by man, the wall-builder?

There are a number of real 'lost islands' around the British Isles. These are islands that have an elusive quality about them, either in terms of physical accessibility (weather-dependent ferry services, tidal causeways), associations (mythic, religious, historical) or actual absence (flooded, subsided, destroyed). Although they *seem* to be empty vessels into which we have poured significance (by centuries of pilgrimage, hermitage, special environmental or heritage status, or sight-seeing) many have an undoubted 'atmosphere', independent of human presence: trees falling in a forest that still make a sound. And yet their nature is constantly shifting depending on our perception and interaction with them. This elusiveness endemic to lost islands could be defined as *ontological uncertainty*: not just in terms of being hard or impossible to find (because most of those featured in this chapter can be pinpointed on a map) but how islands can exist in two or more places at once – in the mythic and in the real.

First though, we must accept their physical presence. The existence of a super-abundance of islands around the coast of the British Isles is plain to see:

> Together, the territories conventionally called England, Ireland, Scotland and Wales comprise over 5,500 islands studding and separating the Atlantic Ocean and the North Sea.

(Macfarlane 2007)

I will not attempt to list or categorise all. Only those that have some kind of legendary nature or status concern us here – through their remoteness, otherness, sanctity or weirdness. Some are no more than rocky outcrops. Many more have been lost, or never were, or exist in other forms, for example, lost villages, drowned valleys, drained lakes and so forth – all of which I interpret as forms of lost island – interpreting 'islands' in its broadest sense (2. 'a thing that is isolated, detached, or surrounded' OED) . Every country has them, but as one that defines itself as an 'island nation' (or is perhaps defined by its insularity alone) we are adept at creating and destroying our own; be it with tourism, pollution or private ownership.

The Norman moat creates an artificial island. Middle English *mote* actually signified a mound – a similar topographical inversion to the Old English origins of the word 'island', which originally meant 'watery'.

Bardsey Island, looking north-west.

According to the cliché an Englishman's home is a castle, but a Brit's home seems to be an island. Britain, before borders, is a nation of island people, at least since the end of the last Ice Age when we were cut off from mainland Europe. Many find this insularity comforting, even more so on a small island (Bill Bryson called Great Britain a 'small island' in his successful travelogue, which has been voted in a 2003 poll the book that best-represented England). Adam Nicolson is the owner of the tiny Shiant Isles off the Isle of Harris, which he praises for its 'inwardness':

> The usual dream of a small island as a place of release is the opposite of truth: it is a place of enclosure – and comforting, restricting and inspiring because of that.

(Nicholson 2007)

This separation gives them their sacredness. Water defines an island, but it seems an intrinsic part of its sanctity, an incessant ablution and libation: 'According to traditional thinking, islands are inherently sacred, being places cut off from unwanted physical and psychic influences.' (Pennick 1996: 105)

Britain's insularity has helped protect it from both the Spanish Armada and the German invasion. Winston Churchill, in his famous speech of 4th June 1940, evoked a sense of patriotic stubbornness, the classic 'British bulldog' attitude: '… we shall defend our island, whatever the cost may be, we shall fight on the beaches… '. In its darkest hour, Britain was nearly 'lost', but its army, navy and air force saved the day, with the help of its Allies, and to this day Britain's Royal Navy is still a force to be reckoned with and respected throughout the world.

Of course, there are many other lost islands around the planet, but we shall continue to remain in British waters to prevent this book being inundated with examples: a twelve volume *Golden Bough* of lost islands! My purpose here is not encyclopaedic, but discursive and lateral. Brigadoons are, by their nature, elusive – they come and go. Trying to spot and list them comprehensively is too literal. With that in mind, let us bag some brigadoons, starting with the 'real McCoy'.

The fabrication of Brigadoon

There are several Brigadoons: the mythical, the musical and the Germanic to name some which bear that name. To begin with the most familiar: the mythical Brigadoon has entered the popular consciousness as any fabled place which has a tendency to fade away. This received notion is based upon the myth of an idyllic Scottish village that is said to appear for one day every century, its inhabitants and their homes magically preserved in a timewarp of quaint 'bonny-ness', of the shortbread tin variety. After the day was up the village would disappear taking any tardy visitors still there with it – not to be seen for another hundred years.

Yet this 'tradition' is invented folklore, based upon the Hollywood musical *Brigadoon* by Alan Jay Lerner and Frederick Loewe, first produced in 1947. The same story is told, but here the doom of Brigadoon is perceived by its inhabitants not as a curse, but a blessing: a covenant with God, according to which no one may ever leave the village or the preserving enchantment will be broken, making Brigadoon and its denizens disappear into the Scotch mist forever. The inevitable complications arise when two American tourists, curious about the fabled village, finally find it when lost in the Highlands. They stumble Brigadoon just as a wedding is about to be celebrated. One of them falls in love with a local lass and is faced with the predictable dilemma.

Yet although the musical coined the name Brigadoon and brought the myth to a wider audience, the idea for Lerner's story was actually based on a much older German story by Friedrich Gerstäcker about the mythical German village of Germelshausen that fell under an evil magic curse. In 1947, memories of the Second World War were too fresh to present a German-themed musical on Broadway, so Lerner reimagined the story in Scotland, complete with tartan kilts, bonnie lassies, droning bagpipes, Highland flings and 'Heather on the Hill'. Lerner's name for his imaginary locale was probably based on a well-known Scottish landmark, the Brig o' Doon (Bridge of Doon), in Alloway, Scotland, in the heart of Robert Burns country. According to Burns' poem Tam o'Shanter, this thirteenth century stone bridge is where the legendary Tam o' Shanter fled on his horse Meg in order to escape from three witches who were chasing him. Only half of the horse got away.

Bardsey Island (Ynys Enlli) looking towards Ireland

An incomplete guide to British lost islands

To attempt a comprehensive gazetteer would be a perhaps fool's errand, like successfully counting the megaliths of the Rollright Stones, Oxfordshire – famously difficult to do. With so many in around our coasts where does one draw the line? When does an islet become an island? And who could tell the difference between a skerrie, skellig, sgeir, eyot, eilean, inis, ynys, inch, isle, ailsa, élan, oilena – to list the native synonyms for the diverse types of islands these shores are blessed with. Accepting the incomplete nature of such a list, I shall provide an alphabetical selection of differing types to give a general overview.

Anglesey
Called the 'Mother of Wales', *Mona, Manna* or *Ynys Môn* is a large, flat, and often desolate-seeming island – swept by sheets of rain from the Irish Sea. For many it is just the route to the ferry terminus at Holyhead: a blurry, sleepy outline at some ungodly hour too or from Ireland. At one point it was an important centre for Iron Age druidry – a fact corroborated by the effort to which the Romans took to crush it. In 61 CE the infamous massacre of Anglesey took place, as vividly reported by Tacitus, by a legion led by Seutonius Paulinus:

> Women were seen rushing through the ranks of soldiers in wild
> disorder, dressed in black, with their hair dishevelled and

brandishing flaming torches. Their whole appearance resembled the frantic rage of the furies. The druids were ranged in order, calling down terrible curses. The soldiers, paralysed by this strange spectacle, stood still and offered themselves as a target for wounds. But at last the promptings of the general – and their own rallying of each other – urged them not to be frightened of a mob of a women and fanatics. They advanced the standards, cut down all who met them and swallowed them up in their own fires. After this a garrison was placed over their conquered islands, and the groves sacred to savage rites were cut down.

So ruthlessly efficient was this destruction a carved hazel rod from the period is all that has been found there. Yet the island has some remarkable monuments from the early Neolithic: the well-preserved Bryn Celli Ddu with its carved stones (one inside the chamber); and dramatically situated Barclodia-y-Gawres, the 'giantesses apronful' on the coast, now covered by a concrete dome to protect the five carved stones there. Fiercely Welsh, the island people are as singular as any insular race, yet are not without their humour. In 2005, a Hoipolloi/Hugh Hughes Production based upon Anglesey's 'oddness' toured Britain. This is from the flyer:

> April 1, 1982
>
> Hugh Hughes prepares to make his first tentative steps off the Isle of Anglesey. Suddenly the Menai Bridge collapses before him and the island begins to shift away from the Welsh mainland. With the islanders celebrating their newfound independence around him, Hugh seems to be the only one desperate to return Anglesey to its rightful home.

To this day, Anglesey maintains its stubborn independence, in spirit at least.

Anthrax island

During the Second World War Gruinard Island, Scotland – near the mouth of Little Loch Broom – was deliberately contaminated with the anthrax bacillus as part of a biological warfare experiment, like a smaller version of the irradiated Christmas Island, original home of the atom bomb tests. It is still not safe to return.

Bardsey

Bardsey is a seemingly austere island of many facets, ones revealed with each subsequent visit. A document written at the time of the consecration of Llandaff Cathedral in 1120 records:

> …it has been for ages a proverbial saying among the Welsh that this is the 'Rome of Britain', on account of its distance – it is situated in the extremity of the kingdom – and the danger of the sea voyage, and also because of the holiness and charm of the place; holiness, for twenty thousand bodies of the saints, both confessors and martyrs, lie buried there; charm, since it is surrounded by the sea with a lofty headland on the eastern side

*View from south tower,
fourteenth century Augustinian
ruin, Bardsey Island (Ynys
Enlli).*

and a level, fertile plain where there is a spring of sweet water on
the western side.

An island like Bardsey readily attracts such myths and legends as its 'sparseness'
makes it a negative space into which pagan and Christian dreams have been
projected. At one point a Culdee sect seems to have settled there – entirely likely
considering it was on the main 'highway' of the sea – the earliest Christians of these
isles whose brand of Celtic Christianity is said to contain remnants of druidry:

> Beyond Llyn there is a small island occupied by some extremely
> devout monks called Coelibes or Colidei, either because of its
> pure air which comes across the sea from Ireland, or because of
> some miracle occasioned by the merits of the holy men who live
> there the island has this peculiarity, that no-one dies there except
> of extreme old age, for disease is unheard of. In fact no-one dies
> there at all unless very old indeed. The bodies of a vast number of
> holy men are buried there, or so they say, among them that of
> Deiniol, Bishop of Bangor. (ibid.)

Its founding saint, St Cadfan, apocryphally negotiated with God that any who were
buried there would go straight to heaven '… to be buried on it became the desire of
devout Christians in Northern Wales, for they believed it to be the very porch of
heaven.' (Adair 1978: 166)

Leaving Bardsey.

Bardsey became 'des res for the dead', and consequently the Isle of Twenty Thousand Saints – probably an over-estimation, but when work was done on the one stone track that crosses the island countless bones were found. In one ruin alone, which a speculator wanted to rebuild, thirty skeletons were found. The building remains a haunted shell.

Another Celtic luminary is said to be 'at rest' there: Merlin. Within his tower of seventy-seven windows, built for him by his sister Ganeida, he guards the legendary Thirteen Treasures of Britain referred to by Geoffrey of Monmouth. The square-towered lighthouse seems to be a modern analogue for this; the refracted facets of its globe like those numerous windows, an inverted crystal cave from where he was said to view the world. The Victorian lighthouse brought some official recognition to the island. The boatman charged with keeping the lighthouse supplied, Love Pritchard, became the most important person on the island, and soon developed delusions of grandeur. He fashioned for himself a tin crown and became the self-proclaimed 'King of Bardsey'. When fortunes waned, Pritchard left with 'his people' in the Twenties – his departure was a nine-day wonder in the press. Some returned, but the viability of Bardsey as a sustainable community was lost.

Now only one traditional farming family remains: their herds of black-backed cattle and sheep are ferried to the island in the summer and returned to the mainland in winter, along with the family. The empty schoolhouse is used for poetic gatherings and a weekly talk on the history of the island given by the long-term poet-in-residence Christine Evans. The island's main income is from retreatants, holidaymakers, bird-spotters and those undertaking scientific fieldwork, who stay in the Bird and Field Observatory. Wandering the island, you could bump into a twitcher, artist, wildlife photographer or dolphin-watcher, but there is plenty of space to avoid company if solitude is what you are after, and plenty of time to stand and stare on an island inhabited by, so locals say with a wink, 'time-eating goblins'. There is no rush, no stress – the gentle days marked by silent dawns and spectacular sunsets over the Wicklow Mountains far into the west. It is a place of deep peace and beauty.

Brownsea Island

Surrounded by some of the most expensive property in the world, in the centre of the world's second-largest natural harbour, the nature reserve of Brownsea was famously home to the first Scout Camp, led by Baden-Powell, it was the inspiration for Enid Blyton's Famous Five books, and currently the sanctuary of native red squirrels, shooed off the mainland by their interloper grey cousins. It is fictional space in other ways. In the BBC Radio 4 programme 'Brownsea Island: For Nature, Not Humans', (broadcast 10 April 2007), Alan Leith told the story of an eccentric recluse, Mary Florence Bonham Christie, who purchased the island in 1927. She banned people from its shores and allowed the animals on the island to roam free. Christie's Brownsea was a human-created micro-wilderness. The island remains an important nature reserve, owned by the National Trust. Day visits are permitted, via Poole.

Caldey Island

Caldey, off Tenby on the Pembrokeshire Coast, is one of a small handful of 'gender islands' still left. Monks first came to Caldey in the sixth century. Pyro, the first abbot, is remembered in the island's Welsh name, Ynys Byr. Pyro was followed by St Samson, from the Celtic monastery at Llantwit Major. Viking raids may have ended this settlement in the tenth century. The island's name 'Caldey' comes from the Viking name *keld eye* meaning 'cold island'. It is now the home to an all-male Cistercian Order, who rise daily at 3.15 a.m. for the first of seven rounds of daily prayer. Public can visit, attend services and buy Caldey produce (perfume, chocolate, shortbread) from the gift shop.

Crannogs

Crannogs are a type of ancient loch-dwelling found throughout Scotland and Ireland (one has been discovered in Wales in Llangorse Lake). Most are circular structures that seem to have been built as individual homes to accommodate extended families. Other types of loch settlements are also found in Scandinavian countries and throughout Europe. Crannogs are also known as artificial or modified natural islands and they were as much a product of their environment as the period in which they were constructed.

The earliest loch-dwelling in Scotland is some 5,000 years old but people built, modified, and re-used crannogs in Scotland up until the seventeenth century CE. Throughout their long history crannogs served as farmers' homesteads, status symbols, refuges in times of trouble, hunting and fishing stations, and even holiday residences. In Highland Perthshire, the prehistoric crannogs were originally timber-built roundhouses supported on piles or stilts driven into the lochbed. Loch Tay has a large cluster of them (at least eighteen) and a reconstruction based upon the 2,600 year-old Oakbank crannog can be visited at The Scottish Crannog Centre, Kenmore. The original Oakbank crannog, which dates from 500 BCE, was a circular timber platform with a large timber roundhouse built on oak piles driven deep into the loch bed. The walls were made of hazel rods, woven together, and the thatched roof was steeply pitched to allow rain to drain off. Inside, the floor was covered with bracken and ferns, with a flat, stone fireplace in the centre which would have been kept burning continuously and would have been the focus of family life.

In more barren environments and in later periods tonnes of rock were piled onto the loch bed to make an island on which to build a stone house. Today the crannogs appear as tree-covered islands or remain hidden as submerged stony mounds. Several hundred have been discovered so far in Scotland although only a few have been investigated.

Perhaps the most dramatic example of a prehistoric artificial island is Flag Fen, near Peterborough – not strictly speaking a crannog, it still shares many similarities. See the chapter 'Stick in the Mud' for information about this and the Glastonbury Lake Village, another crannog-like structure.

Diana's island

In a nod to her mythic name and fate, the late Princess Diana was said to have been laid to rest on an island in a lake at Althorpe, the Spencer estate near Northampton. However, this seems to have been a ruse to throw morbid tourists and potential grave robbers off the scent. She was apparently laid to rest in the family vault at the nearby church, St John's, Little Brington. The watery memorial in Hyde Park was an allusion to this 'Isle of Diana', one that was widely accessible to tourists, similarly diverting them from her actual resting place. The memorial's flowing design was intended to 'reflect Diana's life' and symbolise her 'quality and openness' (www.royalparks.org.uk, accessed 20/0707). Both are modern examples of 'isles of the dead', illustrating the mythic power such places have. Such islands are cut-off from everyday life – we can visit it to pay our respects and then gratefully return.

Grassholm

A tiny, uninhabited island off south-west Pembrokeshire in Wales, lying west of Skomer, Grassholm (Welsh: *Gwales* or *Ynys Gwales*) is the westernmost part of Wales and is known for its huge colony of gannets. It is associated with the legend of Bran from *The Mabinogion*, where it is referred to as Gwales.

In the story, seven survivors of the raid on Ireland to win back Bran's sister, Branwen, from Matholwch, carry Bran's head first to Harlech, Cardigan Bay, where the war-weary warriors are consoled by the magical birds of Rhiannon. They then continue their journey south – for they have been tasked to take their leader's head to the White Mount in London to be buried. On the way they stop at Gwales, finding a strong-doored chamber. They enter and their leader's head miraculously comes to life and sings to them. For eighty years they are under its spell until one of them opens a forbidden door – breaking the enchantment and causing all their woes to

The Isle of Man's famous Laxey Wheel with its 'legs of man' insignia.

come flooding back. Unaged, the seven resume their quest, taking the head to the White Mount, where it was buried facing France – to defend the kingdom from its sea-borne enemies, until King Arthur dug it up (one of 'Three Unfortunate Disclosures'). Gwales is one of many similar examples of mythological topography – from *The Mabinogion,* The Matter of Britain, and many local folktales – creating a British Dreamtime, the analogue Rainbow Serpent being the glacial Würm.

Iona

A small island, located in the Inner Hebrides, Scotland, the name itself evokes an atmosphere of otherworldliness. Mike Scott of The Waterboys chants it in his song, 'Peace of Iona' (released on the album *Universal Hall* in 2003). Iona has an important place in the history of Christianity in Scotland and is popular for its tranquility and natural beauty. Its Gaelic name is *Ì Chaluim Cille* (Saint Columba's Island), or sometimes jus t *Ì* or *Idhe*. When St Columba founded his monastery there in 563 CE, St Oldham (otherwise known as Brother Oran) volunteered to be buried alive in the new cemetery as a foundation offering. After a while he emerged, and mysteriously spoke the following – 'Hell is not as it is thought to be' (Palmer 2008: 44) – before descending once more for good. It remains a place of pilgrimage and sanctity.

Isle of Man

The Isle of Man, in the middle of the Irish Sea, known in Roman documents as *Monapia, Manavia, Manavi* and as *Ellen Vannin* in Manx. It is 33 miles long, 14 miles wide, and 227 square miles in total and said to be named after its tutelary deity, Manannan Mac Lir, who protects the island with a cloak of mist.

Man has a legend of a strange inland sea. Nennius, (a.k.a. Gildas) describes it as 'a strand without a sea… a ford which is far from the sea, and which fills when the tide flows, and decreases when the tide ebbs' and 'a stone which moves at night in Glen

Left: *A Manx police officer guards Tynwald Hill.*
Right: *Tynwald Day, July 5th. Manx parliament in session.*

Cinden, and though it should be cast into the sea, yet at morning's dawn it would be found in the same valley' (cited in Moore 1891). Man also has more than its fair share of fairy lore, with a cast of peculiar characters unique to the island. Its language is distinctive, a kind of phonetic Gaelic; and its place-names are a blend of Celtic and Norse. It is a singular place, stuck in many ways in a Fifties time-warp, with horse-drawn trams, seaside old-fashionedness and strange customs. Famed for its tail-less cats; the three-legged man, the Triskel, the national symbol; and the TT motorcycle races, it has the longest-running parliament in Europe, which convenes on Tynwald Day, 5 July, every year. All laws must be proclaimed from Tynwald Hill in Manx and English, and any petitions to the government, a Crown Sovereignty, are made on that day.

As well as its own laws (as symbolised by the policeman sporting white pith helmets), it has its own tax system, making it a popular haven for the rich. The well-heeled rub shoulders with bikers – who flock to the island in their hordes for the races – and Vikings attending the annual week long Peel Viking Festival. It has an abundance of impressive prehistoric sites. See the 'Stick in the Mud' chapter for the archaeology of Man, and the 'Phantom islands' section of this chapter for further discussion of its legends.

Isles of Scilly

Dedicated to the goddess Sillina (possibly connected with Sul of *Aquae Sulis*, Bath), referred to as the Fortunate Isles by the Greeks and Romans, and even called by some archaeologists the 'isles of the dead', the Isles of Scilly have attracted romantic speculation for a long time. They have an agreeable sub-tropical climate, sitting right in the Gulf Stream, making it feel Mediterranean with its palm trees, warm, pellucid waters and fine white sands. Like the Isle of Man, the Scilly Isles seem stuck in a Fifties time-warp, with few cars (unlocked at that). There are many burial chambers,

The original Troy Town maze, St Agnes, constructed circa 1729. Many others now litter the Isles of Scilly.

hence the archaeologists' appellation, including two for King Arthur (in case one was not enough!). Until the end of the Ice Age they were connected to the mainland of Cornwall, and until the end of the Roman era it was one island. Now it is an archipelago of hundreds of islets, some that could fit no more than a seagull. Stories of a drowned land – Kêr-Ys or Lyonesse, with bells beneath the deep – are less likely to be ancient folk memory than inspired by the occasional glimpse of submerged forests and the ship bells of the many shipwrecks in those notoriously treacherous waters now guarded by the Wolf and the Bishop's Rock lighthouses. The Neolithic stone rows on the beach of Bryher, exposed at low tide, attest to its former coastline, and its distinctive pebble-lined miz-mazes, known as Troy Towns, prove to some that it is a colony of Atlantis – although the first was made by a lighthouse keeper *circa* 1729.

From the remote campsite on rugged St Agnes, gazing out over the wild Atlantic towards the setting sun, it is easy to succumb to the enchantment of the place, especially after a pint or three in The Turk's Head, Britain's most south-westerly pub.

Kimber

On Salisbury Plain, Wiltshire, there is the lost village of Kimber, evacuated and used for Second World War training. It remains frozen in time, untouched by normal human habitation. It is off-limits except for a brief window every year, when it can be visited by those willing to hike across MOD land. It stands eerie and silent, like something out of the Quatermass Experiment or a John Wyndham book, a military Brigadoon.

Lundy

Called by some the 'Isle of Avalon', this small island in the mouth of the Severn has accreted its own legends. In *The Measure of Albion: The lost science of prehistoric Britain* (2004) John Michell and Robin Heath reveal that if a bearing is taken from the exact centre of Stonehenge due west it hits Lundy at a point marked precisely by a round barrow – and if a line of the same distance is taken north from this point of the same length, it intersects with the Preseli mountains in Pembrokeshire, where the

Looking towards Steep Holm from Brean Down, Somerset, where Dion Fortune set the temple in her 1920s novel The Sea Priestess:

> Bell Head sticks straight out into the sea, pointing towards
> America, and when the wind is westerly the great Atlantic rollers
> come driving in without let or hindrance, which is why we have
> such heavy seas on the point. It is formed of cocked-up strata,
> lying slab-like one upon another; this gives a steep drop along the
> exposed edges of the strata, formed a ledged precipice. The top is
> weathered fairly flat, and rises whale-like to the highest point
> above the precipice that faces the land. Then there is a narrow
> neck of detritus connecting what was probably once an island
> with the mainland, beside which lies the ancient channel of the
> river Dick, now a runnel in wet weather and dry at other times,
> being fed from no source.

bluestones of Stonehenge come from, forming a right angle with Lundy at its corner, and apparently Lundy was known as the 'Angled Place', although its name actually means 'puffin island'. It is now owned by the Landmark Trust, who let out a number of quirky properties, including a castle, lighthouse, pig sty, radio room and barracks. There is a pub, shop and post office, and a regular turnover of tourists, brought by the SS Oldenburg from Ilfracombe and Bidecombe. It has been designated an official 'no take' zone, with the consent of local fisherman, to protect its varied marine life.

Phantom islands

Brigadoon is akin to many 'phantom islands'. The Isle of Man has an abundance, mainly off the south-east coast, around the Langness peninsula and off Jurby. The common legend of these submerged islands goes:

> Once in seven years it rose to the surface and it was said that, if it stayed long enough for someone to place a Bible on it and so sanctify it, the enchantment that held it submerged would be broken and it would never disappear again.
>
> (Killip 1986: 138)

Yet it seems not even the Church is immune to such fabulating, for a phantom island is enshrined in the Diocese of Sodor and Man, the 'See of Sodor' being a place of negligible existence possibly off Langness, but the Bishop would have to get his cassock wet to visit it (Killip 1986: 139–40).

The 'Western Land' can apparently be glimpsed in the Irish Sea in certain weather conditions – 'especially at sunset', a dark silhouette on a second horizon over the sea. There are many recorded sightings from the west coast of Ireland, as D.R. McNally recount in his *Irish Wonders*:

> At his own sweet will it comes and, having shown itself long enough to convince everybody who is not an 'innocent entirely' of its reality, it goes without leave taking or ceremony, and always before boats can approach near enough to make careful inspection. This is the invariable history of its appearance.
>
> (McNally 1981)

Changing location and appearance, sometimes a woodland or a shining city, 'attest to the skill of the enchanter who controls it' (McNally 1981). One can almost smell the blarney here, as though some winking locals are winding up a visitor with tall tales, to milk another jar, or more tourist dollars from them with such fairy gold. Yet who knows, perhaps Ireland, alone in the world, is favoured by vanishing islands, in the same way perhaps Wiltshire seems particularly favoured by people who believe in alien intelligences communicating in crop circles?

Yet Wales it seems has its fair share of disappearing islands too. From Pembrokeshire comes the legend of the 'green isles of the sea':

> A century ago, so the tradition says, sailors on the coast of Pembrokeshire had actually landed on islands out at sea where the Plant Rhys Ddwfn, children of Rhys the Deep, lived. This was the name given in West Wales to the Fair Folk, the Ty'wyth Teg, or, if you like, Fairies. The curious thing was that when the sailors returned to their boats, the islands simply vanished from view.
>
> (Roberts 1974)

Similar phantom island were recorded by Gerald of Wales in his tour, the *Itinerarium Cambriae*: Llangorse Lake, which had red and green oracular currents (apparently caused by myriads of water beetles), opulent fish and occasionally, its surface covered with buildings or gardens and orchards...In effect, a mobile Rorshchach test: the gazer projects whatever they wish onto it. Or is this a case of place memory? For actually it seems to have been a crannog. Lake Bala (or Llyn Tegid) in north Wales, is said to be bottomless and has a similar legend of a lost village – the bells heard at certain times – and a monster to boot, of the Loch Ness variety. It seems the deeper the lake, the more we project into it. We see what we want to.

Priest islands

The cult Irish sitcom *Father Ted* is set on the fictional 'Craggy Island' and however absurd, is only the latest in a long line of actual 'priest islands', many of which have the tag of 'papa':

- Priestholm, Anglesey

- Priest Island, north of Loch Broom

- Papa Little, Papa Stour – Shetlands

- Papa Stronsay, Papa Westhay (where the last Great Auk was shot in 1813) Orkneys

- Pabbay, close to Barra, Hebrides

Also many bear the names of saints:

- Barry Island, near Cardiff – St Barruc (buried there)

- St Patrick's Island, close to Peel, Isle of Man

- St Tudwal's, two islands which lie two miles south of Abersoch, off Llyn

- Inishceatha (dedicated to St Caimin) Lough Derg, County Clare

- Our Lady's Island, South of Rosslare in County Wexford

- St Patrick's Purgatory, Lough Derg (both pilgrimage places)

An amusing 'footnote': the remote Arran islands of Inis More and Inis Oirr off County Galway competed for the dubious accolade of the 'real Craggy Island', with its attendant lucrative tourist trade. The matter was disputed vigorously, becoming a media-fuelled feud – finally settled in a suitably Ted-esque way, over a five-a-side football match. Inis More won and hosted the first Tedfest, complete with Funland and 'lovely girl' contests. Due to the success of the match, which attracted wide interest, it was decided to make it and the festival an annual event, with the winning side, comprising of the respective islanders, being awarded 'the real Craggy Island' for that year. (Brown 2007)

Lyn Tegid, or Lake Bala, is claimed to be bottomless, haunted by a monster, and the location of a lost village. It certainly has a numinous quality, fed as it is by mythic streams – Aber Gwenwen y Maych (the Stream of the Poisoned Horses) feeds into it – as featured in the legend of Taliesin.
Photo: Bob Trubshaw

Private islands

When an island becomes privately owned it becomes 'lost' to the public, with rare exceptions where limited public access is allowed, for example, by the Duchy of Cornwall. The smaller ones are firmly 'off limits', for instance Adam Nicolson's Shiant (mentioned above). Some you take your life into your hands if you dare to trespass. Sealand, is a rusting gun platform in the North Sea off Suffolk. Built in 1942 to shoot down German aircraft, it stationed up to 300 servicemen. Abandoned ten years after the war ended, in 1967 a former British Major, Paddy Roy Bates, occupied the fort after ejecting some competing pirate broadcasters. Bates claimed sovereignty and after firing a shot across the bow of a passing Royal Navy shop, the British court held that the platform was in international waters and outside its jurisdiction, giving Bates a de facto claim to independence, so it became a self-declared principality (with its own currency and flag). Still occupied, it has just started to host visitors again, but do not go calling uninvited.

However elitist, there is an undeniable appeal in the notion of owning an island, so international island broker, Farhad Vladi suggests:

Mont St Michel, Brittany – the sister site to St Michael's Mount, Cornwall.

'There is a sense of romance in buying islands…It is the ultimate purchase you can make, a complete miniature world of which you can become king… '

(cited in McIntosh 2004)

But what if there's a revolution? Off the Western Isles, the Isle of Eigg was owned by a wealthy Dutchman, Keith Schellenberg, until the laird was ousted by the locals who bought back their island and now run it collectively – for once a victory for the 'little guy' as recorded inspiringly in Alastair McIntosh's *Soil and Soul*.

Tidal islands

Islands separated from the mainline twice a day always have a Brigadoon-like quality to them. At high-tide they are out of reach to all but boats and helicopters, then suddenly the intrepid pedestrian can access them – but take too long and you can be stuck there! There are several off the coast of Britain including Northey (Essex) – site of the Battle of Maldon in 991 CE when an army of Danish raiders challenged the locals and lost; Cramond Island (Firth of Forth); the holy island of Lindisfarne (Northumberland) where the ruins of the eleventh century priory are said to be where the remains of St Cuthbert were discovered in 698 – undecomposed eleven years after he was buried there; St Michael's Mount, Marazion, Cornwall; and Gugh (Isles of Scilly), with its cluster of Bronze Age sites and three residents.

Worm's Head at low-tide, Gower Peninsula.

One of my favourites is Worm's Head on the Gower Peninsular, a serpent-like isthmus of land that can only be reached at low-tide. The energetic can reach all the way to the 'head' but you have to watch your step – there are lots of hairy drops, especially the sea-arch – and watch the time, because there is a risk, as on all of these tidal islands, of being trapped. Time and tide wait for no one.

Seeking the archipelagic

There are many other islands around the shores of Britain and Ireland, each with its own layering of myth, legend, history, folklore and fact: both sets of Arran Isles, the Channel Islands, Faroe Isles, Lindisfarne/Holy Island, Orkney, the Shetlands and the Western Isles. All are within reach to the intrepid island-hopper. Here we have looked at only a handful but if nothing else I hope this selection has provided an appetiser for you to explore and experience these places yourself and create your own incomplete guide.

Robert Macfarlane discussed the difficulty in describing the body of writing about such littoral territories as islands in his article 'Go Wild in the Country' (Macfarlane 2007). 'Nature writing', 'pastoral' or 'environmental' do not serve he complained:

> Perhaps the adjective 'archipelagic' might serve, catching as it
> does at imaginings that are chthonic, marine, elemental and felt.

Seekers on the Gower Peninsula.

Macfarlane claimed 'a tradition of archipelagic writing goes as far back as the Celtic peregrine of the sixth to tenth centuries AD: the monks, solitaries and pilgrims who travelled west to live on the remote littorals of Britain and Ireland, and who left behind them a literature that is devotedly alert to place' (Macfarlane 2007). This celebration of place through culture – poetry, painting, music – helps to forge a sense of belonging, of community and nationality. As Simon Schama pointed out, 'National identity… would lose much of its ferocious enchantment without the mystique of a particular landscape.' (Schama 1995: 15)

Numerous kinds of cultural 'lost islands' – that is rare and wonderful things, or just plain peculiar (postboxes, village jails, Morris dancing, white horse hill-figures, even cooling towers) – are listed in Sue Clifford and Angela King's brimming national miscellany, *England in Particular* (2006), which celebrates what they call 'local distinctiveness', something their organisation, Common Ground, campaigns for: the biodiversity of English culture, not in competition to anything else, but to be recorded and preserved. Like types of apple or ale – if we were limited to one choice, life would be considerably blander. 'Local distinctiveness' aims to stem the tide of homogeneity.

This tradition of the 'archipelagic imagination' has ebbed and flowed over the centuries, but Macfarlane believes it is presently 'unmistakably surging'. The tide which draws us to these places today flows against the mainstream. Like the monks of old, tomorrow's ardent lost islander will be driven to increasingly more inhospitable and inaccessible places to get 'away from the tourists' (wildcamping being the latest craze). But it is a doom we take with us. All we can do is travel consciously if we must. A journey with a deeper purpose than just recreation, especially a spiritual one, becomes a pilgrimage.

But the pilgrim does not embark unless they are prepared to be changed, so be warned. The place we arrive at will be altered by our experience of travelling there.

By now you should have itchy feet and wish to visit at least one of these brigadoons – but mind your step as you take to the pilgrim's road...

Chapter four

To be a pilgrim

Oisín couldn't believe he was finally here. Walking on the beach of Tir nan Og. The sand, the sea, the waves, the wind, the warm sun – all seemed real enough, but for all of his life the Island of the Ever Young had been a legend, a place souls were said to go to in death – but nobody knew for sure. He waxed lyrical about it as poets are wont to do, and made the listener yearn for it, as Niamh had done to him with her song, but even Oisín had doubted at times. And then the call had come. It had been the most spontaneous of pilgrimages, although it was less for divine love, as for love of Niamh and her golden hair. How many others had alighted on these shores on the ultimate journey – the final pilgrimage of death? Would dearly missed friends, loved ones, ancestors, even enemies be here – in this place beyond the setting sun? The Fenian poet knelt and sank his hands into the sand, scooping it up and watching it trickle through his fingers in delightful fascination. Each one seemed to contain a world.

'Poet, stop playing in the sand and get up!' Niamh commanded briskly. 'We've got company.'

~~~~~~~~~~~~~~~~~~~~~~~~~~~~~~~~

Pilgrimage has been a popular activity for millennia. It was well-known in Classical Greece and Rome. Chaucer's pilgrims in the fourteenth century could not resist the call, the stirring of the blood and soul that spring brings in northern Europe:

> Whan that Aprill with his shoures soote
> The droghte of March hath perced to the roote
> And bathed every veyne in swich lycour
> Of which vertu engendred is the flour;
> When Zephirus eek with his sweete breeth
> Inspired hath in every holt and heath
> The tendre croppes…
> Than longen folk to goon on pilgrimages.
>
> (*The Canterbury Tales*)

Grave of John Bunyan, author of The Pilgrim's Progress, *Bunhill Fields Dissenters' Cemetery, London*

The word 'pilgrim', so Jennifer Westwood tells us in her book on pilgrimage, *Sacred Journeys* (1997), derives from the Latin for 'wanderer' or 'stranger', *peregrinus*. The deeper definition of a pilgrim is a person who makes a journey, usually over a long distance, to a sacred place as an act of religious devotion. Tellingly, it is a noun *and* a verb: it is only through action and intent one becomes a pilgrim. This earnest and immediate calling is part of its appeal '… a pilgrimage could be done: it was devotion pitched in the language of action rather than belief.' (Adair 1976:14)

The act of pilgrimage transforms the pilgrim, and also his or her perception of the final destination. To arrive at say, Santiago de Compestala, perhaps the most famous pilgrim route in the West (as made even more famous by Paulo Coelho's book, *The Pilgrimage,* 1987) after a 900 km trek across Spanish mountains is to arrive in an altered state of consciousness. This is what the pilgrimage is meant to do. Those who arrive by coach or train – as at Machu Piccu, Peru, circumventing the four-day Inca Trail – miss out in more ways than one. They arrive, but fail to experience it as a pilgrim should. Their perceptions have not been altered by the rigours of the journey. They are not exhausted, emotionally and physically – feet blistered, sunburnt, drenched in sweat, kneeling and kissing the ground in gratitude, in a state of euphoria. They fail to connect. They tick off another item on their itinerary, take some photographs in a vain attempt to steal the soul of the place – to take away some of its 'magic' but when they get home and get them printed, the pictures they have taken never do it justice. They have come away with fairy gold – crumbling dry leaves in their hands.

To such tourists, these sites remain 'lost islands' – they travel to them, pay the admission fee, but actually fail to find them. Such places hide in plain site and only reveal their mystery to the initiated – to those who have taken the initiatory journey, who have altered states of consciousness through fatigue, hunger, oxygen-starvation, and silent communion with nature.

Compounding this is the mindset of the devotee. To all but the devote Muslim, Mecca seems to be a giant dark box – the black box recorder of the Muslim world, absorbing the countless prayers of the devoted – which the pilgrims circle in an awe-struck daze, rather like the apes around the alien monolith in Stanley Kubrick and Arthur C. Clarke's *2001: A Space Odyssey*. That is not to say it is not a sacred place, of course, or that the pilgrims are ape-like! Both Clarke and Kubrick may have had this iconography at the back of their minds when creating the famous scene, in effect an alien cargo cult.

Far more ridiculous is when tourists flock to pay homage, in a pseudo-religious way, to such landmarks such as Mount Rushmore in North America with the Presidents' faces carved into it, or some giant Technicolor statue of Johnny Appleseed, the Jolly Green Giant, Michael Jackson, or Saddam Hussein, Stalin, the North Korean President or their ilk. Kitsch icons, which act as substitutes for the genuine 'pilgrim fix'.

Yet all pilgrimage is an act of madness, of folly – and that is not such a bad thing, and in comparison to the insanity of 'the real world', a small craziness – and each pilgrim becomes a holy fool, as epitomised by the tarot card of The Fool.

The visionary artist Cecil Collins wrote eloquently about 'The Vision of the Fool' in his book of that name (1981), illustrated with several of his faux-naïf fool paintings:

> Our society has rejected the Fool, not only because he cannot be
> exploited, not only because he cannot be exploited, not only
> because they judge everything by its usefulness; but they are
> frightened and disturbed by the Fool, because he is the child of
> life, and of abstract virtue. The Fool is purity of consciousness.

(Collins 1981 (1994: 74))

To wander is to wonder. The pilgrim becomes the child of the world with a freshness of perception akin to the boy in Hans Christian Anderson's fairy tale, 'The Emperor's New Clothes', who sees the folly of authority for what it is because he is the only one not programmed to see what he is told to see, the only one who dares speaks the truth.

When people refuse to listen to the truth sometimes we must do the opposite, like John Francis who stopped talking and started walking for seventeen years – literally walking his talk. Francis started his journey in protest of against the oil industry, triggered by the devastating collision of two oil tankers near Golden Gate bridge, the Exxon Valdez disaster. San Francisco Bay became an environmental rescue zone. At first Francis stopped using motorised transport in protest, then he stopped talking to

Keeil, Isle of Man – still in use as a sacred site with 'offerings'

disengage from the endless arguments his action caused. He found silence was the best way of communicating his message: 'I realised if there was something worth doing I'd better do it now because there was no guarantee there would be a tomorrow.' (Rowe 2007)

Francis got a PhD in environmental science during his years of silence, and wrote about his experiences in his book, *Planetwalker: How to Change Your World One Step at a Time* (2005). People turned to him for advice, including the National Coast Guard who asked him to rewrite their oil-spill regulations. He had become a wise fool.

On the road

The act of pilgrimage appeals to us because it is a primal urge, a return to the basics of life: 'The wandering man becomes the primitive man in so many ways.' (Hesse 1920 (1975: 11)). To set aside worldly concerns, to renounce the comforts of home, the security of family, friends and the familiar, to endure the ardours of the road, is to enter sacred time – to value the spiritual over the material. In India, and other buddhist countries, when people reach the age of sixty they give up everything and hit the road: they take the 'road trip of the soul'.

Taking to the road took on a new form in the Sixties when those disenchanted by the West dropped-out and headed for India. This movement, from the Occidental to the

A simple Christian altar for modern pilgrims inside the ruined tower of the fourteenth century Augustinian ruin, Bardsey Island (Ynys Enlli – 'the island of the strong currents', which took its toll on medieval pilgrims). Safe arrival was never guaranteed.

Oriental, had begun in earnest with Madame Blavatsky and the Theosophists in the late nineteenth century (although there had been precedents with the translations of the *Rubaiyat*, Rumi, *A Thousand and One Nights* and the *Kama Sutra*). Such feelings had become immortalised in Herman Hesse's *The Journey to the East* which, although written in 1932, became a Sixties classic for those on the trial to Kashmir or Marrakech. This echoed the sixteenth century novel by Wu Ch'êng-ên, *Xiyouji*, *'Journey to the West'*, a.k.a. *Monkey* (published anonymously in 1592), in which the simian trickster hero undertakes a pilgrimage of atonement – helping the monk Tripitaka deliver the Buddhist scriptures to India.

In the West, the mundane equivalent to the Indian forsaking of worldly wealth and hitting the road is the retiree purchasing a mobile home and wandering, as depicted memorably in the 2002 film *About Schmidt* when Jack Nicholson buys the biggest Winnebago imaginable and hits the road, in search of an enervating experience to ameliorate his ennui.

Robert M Pirsig's seminal classic, *Zen and the Art of Motorcycle Maintenance* (1974) is a pilgrimage of meaning, 'an inquiry into values', written in the form of a Chautauqua, a peripatetic medicine show. The Greek philosophers deconstructed by Pirsig taught in this manner, on the hoof.

In her 'history of walking', *Wanderlust*, (2000) Rebecca Solnit discusses the meaning of the journey:

> Travel can be a way to experience this continuity of self amid the flux of the world and thus to begin to understand each and their relationship to each other.

(Solnit 2000: 27)

A true journey changes you, either externally or internally. Think of Odysseus, searching for his Ithaka – learning to appreciate what was on his doorstep the hard way, just as Dorothy in the Wizard of Oz realises 'there's no place like home'. A sacred journey transforms even more. Such journeys are a form of sacrifice, made meaningful by the hardships endured. Martin Palmer, in his foreword to *Sacred Journeys*, says true pilgrimages need to be 'costly, risky and unpredictable' – costly not necessarily in a financial way but in terms of the investment of time, energy, health, even sanity. Palmer suggests '… only when you are prepared to chance the deepest dangers of risk or joy do you become a true pilgrim.' And the ultimate risk is that 'you might not return as the same person who set out.' (cited in Westwood 1997: 8)

Although genuine pilgrimages still occur, modern equivalents are the popular sponsored charity treks to exotic climes – the Great Wall of China, Mount Kilimanjaro – the fundraiser going on a journey to win 'virtue', and paying for the privilege: the modern version of 'papal pardons' or indulgences. Round the world trips are less conscience-based, but gap years can be times of real growth – a rite of passage for those on the cusp of the world of adult responsibility. And long solo journeys by the likes of Ted Simon (by motorcycle), Ffyona Campbell (by foot) or Ellen McArthur (by boat) are also a kind of pilgrimage where the protagonist must tap into inner reserves of strength and stamina, discovering if not 'revelation' then the odd epiphany, and often a renewal of values, a rediscovery of the familiar, on the return home. Often we must go far to appreciate the simple pleasures on our own doorstep.

Eventually, for the determined pilgrim meaning is reached, or at least a state of grace, of contented stillness as Hesse expresses in *Wandering*:

> Many detours I will still follow, many fulfilments will still disillusion me. One day, everything will reveal its meaning.

> There, where contradictions die, is Nirvana. Within me, they still burn brightly, beloved stars of longing.

(Hesse 1920 (1975: 89))

Hesse's phrase 'where contradictions die' sums up the vanishing point all seek, a state of Nirvana within not without. It seems it is the journey not the destination after all.

St Cybbi's Well. One of the pilgrim wells along the Llyn Peninsula.

In his book on the subject of pilgrimage, John Adair, says: 'The pilgrim instinct must be deep in the human heart.' (Adair 1976: 9)

Many pilgrim routes are on an East-West alignment, often on a peninsula, heading West towards the ocean (Santiago de Compesta, St David's, Bardsey, Croagh Patrick) corresponding not only with the direction of the setting sun, but also the *Via Lactea*, the Milky Way, thus suggestion a synchronisation of Heaven and Earth – the secular and the sacred coming into alignment through an extended act of intention. It is a literal manifestation of the Hermetic dictum: 'As above, so below.'

In Darren Aronofsky's visionary film *The Fountain* (2006) the quest for the Tree of Life begins in the Mayan jungles of the fifteenth century and ends in the distant reaches of space, as the last human journeys towards a dying nebula – Xibalba, the Mayan Underworld – in the hope its death will give birth to new life. The film's central notion that 'death is the road to awe' is mirrored in its structure – that of a journey from darkness to light. When the quest is complete, the waters of life are released.

The trope is familiar from *2001: A Space Odyssey*, and also harks back to the experience of a medieval pilgrim finally reaching one of the shines of Christendom – whether Jerusalem, Constantinople, Rome, Santiago or Canterbury – with their lavish gilding reflecting the light of multitudes of candles. Pilgrimage is a timeless human experience.

Starting at the source

Along the pilgrim route that stretches across the length of the Llyn peninsula, north-west Wales, to Bardsey Island there are chapels and wells for the pilgrim to refresh themselves. One of the best preserved is St Cybbi's Well.

Others wells, like St Modron's in Cornwall became pilgrim sites in themselves. In recent years 'clooty trees', where visitors tie rags to the branches with a prayer, have come to dominate sites like St Modron's. Such practices can be invented from scratch, as at Swallowhead Spring, birthplace of the River Kennet, by Silbury Hill, with its makeshift shrines and intimate offerings – private messages between the

Source of Aber Gwenwen y Maych, the 'stream of the poisoned horses', above Llyn Tegid, North Wales.

pilgrim and spirit. Now a place of powerful metaphorical significance the birthplace of this river was entirely unmarked and unrecognised before the publication of Michael Dames' influential books in the late 1970s (Dames 1976, 1977, 2007).

Here, at the source, the journey begins.

Pilgrimage is a microcosm of the soul's journey through life, one which John Bunyan immortalised in his allegory, *The Pilgrim's Progress* (1678), and his famous hymn, *He Who Would Valiant Be*, with its refrain 'To be a pilgrm.' We are all on that journey, to the final pilgrimage site of death. Often we feel we have 'lost our way' and so a conscious pilgrimage can help to re-align us to cosmic or spiritual forces.

> Pilgrimage has become a metaphor for life itself, the journey we
> set out on the moment we are born, the road to the Otherworld,
> the Celestial City.

(Westwood 1997: 20)

A holiday is a pale imitation of this – taking one we hope to feel rejuvenated in some way, with hopefully a renewed enthusiasm (from *en theos* 'the god within') for life. Sun, sea and sand is the mantra of Western hedonists, although many find nourishment and inspiration from many other things beside burning skin on a beach.

Modern pilgrim stone bearing the traditional sign of the scallop shell, Old Wells Road, Glastonbury

A pilgrimage is about reconnecting with the source, whatever we deem that to be – the font of our inspiration, the well that is often capped in our daily lives, thus making us stagnant, disillusioned or depressed.

There is an Arthurian story of the Maiden of the Wells, who once refreshed travellers with draughts of their healing water from a golden chalice. A greedy king called Amangons wanted the chalice and the well for himself, so he seized it, and his knights despoiled the maidens and desecrated the wells. The chalice became a poisoned one for it brought Amangons no bliss – he sickened but could not recover. He lived on and on like this, unable to live in health, but unable to die – he had become the Fisher King, who could only be healed by the Holy Fool.

Every pilgrim is a potential 'freer of the waters' who attempts to 'pierce-the-veil' of mundane reality like Parsifal, and heal the inner Fisher King and their own Wasteland. Every pilgrimage is a call to action – from the inertia of daily life, a life often led without full consciousness. When on the road we are strangers in strange lands. We must think on our feet, making decisions in the moment. Everything we experience, everything our senses imbibe, is something new, something that makes us pay attention to the here and now.

'...begin a journey without delay.'

The ancient advice is 'to begin a journey without delay'. Why delay enlightenment? Why fritter your life away with mundanities? The joy of pilgrimage is that it is a very practical and empowering form of consciousness-raising.

The true pilgrim walks counter to the world but in harmony with cosmic forces. Forced to travel light, he or she is a living symbol of a 'turning away' from materialism towards something higher. The devote pilgrim is, as Bunyan advises, '... one who strives to obtain salvation of their soul through a physical journey in which *caritas*, love for God; and not *cupiditas*, love for material things, drives them.' It is a journey towards love, towards oneness, like one undertaken by the Moorish hero of the medieval tale *The Pilgrim of Love* (retold in Irving 1832).

In contrast to such medieval ideals, modern day 'pilgrims' refresh their weary steeds at garages bearing the scallop shell, ancient emblem of the pilgrim but now a signifier for doomed fossil fuels – twenty-first century fools on a road to nowhere.

In the next chapter we shall finish our tour of British brigadoons with the most famous one of all – Avalon, which some claim to be found in deepest Somerset at Glastonbury. It has been a pilgrimage place for centuries, and still today 'new pilgrims of all kinds journey here.' (Clifford and King 2006: 22)

Chapter five

Inventing Avalon

The Fenian poet had never seen such an airy-fairy bunch. What a contrast to the rough and ready Fianna! To become one of his father's famous warband you had to fend off spears while buried to the waist in the ground, compose poetry, throw a Gae Bolg with your foot, and be able to perform the deadly salmon leap. These Tír nan Ogians looked like a load of hippy drop-outs. Going by their high spirits and strange clothing it seemed like a festival had been going on for some time...

Led by Niamh and her camp followers, who greeted them with garlands and bowls of ambrosia, Oisín ventured further into the interior.

'Welcome, poet of the Fianna,' smiled the golden-haired princess, 'to the Land of the Ever Young.'

~~~~~~~~~~~~~~~~~~~~~~~~~~~~~~

Within the British Isles Avalon is the lost island *par excellence*. Apart from Atlantis it has been written about more than any other. It haunts Western literature, cropping up time and time again in poetry, fiction, obscure tracts, pseudo-histories and other esoterica and cultural miscellanea. These include Bryan Ferry's song 'Avalon'; Van Morrison's 1989 album *Avalon Sunset*; the Japanese virtual reality fantasy *Avalon* (2001); and the film *Finding Forester* (2000) about a grumpy novelist, played by Sean Connery, who is the unlikely winner of the Pulitzer Prize for his one-hit wonder, *Avalon Landing*.

Avalon takes on a sublty-shifted meaning the 2006 French animated film, *Renaissance* set in Paris 2054, in which the sinister Avalon Corporation promises eternal youth – at a price. The tech-noir film uses advertising on airships and moving billboards, à la *Blade Runner* (1982), to tout the Corporation's product:

> With Avalon, I know I'm going to stay beautiful
> Health... Beauty... Longevity... Avalon.
> We're on your side
> for life

Avalon has come a long way from its obscure roots. It now has entered the public domain as a metaphor for anything otherworldly. Whatever its origins – as hard to trace as the place itself – it is commonly believed to be an otherworldly location, perhaps faerie-land, and the final resting place, or place of convalescence, of King Arthur: a nursing home for heroes. Ironically several nursing homes, as well as bungalows, canal boats, OAP coach companies and yachts are named after it! It seems to have become synonymous with a pleasant retirement more than enchantment!

But where did the myth begin, and why has it been associated with a small town in Somerset for so long?

Firstly, let us look at the word itself. Etymologically 'Avalon' is known in French and Welsh sources, and refers to at different times a personal name (Avolloc/Afallach) or as 'Island of Apples'. According to David Dom, 'Afallach was the name of a Celtic King in North Wales' and seems to have given his name to 'Ynys Afallach': the island belonging to Afallach, or perhaps just the 'realm of Afallach bordered by water' (Dom 2005). In North Wales, by the banks of the River Dee, there is in fact a Caer Afallach, an Iron Age hillfort now known as Moel Y Gaer, so this seems to suggest an actual Afallach existed – either as a tutelary spirit, or as a real chieftain, possibly around 45 BCE – the supposed son of Lludd Llaw Ereint (Ludd of the Silver Hand; the Welsh variant of the Irish Nuadu), although this could be a pseudo-spiritual lineage, as with Geoffrey of Monmouth's sequence of British kings going back to Brutus.

Returning to Afallach and Avalon, there is an interesting link here as the Welsh word for apple is *afal*, and so Ynys Afallach can easily be interpreted as the 'Island of Apples'. Because of the association in the Celtic mind with apples and the otherworld (the apple branch of Emhain, etcetera) it is easy to see why this became an analogue for the Celtic paradise. Seemingly the French Romance writers in the late middle ages confused Avalon with an actual place, and then it became fixed in the canon of the Arthurian Tradition as the place 'where Arthur goes'. Avalon has come to mean many more things since. Here are some 'definitions' of Avalon:

1. 'Avalon may mean island of apples, and/or it may refer to a 'pointed rock', perhaps that of Glastonbury Tor, a numinous island-hill visible for many miles across the watery levels of Somerset – summer land.' (Clifford and King 2006: 21)

2. 'A beautiful lake and rock island, surrounded by deep meadows with orchard lawns and wooded hollows...' (Manguel and Guadalupi 1999: 46–7)

3. Fairyland

4. An otherworldy island of rich enchantment and resting place of King Arthur, presided over by nine priestesses or goddesses, chiefly Morgen/Morgan le Fay.

5. A colony of Atlantis (Bradley and Paxson 2005).

6. A state of consciousness.

Although the concept of 'Avalon' itself may relate to something far older and more authentic, Glastonbury-as-Avalon is a relatively recent invention. It is not associated with the town until the early twelfth century. The first association recorded is by William of Malmesbury, *circa* 1135.:

> This island was at first called Ynys Wytrin by the Britons, then by
> the Angles (when they had conquered the land), Glastonbury... it
> was frequently called the Island of Avallonia.

Giraldus Cambrensis, Gerald of Wales, is the next to mention it, in 1195:

> The place which is now Glaston was in ancient times called the
> Isle of Avalon... and Morgan a noble matron and ruler and lady of
> these parts and kin by blood to King Arthur, carried him away to
> the island... that she might heal his wounds.

What Gerald of Wales's actual sources were remain unknown – he claims to have been influenced by a 'lost book' like Geoffrey of Monmouth and Iola Morgannwg. Was he drawing on oral tradition, or making it up? He would not be the first meddling monk or the last. The twelfth century was especially important for forging monastic 'histories'. (Rahtz 1993: 31)

'Ynys Wytrin' is mentioned by William of Malmesbury – a slippery name, both in spelling, definition and origin – and is supposedly equated with Glastonbury in a charter of 601 – but modern historians regard this as spurious.

'Ynys', 'Inys' and 'Inis' all mean an 'island', as mentioned above; whileas 'Wytrin', 'Witryn' and 'Witrin' are connected to the fifteenth Latin *vitreus,* 'glass', thus 'Isle of Glass'. So one can see why people have made the obvious, but etymologically incorrect, connection between that and 'Glastonbury'.

Glastonbury seems to be Anglo-Saxon in origin: 'Glestingaburg'. The town's current name has the classic suffix of 'bury', a common place-name element designating a 'strong place', such as a fort or a monastery. The 'Glaston' prefix is thought by place-name experts to be a Celtic name, possibly meaning 'woad place', although there is no shortage of alternative theories, which accrete around such places like flies to honey.

There is a particularly ludicrous folk tale which is worth sharing here for entertainment value:

> There was once a man from the North called Glasteing, who
> seemed to be a swineherd, but not a very good one, for his lost
> his prize sow. He pursued her to Glastonbury, and found her
> suckling her piglets next to the Old Church under a fruit tree, and
> so Glastonbury was so named!

Perhaps the sow had merely gone there for the cider apples, maybe to ease the pain of her labour! Arthur was said to have found 'apples of the most precious sort' there

The 'Glastonbury Thorn', Wearyall Hill, looking towards the Tor.

– Otherworldy apples from a West Country Hesperides, or just the produce the West Country is famous for?

However absurd this story may seem there are interesting mythic resonances. Merlin, in the guise of Myrddin Wyllt (Wild Merlin), communed with a pig in his 'madness', as recorded in an obscure poem. Also, in the story of Lleu Llaw Gyffes in *The Mabinogion*, Gwydion the magician tracks down his nephew, betrayed by Blodeuwedd and turned into an eagle, by following a pig which eats his rotting flesh as it falls from the oak tree he languished in. And there are other magical pigs, boars and sows in other parts of *The Mabinogion*: Henwen, a fructifying sow; and Twrch Trwyth, the destructive opposite, a monstrous boar who lays waste to half of Britain.

Closer to Glastonbury, there is a folk tale which the Glasteing story echoes: that of Bladud and the swine, the 'creation myth' of the city of Bath, twenty-two miles to the north. Like Glasteing, Bladud is a swineherd who founds the city when he finds his erstwhile pigs – bathing in the hot springs. Could Bladud be the same 'man from the north'? Bath is on the pilgrim route between Malmesbury and Glastonbury – pilgrims would have passed through the city on the way there, and could have carried the 'swine virus', in the form of the folk tale, with them.

The boar crops up as a heraldic totem all over Britain – as in Winchester – but there seems to be a concentration around the West Country: Swindon (possibly the 'Dun of King Swain'; Swainswick, a valley near Bath (both possibly named after Svein), and Swinford, a hamlet between Bath and Bristol which was 'the pig crossing place'.

Glastonbury Tor, a nexus of legend.

Glastonbury Tor

Even to this day, there are many pig farms in the Wiltshire-Somerset area, and just a little further north, the Tamworth Two gained celebrity in January 1998 when they absconded in Malmesbury and escaped the chop.

This all seems a long way from the romantic associations of medieval literature, for instance, the thirteenth century romance, *La Mort Le Roi Artu*, which connected Avalon with Glastonbury. Avalon, rightly or wrongly, is forever associated with Glastonbury.

A small town in Somerset

The problem with seeing Glastonbury as Avalon is right in front of the eyes: it is, undeniably, a small town in Somerset with its share of traffic congestion, supershed industrial estates and supermarkets, derelict homeless on the aptly-named High Street, drug problems, crime, parochial politics, and so on – all the problems that affect most modern communities.

Glastonbury happens to have an unusually-shaped hill and at least two good springs, plus an amazing heritage, but it seems far removed from the vision of the otherworld which Avalon epitomises. There is no denying its romantic charm, and to wander its orchard-filled slopes in spring or autumn, or to stand on one of its hills at dawn, or under a full moon, makes it is difficult not to be caught under its spell. But there is no escaping it is a modern town with its attendant infra-structure, environmental impact, problems and a community divided between the hippies and the more prosaic locals. The number of businesses cashing in on the tourist trade illustrate its

A road sign in Glastonbury.

'worldliness' more than its 'spiritualness'. Here capitalism and 'Babylon' have not been held at bay – they have set up their stalls in the temple itself.

The curiously-shaped hill draws the eye, visitors, businesses and the wildest theories – all because of, it seems, an accident of geology. One of the key things that debunks the myth of it being the 'Isle of Avalon', as the optimistic road sign says, is the inescapable fact that Glastonbury is *not* an island. It is surrounded by land not water – much of which was once regularly flooded, granted, but *not all of it*, for the Tor itself is linked to higher ground. The 'isle of Avalon' is not in fact an 'isle' but '… a peninsula, linked to higher ground to the east by a neck of land nowhere lower than 10 metres (33ft) above modern sea level.' (Rahtz 1993: 12) This earthwork is known as Ponter's Ball: a kilometre long, ten metres wide and 3.3 metres high, it runs across the neck of land linking the Tor to the Mendips. This would have been the only dry way in or out of what would become Glastonbury, and so an important route, one that needed defending.

Rahtz, in his geological and archaeological survey goes onto say: 'To travellers from the west, coming by water, it may have *looked* like an island, with water or watery moors on three sides.' (Rahtz 1993: 12) But that illusion is soon dispelled when you arrive. On a misty morning, with the Tor rising over a soft grey sea, it may *seem* like an island, but the fact remains: 'Glastonbury is not an island and has not been one in recent geological time.' (Rahtz 1993: 12)

In 1723 the antiquarian William Stukeley commented: 'Hence let us go, as in pilgrimage, to the famous Glastonbury; for it is a very rough and disagreeable road, over rocks and the heads of rivers.' For the modern traveller breaching the summit of the Mendips, the first sight of the Tor standing proud from the levels is a gladdening one.

The Somerset Levels of course flood, as such wetlands are prone to do, and have been under water in the past – either from heavy rains or what are known as marine transgressions, when the sea inundates low-lying land: 'It is… generally agreed that there was severe flooding in the second and first millennia BCE and again in the early medieval period.' (Rahtz 1993: 12) Storm surges such as these coupled with heavy rains can have devastating consequences as in the notorious flood of 1606, worth mentioning here in more detail. Rahtz, quoting local archives, describes how on 20th January of that year:

> ... the sea, at a flowing water, meeting with land floods, strove so violently together that heaving down all things it was builded to withstand and hinder the force of them, the banks were eaten through, and a rupture was made into Somersetshire.

> (Rahtz 1993: 12)

Rahtz goes onto describe how: 'The whole of the Brue Levels were 3–4m (10–13ft) deep; ricks floated away, 'but the company of Hogs and Pigs went on eating on top... rabbits on sheeps' backs were drowned with them. Floodwater extended up to St John's Church in Glastonbury, with water 2m (over 6ft) deep in the streets. The same thing happened in 1703. Babies were drowned in their cradles of willow bark; this led to the invention of cradles with raised joists to keep them above the water.' (Rahtz 1993: 12).

With global warming, such flooding will become increasingly common. Glastonbury once more may become a 'lost island' – a place reached on the main by boats – except along Ponter's Ball, stubbornly unyielding to the myths of Avalon even to the end.

Other Avalons

Avalon is thought to reside in a number of locations, including north Wales (as suggested by David Dom, above); Mont St Michel; Isles of Scilly (with its *two* Arthur graves); in the wild Atlantic, and more locally Bath, Somerset. The *Vita Merlini* suggests Avalon is accessed not from Glastonbury, but from *Aquae Sulis*, a.k.a. Bath, twenty-two miles to the north-east. With its four kilometre fault in the oolitic limestone creating the geothermal springs, and a name which means 'Waters of the Gap', – suggestive of an otherworldly entrance as well as a very real entrance to 'the underworld' – it is perhaps a claim with some merit.

Like Glastonbury, Bath borders the Mendips, which are riddled with caves (at Cheddar and Wookey Hole – inspiration for Coleridge's 'caves measureless to man', as well as local author H.G. Wells' Morloch civilisation in his 1895 science fiction novel *The Time Machine*); actual 'hollow hills', and ones that are littered with barrows – regarded, it is clear from such evidence, as the Hills of Peace to our ancestors, and thus more accurately the 'place where the dead go' than Glastonbury (the burial site of the prehistoric Glastonbury lake villagers is yet to be found).

There are many Glastonburys

Glastonbury has attracted more than its fair share of theories, ranging from the sober to the outlandish:

Burrowbridge Mump – another ruined church on a hill in the middle of the Somerset Levels, but without the tourist industry. Reputedly on an energy line connected to the Tor.

The potent myth – or is it story? – of Arthur and his grave, where the tissue between this and the other world still seems so thin, laps around the Christian and pagan, ancient and modern fragments of Glastonbury with ease.

(Clifford and King 2006: 22)

The town has a long and fascinating history. It is said to be the site of the first Christian church in Britain – a humble wattle-and-daub affair, probably sixth century. Subsequent Christian activity expanded the site – leading to the now magnificent ruins of Glastonbury Abbey. A major religious centre, it was a famous pilgrimage site for centuries, as Malory mentions: 'Thus Sir Lancelot and his eight fellows went on foot from Almesbury into Glastonbury.' (*Le Morte d'Arthur* Book 21, Ch. 11)

Yet Glastonbury started out as a far humbler collection of beehive cells and a simple chapel, perhaps the first in England. Malory's tale recounts: 'Thus I leave here Sir Bedivere with the hermit, that dwelled that time in a chapel beside Glastonbury, and there was his hermitage.' (*Le Morte d'Arthur* Book 21, Ch. 8) When Guinevere dies, Lancelot escorts her to Glastonbury – seen also as an isle of the dead in Malory's treatment – 'where she was curiously put in a 'web of lead, and then in a coffin of marble'. (*Le Morte d'Arthur*, Book 21, Ch. 8)

There is the persistent, if unsubstantiated, legend of Joseph of Arimathea, Jesus' uncle, coming to Britain, making landfall on Wearyall, or Wirral, Hill, where the Glastonbury Thorn grows to this day – said to have sprung up from his staff as he plunged it into the soft English soil. Every year, local school-children send a cutting to the Queen from one of the several 'Glastonbury Thorns' dotted about the town. Joseph may have even brought a young Jesus to England, during his extended 'gap' year, where he bummed about for a bit (the reluctant messiah), as Blake immortalised ('and did those feet in ancient times walk upon England's pastures green?'). This mythologizes the landscape, and is at the same time, a mystification – for the sources are obscure and ambiguous. We can read whatever we like into them. The past accommodates a multitude of scenarios.

Glastonbury has become a dreaming space, a liminal zone, on the borders of reality, or at least the mainstream. No train station or motorway connects it to the rest of Britain. It has become a Mecca for British counter-culture and more besides: all things to all people, where different narratives collide and engage in a renegotiation of reality. It attracts droves of lost souls, wounded healers, mystics, visionaries, poets, artists and musicians – the disenfranchised of consensus reality, as well as New Age entrepreneurs, hippy capitalists out to cash in on the 'purple pound' with their crystal shops and pagan retail therapy. In Glastonbury, multiple paradigms co-exist, perhaps analogous to Jerusalem (an analogy Blake would have liked), with all the different temple-traders selling their brand of the same product, the God/dess Stuff – wiccan, Hellenic, sufi, Greek orthodox, buddhist, Gardnerian, druid, heathen, hindu, Hari Krishna, chaos, Crowleyanity, Mayan, qabala, Yoruba... You name it, there's a treatment, course, book or cult for it there. A healthy mix, some would say. If only all places were so tolerant.

Yet it is place not to engage with reality, but to escape from it, it is a *refugium*, a polder, where countless 'Arthurs' can lay low, lick their wounds, nurse their egos, or plan their revenge on the world. '... for I will into the vale of Avilion to heal me of my grievous wound.' (Malory, *Le Morte d'Arthur*, Book 21, Ch. 5) This woundedness has become almost institutionalised here, in endless therapy sessions where everyone is encouraged to explore their 'issues' ad nauseam. It seems there are more healers than patients, more therapies than conditions to treat. At its worst it is vortex of madness, drug-abuse and power-trips; a honey pot for the spiritual tourist. At its best, it is a creative field of potential that attracts shining souls, imagineers, pioneers of spirit, true teachers, genuine healers – but trying to discern them from the charlatans, hucksters, black magicians and nut-cases is often a treacherous past-time!

> It has become something of a magnet for idealistic visionaries who see the place as having some intrinsic power apparently quite distinct from its history.

> (Rahtz 1993 Introduction)

Yet even the likes of Rahtz, who attempt to depict the 'true rather than the bogus Glastonbury' admits that in his book 'discussion is restricted to what would nowadays be called a 'reductionist' or 'minimalist' summary of what are generally believed to be 'true' facts and interpretations. (Rahtz 1993: 11)

'Interpretations' is a telling word – what are presented as the facts are often just one person's interpretation of the available material. Who knows what evidence may yet come to light, proving or refuting the various claims? Even Rhatz admits:

> What has been discovered to date is a small fraction of what still
> lies beneath the ground.
>
> (Rahtz 1993: 41)

What is the 'true' Glastonbury then? Surely Rahtz' reductionist, if useful, survey is only another layer to the multi-faceted cultural construct of Glastonbury. Scepticism can be just as myopic as blind faith, and perhaps the best strategy at the end of the day is to maintain an open mind. Orthodoxies are always been overturned by the latest discovery, and so it is wisest to enjoy all sides and expect to be surprised! Many more Glastonburys may yet see the light of day.

The Glastonbury 'Avalon' industry

So when did this 'Avalon' industry and air of credulity begin? With, it turns out, the meddling monks of Glastonbury Abbey in a cunning piece of medieval public relations. It seems to have been a common phenomenon that when an abbey was struggling for funds a relic was found. Even in the glory days of the Church, such venerable institutions would have to do much hustling and political manoeuvring for funds:

> Dunstan had made this the prime shrine of the tenth century and
> the wealthiest abbey in a newly emergent England. The monks
> learned much about promotion and power from him, turning to
> myth-making to help rebuild the attraction of the abbey.
>
> (Clifford and King 2006: 21–2)

With the Devil-beating Dunstan as their Richard Branson-esque role model, the monks were set for their own form of rebranding:

> …Henry II encouraged the monks to search for the great king's
> grave a few years after their abbey had lost everything in a fire.
> The monks discovered not only the supposed remains of Arthur
> and his wife in 1191, but the remains of the St Dunstan and a
> manuscript of St Patrick.
>
> (Clifford and King 2006: 22)

This PR hat trick certainly worked, raising the necessary funds for the refurbishment and filling the coffers as pilgrims predictably flocked to see these astonishing treasures. The most sensational discovery was that of Arthur's grave. According to the chronicler Gerald of Wales and others, the abbot Henry de Blois commissioned a search, apparently discovering at the depth of five metres (sixteen feet) a massive oak trunk or coffin with an inscription *Hic jacet sepultus inclitus rex Arthurus in insula Avalonia.* ('Here lies King Arthur in the island of Avalon'). The remains were reinterred with great ceremony, attended by King Edward I and his queen, before the high altar at Glastonbury Abbey, where they were the focus of pilgrimages until the Reformation.

Suddenly Glastonbury became the hottest ticket in town. Visit King Arthur's grave! See Dunstan's remains! Behold St Patrick's manuscript! Walk where Joseph of Arimathea and (possibly) his famous nephew walked! Take home some of the Glastonbury thorn and well water! The Glastonbury industry was born.

Although pilgrimages died off after the Reformation, the creation of the tourism industry in the late nineteenth and early twentieth centuries meant that the wheels of the PR machines needed oiling once more. Suddenly 'evidence' sprang up all around Glastonbury. The 1920s were an especially fertile period. Katherine Maltwood 'discovered' the Glastonbury Zodiac layed out around the Tor in field shapes and topographical features from different periods; and a 'sacred' blue bowl was found in what became Chalice Well by Wellesley Tudor Pole. Violet Firth (better known as Dion Fortune) moved to town and the Chalice Orchard Club was set up. The earthwork of Ponter's Ball, also known as Ponting's Ball or Fonter's Ball, suddenly in 1923 became Arthur's Causeway the route 'from Camelot to Avalon'. It is easy to imagine romantic Edwardians associating it with the scene evoked in Tennyson's *The Lady of Shalott*:

> On either side the river lie
> Long fields of barley and of rye,
> That clothe the wold and meet the sky ;
> And thro' the field the road runs by
>   To many-tower'd Camelot;
> And gazing up and down the people go,
> Round an island there below,
>   The island of Shalott.

The roadside plaque on the Glastonbury-Shepton Mallet road buys into this myth, giving it even another name:

> This is the site of *Pontis Vallum*, the Fort of the Bridge,
> which defended the Isle of Avalon from the mainland.

And just in case the traveller was in any doubt the municipal council helpfully placed signs on the way in, 'Welcome to Glastonbury, the Isle of Avalon'. The 'fact' that Glastonbury was Avalon was now enshrined in its official identity, its 'branding' of itself. The glamour of Avalon was good for business. In the 1960s one local businessman would use this 'Glastonbury trade mark' with unexpectedly fruitful effects.

Left: *The chalybeate spring stains the stone red from the iron deposit, giving birth to the nomenclature, 'the red spring'. Chalice Well, Glastonbury.*
Right: *Chalice Well head, Glastonbury*

Glastonbury™

An enterprising Methodist farmer, Michael Eavis of Worthy Farm, started the world-famous midsummer festival in 1971, after visiting the Bath Blues Festival on the Bath recreation ground the previous year – where the young farmer and his wife saw the likes of Led Zeppelin and Fleetwood Mac. The following year, with the help of Andrew Kerr and the late Arabella Churchill, Eavis booked Marc Bolan to perform on his farm and he gave away free milk. (See Worthington 2004: 34–7 for details of the early Glastonbury Festivals.)

Since its low-fi origins the Glastonbury Festival has ballooned into the largest festival in Europe, and requires year-round planning, a massive and expensive infrastructure, a huge police and media presence, and yet remains one of the 'Greatest Shows on Earth'. It has even trademarked the name of the town, preventing local businesses from using it.

The Glastonbury Festivals are actually held near Pilton (or 'Pill town', appropriately enough, to locals) eight miles from the town of Glastonbury But it still cashes in on the mystique of 'Avalon'. Eavis has used Tennyson to evoke the mysticism of Avalon. He recited this extract, as used on the publicity, in the Poetry and Words Tent one year:

To the island-valley of Avilion;
Where falls not hail, or rain, or any snow,
Nor ever wind blows loudly; but it lies
Deep-meadowed, happy, fair with orchard-lawns
And bowery hollows crown'd with summer sea,
Where I will heal me of my grievous wound.

(*Morte D'Arthur*)

In the film of the festival by Julian Temple, *Glastonbury the Movie* (2006), Billy Bragg describes the event as 'brigadoon: it's here for a few days and then it's gone', as does the huge media circus which goes with it.

Viva Glastonbury!

Glastonbury should be cherished as a meeting place of paradigms – an ongoing conversation of reality, a place where virtually anything is permissible, or at least you can 'live your illusion', a town-sized playground for colourful souls.

There is something heart-warming about having the Otherworld so close, so 'down to earth'. And why not? To always see the sacred as elsewhere, as beyond, as separate from matter is to buy into the Descartian divide, rather than seeing the sacred as immanent. Other cultures manage to; not to is a particularly Western hang-up. Shed this hang-up and this land becomes our Dreaming.

However ludicrous the assertion that Avalon exists in Somerset, there is still a tiny possibility that it might be so – in an infinite universe all possibilities are realities somewhere. Maybe Glastonbury's purpose is to annoy the 'reality police', rationalists, reductionists and other agents of 'the matrix' by its very presence – a 'violation of border' as C.S. Lewis would have it – an intrusion of a shape from another dimension, a 3-D object into a 2-D world. Something to give the Flatlanders night terrors, which is no bad thing; but more positively, a place that gives people hope that other realities do exist. It offers, if nothing else, a gateway.

The Star Cults of Somerset

A popular prevailing idea amongst the ageing New Age population of Glastonbury and its environs is the notion of 'starseed' people – that some have chosen to incarnate on Earth at this time of global peril to help humanity. Common sources of these alien avatars include Sirius and Andromeda. Groups gather in living rooms on housing estates to share messages from cosmic guides. This activity – which seems to be increasing in popularity (although these spiritual fashions go in waves through the town) – seems to be connected to the Mayan prophecies of 2012, when the 26,000 year cycle of the Precession of the Equinoxes is due to come full circle. This has turned attention to the stars and to cosmic time – perhaps as a consoling fiction to the very real threat of Climate Chaos. Some believe a gateway to have opened between Glastonbury and the heart of the galaxy in preparation for this cosmic alignment. Where once it was content to see itself as heart chakra of the Britain, if not the world, it now sees itself as something of universal significance: Stargate Glastonbury. This is nothing new: Katherine Maltwood created her own version with the 'discovery' of the Glastonbury Zodiac in the Twenties. The signs are always there for those who (make-)believe.

Mutually perpetuated illusion

Glastonbury offers a mutually reciprocating reality, a never-ending role-play: 'You can be Gawain if you accept me as Guinevere', 'You can be Pleiedian if I can be a pirate', and so on. We can all have a role in the Masque of Britain and keep reality at bay. It is place to opt out of consensus reality: not a place to engage with the world, but to escape from it.

And thank goodness! Life would be less interesting without Glastonbury and its like. It is undoubtedly a 'weirdness zone' where normal rules, and judgement, breaks down – Britain's answer to the dream factory of Hollywood perhaps, with its own pantheon of stars, celebrities, legends, rumours and scandals. 'Many claims that appear to make Glastonbury extraordinary are seen to be commonplace when place in a wider historical perspective.' (Rahtz 1993: 31)

And yet, and yet, on a misty day it is easy to succumb to the spell of the place. The hills have an undeniably fey atmosphere. The hills, the springs, even the abbey grounds – they are real, they are sacred. Anything else is frippery. There *is* something genuine there, beneath the glittering surface. Maybe it is just a matter of perception.

To paraphrase the classic saying of Voltaire's: 'If Avalon did not exist, it would be necessary to invent it.'

The allure of the imaginary has led many to seek lost islands, or failing to find them – as they must by definition – to invent their own. This does not make them any less valid. As a phenomenon, like the creation of crop circles, the invention of lost islands is fascinating in its own right because of the very fact *it happens*, whatever the causes. And yet there are actual causes of actual lost islands, which we turn to in the next section, as we look at lost islands in the cold light of day.

PART TWO

The cold light of day

Chapter six
Did the Earth move?

Oisín woke up. He lay in a bed, a very soft bed. Sheets smooth as cream, cushions soft as moonlight. It was an extravagant affair, a vast four poster thing. But it didn't just have posts – it had *columns*, made of swirling marble around which ivy and vines grew, laden with dark bounty. He heard a contented sigh and turned to see Niamh laying next him, hair curled in question marks around her head, her milk-white body naked beneath the thin sheets. She stretched like a cat, and opened her astonishing eyes.

'Good morning, my poet.'

Oisín quickly tried to remember what had happened the night before. There had been endless carousing – they liked to do that a lot around here, he had noticed, and little else. Dancing, music, mirth. Mirth, music, dancing. They'd had too much mead. Staggered upstairs. Tumbled into bed.

Had they? Did they?

'How was it for you?' she smiled, noticing his questioning eyes.

Then he noticed he was naked too, his clothes slung over a carved chair, bucket boots sagging by tipped over goblets.

Oisín had a pounding ache behind his eyes. Mental note: not to mix the mead with the ambrosia. He tried to sit up, and immediately regretted such a rash action.

Rubbing his temples and groaning he noticed the ring on his hand. Left hand. One. Two. Three. Third finger.

Niamh had one that matched, although it held a diamond the size of a strawberry. 'Darling husband,' she presented cherry-full lips, 'You may kiss the bride.'

~~~~~~~~~~~~~~~~~~~~~~~~~~~~

The world has not always been the same shape. Putting aside, for the time being, the various ideas about the Earth and its place in the universe, let us consider the actual fabric of the planet itself, its *prima materia*, rock, the bones of the world. The Earth is approximately 4.65 billion years old – a date scientists arrived at by radiometric dating of its Hadean rock. And the elements it is formed from are even older – harvested from vast gas clouds and the flotsam of space, asteroids, comet trails, star dust, the ashes of dead stars, the debris of the Big Bang. The Earth is formed from the lost islands of space.

Our world was meant to have been formed by the destruction of its twin – another potential planet side-by-side to ours (in its embryonic phase), from which the stronger planetary embryo began to steal, increasing Earth's mass, increasing Earth's gravity, and draining it into oblivion – it died so Earth could live. We live on the planet of Cain, which like the doomed wanderer killed its brother. But even after the planet congealed into its 'final' shape things were on the move. The sphere was settled on as the optimum Platonic solid, but the details of its surface were still being worked out, as if by a perfectionist artist. The world, as we have come to know it, is the result of many 'early versions'. It would take many millions of years before settling down into its current configuration. And the world continues to be a work-in-progress, not only in its 'surface details', but chiefly because continents are moveable feast-tables.

Lost islands are not a new phenomenon. The Earth's continents (properly called 'lithospheric plates'), float on the planet's core of magma like skin on a milky drink. These largest of landmasses have been floating, rising and falling since the formation of our planet. In a process called continental drift that takes place over millions of years these continental plates have been moving about like pieces of a gigantic jigsaw puzzle trying to fit itself together. When dealing with geological timescale, we are talking big numbers, so take a deep breath as we plunge into the chasm of time.

The largest lost island

Originally, all the world's continents were congealed into one vast lump, called Pangaea, a term hewn from Greek ('Pan': all; 'Gaia': Earth) by the German meteorologist Alfred Wegener, who devised the theory of continental drift in 1915 by palaeomagnetic testing of rock, which can pinpoint where the pieces of the jigsaw puzzle 'joined up' in the vast past. As with many paradigm-shifting discoveries, his theory was heavily contested at the time, but has since been widely accepted. Now it is difficult to believe otherwise.

Pangaea existed during the late Palaeozoic and early Mesozoic Eras (about 300 million to 200 million years ago) from the time of insects to the time of mammals on the evolutionary tree. This supercontinent consisted of two large continental masses: Laurasia to the north and Gondwana to the south.

Before Pangaea these two large lost islands existed separately: 500 million years ago Gondwana straddled the equator in the eastern hemisphere, with its southern

Kilve, East Quantoxhead, Somerset.

portions near the South Pole. It consisted of the continents of South America, Africa, Australia and Antarctica, as well as the Indian subcontinent.

To the west of Gondwana were three large continental plates: the North American plate (including Greenland and Scotland); the North European plate (Baltica); and the Scandinavian plate. Over the next 200 million years these plates, plus minor and micro plates, converged to form Laurasia. This was thrust against Gondwana by continental drift. From this 'coupling' the seven continents broke off: Africa, Asia, Europe, North America, South America, Australia and Antarctica. These could be seen as the 'children' of Laurasia and Gondwana – the Man of the North and the Woman of the South, as it were, who 'came together' in blissful union as Pangaea: a continental chymical wedding, which lasted a hundred million years! Pangaea formed a sideways 'V' shape, with its apex towards the west. In the east it was sundered by the Tethys Sea, and around it was the primal ocean known as Panthalassa. Where continental plates pushed together, mountain-building occurred, called 'orogeny'. These 'orogenous zones' would become the world's great mountain ranges. Around 240 million years ago, during the Triassic Period, Pangaea began to split apart. The dance of plate tectonics caused the supercontinent to rotate as well as move north. They and their children have been sundered ever since.

This tremendous event was not unique in Earth's history. Many researchers believe an earlier supercontinent existed before Pangaea – Rodinia, 'Gondwana's grandmother', which existed in the southern hemisphere and split up about 750 million years ago. And geo-scientists believe a new supercontinent is slowly forming in the Northern hemisphere: so watch out for the 'Son of Pangaea' – coming in the next hundred million years or so!

As a footnote to this geological epic, the micro plate consisting of England, Wales and Southern Ireland was named Avalonia in the Victorian era, thus it can be said truthfully that Avalon does exist. However, before Avalonians get excited, it is wise to consider the popularity of all things Arthurian to the Victorians – so the Adamesque geologist was probably inspired by the romance in his choice of name, not the other way round.

Legends of Lemuria or Mu seem to derive from this notion of a geological 'lost continent'. Such theories became very popular in the late Victorian age, just as Darwinism and discoveries in geology were redraughting the map of the world. They cannot be the product of ancestral memory, because humans have only existed for a fraction of this geological time – certainly not 200 million years ago. Besides which a continent is not something easy to lose! When dealing with hundreds of millions of years, things can 'appear' and 'disappear' – but they do not vanish overnight, as some claim Atlantis did. The painstaking processes of geology take aeons to implement, and leaves plenty of evidence, otherwise we would not know about the largest 'lost' island at all.

Cauldrons of fire

Plainly, geological factors are responsible for a large number of lost – and even 'found' – islands. The most spectacular of these factors is volcanic. One could argue that all continental drift is 'volcanic' as it is linked to the ocean of magma the plates float upon, and the convection currents therein, which generate the Earth's magnetism. The Pacific 'Ring of Fire' is directly related to this – all around the Pacific Rim there is a prevalence of volcanic and seismic activity caused by the collision and subduction of the world's chthonic gods – the continental plates. Off the coast of Japan is the deepest place in the world's oceans, as recorded thus far: Tuscorora, a staggering 32,636 feet below sea level.

Undersea volcanoes are evidence of this planet-forming process still continuing, for example Surtsey Island off the coast of Iceland and the Galápagos Islands where new land is being formed (for more on both see below). Another spectacular example is Hawaii, which is the summit of massive marine volcanoes, the largest being Mauna Loa (4,169 metres; 13,677 feet), the most massive single mountain in the world, rising about 10,000 metres (33,000 feet) from the sea floor.

When a supervolcano erupts it can leave a caldera – Spanish for cauldron, which they resemble on a vast scale, often miles across. Land-based calderas can contain wide lakes with the old summit forming an internal cone-shaped island (as in Wizard Island, Crater Lake, Oregon); while sea-based ones can form rings of small islands, such as Santorini and its surrounding islets in the Aegean, which form the rim of an ancient drowned volcano that exploded in about 1500 BCE – burying the island of

Thira and possibly inspiring Plato's Atlantis. At the other end of the volcanic island scale are atolls.

Nothing Atoll

Atolls are the last gasp of the volcano god, the haloes of drowned saints, floating it seems like lifebuoys on the brine. Their creation by volcanic processes was first postulated by Darwin. Though these coronas of coral are being continually eroded, like the crescent of the waning moon, many of these fragile islands are now threatened by sea levels rising and could disappear in decades rather than millennia.

Sadly, such island paradises have become synonymous with nuclear testing. America used Bikini Atoll to test an Atomic Bomb in 1946. And there have been numerous test explosions since – rendering many of the islands uninhabitable. Whole populations had to be moved, and there has been a recent case about a Polynesian tribe fighting for its right to return to its native island after it was turned into a military base – owned by the UK, and leased to the USA. The impact of such tests of marine life would have been devastating, and will leave seabeds polluted for centuries. As recently as 1997 France tested a nuclear weapon in the Pacific (on the Moruroa Atoll) – its secret service infamously blowing up the Greenpeace ship *Rainbow Warrior* in a New Zealand harbour, after its direct action campaign to stop them in 1987. Decades of tests have caused the Moruroa atoll to begin sinking— some 5 metres (16 feet) by the mid-Eighties. Tests at both the Moruroa and Fangataufa atolls were conducted at the bottoms of shafts bored to depths of up to 1,200 metres (4,000 feet) into the basalt core of the atoll. Who knows what earth-shattering consequences these tests will have? Such folly jeopardises the *fabric* of life on this planet: the continental plates. A nuclear test was reported to have taken place just before the Indian Ocean Tsunami, 26 December 2004 – was the marine earthquake which caused the devastating wave (resulting in the loss of at least 75,000 lives) the direct result of this?

Immovable objects, irresistible forces

All this tectonic moving about can create as well as destroy. Where continents collide the plates can be *both* pushed up, as in when the Indian subcontinent 'crashed' into the edge of Asia 200 million years ago to create the Himalayas. When one continental plate is pushed underneath another one it is known as a 'subduction zone'; for example, where the Andean Plate pushes into Chile and creates the Andes. The Mariana Trench, the world's deepest ocean trench, is formed by the collision of two oceanic crustal plates and from the subsequent volcanic activity the Mariana Islands have been formed along the western margin of the trench.

On the rebound

When an ice sheet melts the vast weight pushing the continental plate down is released, and consequently it slowly rises, returning to its pre-Ice Age level – in a process known as 'isostatic rebound'. This creates raised beaches, shore platforms and marine trenches and is still happening in Britain, with Scotland slowly rising a

The end of the road. Lyme Regis, Dorset. Photo by C. Williamson

couple of centimetres each year. Oban, on its west coast has a fine example of a raised beach, 35 to 40 feet above sea level. This displacement and 'stranding' can also occur through global sea level changes, known as 'eustasy' – which can be caused by movements of the Earth's crust, as well as other factors explored in the chapter 'When the Levee Breaks'. Britain is both emerging from and 'sinking' into the sea, but is not the only island where work still is in progress.

Islands freshly forged

Geologically the new kid on the block, but with the oldest parliament in Europe, Iceland lies atop one of the major fault lines in the Earth's crust, the vast wound in the world known as the Mid-Atlantic Ridge, where crustal plates move apart at about two centimetre a year. As a result Iceland, straddling its northern reaches, is one of the most tectonically-active places on Earth, with a plethora of volcanoes, thermal springs, and solfataras (volcanic vents emitting hot gases and vapours) rendering most of the centre uninhabitable. The majority of the population live on one quarter of the land – the lowlands, mainly around the coast, and three-quarters of those in its capital Reykjavik. The Gulf Stream ameliorates the climate, making Island a prize for seafaring explorers. It was finally settled in 874 CE by the Norwegian chieftain Ingólfur Arnarson.

Life on such a hot spot is predictably precarious. In 1783, when the only known eruption of Laki occurred, molten lava, volcanic ashes and gases, and torrential floods resulting from melting ice and snow led to the deaths of more than 9,000 people, ruined large tracts of arable land, and destroyed about eighty percent of the livestock on the island. And yet geology can be generous. In November 1963 submarine volcanic action resulted in the birth of Surtsey (Icelandic for 'Surtur's island', named appropriately after the Norse god of fire, Surtur). This small island emerged from boiling waters, clouds of steam and jets of fiery lava off the southern coast. Two years later, the lava flow ceased and the new island, about one square mile in area and 560 feet above sea level, was designated a nature reserve. Biological, geological and meteorological research is conducted on the island.

Nature's war of attrition

The inexorable processes of geology continue. The world may seem to have 'settled down' into its current shape, but that is only how it seems to us. Nature never sleeps. Continents continue to rise and fall and drift. New islands are still being born, while others are being lost (see Galápagos Islands below). Coastlines are under a state of constant negotiation between the land and the sea. Coastal features are being formed or eroded all the time. Today's headland or promontory becomes tomorrow's natural arch, (for instance, Durdle Door, Weymouth) then stack (Old Harry and his wife, Purbeck), then rocky islets, and so on. Sand spits caused by longshore drift (Chesil Beach, Dorset, being the longest example in the world) can connect islands to the mainland or sever them. The islet of Koh Nang Yuan, off Koh Tao in the Gulf of Siam, consists of three rocky outcrops joined by three spits of sand – like a natural triskel – unique in the world. How long this natural wonder will last, who can say? The mightiest mountains, formed by these huge geological forces, eventually end up as grains of sand blown along a beach, or absorbed into the endless ocean. The world is constantly being worn away, as it is dissimilated to its elemental particles, its stardust – a vast hourglass consisting of millions of year's worth of sand. And within each grain of sand there is evidence of, if not an entire world, as Blake saw, then at least a lost island.

Islands on the move

> The Galapagos islands are in a constant state of flux…

> (Stewart 2006b: 22)

If there was ever a place on this planet that was the living embodiment of all the lost island myths it is the Galápagos Islands. Almost as isolated as Easter Island, yet close enough to the prized shores of South America to be useful for whalers, pirates, navies and determined settlers, approximately ninety one degrees west, one degree south, these thirteen or so islands now belonging to Ecuador. They were called the Encatadas, the 'Enchanted Isles', by Spanish sailors who thought they moved: they weren't wrong. The islands are a prime example of how the forces of geology are shaping – and destroying – the world still.

Paul Stewart in his recent book on the isles (accompanying the 2006 BBC2 series, *Galapagos*) renders it as: 'an earthly Tartarus at the edge of the known world.' Echoing the Lost World of Professor Challenger, from Arthur Conan Doyle's famous adventure story, Stewart further describes it as:

> A lost world for the imagination to play on and science to work on.
>
> (Stewart 2006b: 163)

Warming to his subject, Stewart pursues the metaphor further:

> If this phrase, [a lost world] means anything, then it is here on Galapagos. There is evidence that the very first Galapagos islands may have emerged and disappeared during the Cretaceous – the age of the ruling reptiles. If so, then half-drowned dinosaurs may once have found salvation on Galapagos shores…Sadly the earlier Galapagos islands, and any fossils of creatures that occupied them, have long since been dragged beneath the ocean…
>
> (Stewart 2006b: 89)

The Galápagos Islands had a far more prosaic name than Challenger's zone of evolutionary anachronism, being derived from the name of a type of saddle, which the Spanish explorers were reminded of by the scalloped shell of the famous indigenous turtles: it could not have been more appropriate, as the islands are like gigantic turtles, making their slow determined way east, towards the subduction zone of the Andean Plate, real Turtle Islands:

> Across great spans of time these islands have wandered, like so many giant tortoises bathing in a pool.
>
> (Stewart 2006b: 89)

The Galápagos Islands crawl four centimetres a year towards South America – riding the Nazca plate south-east towards the subduction zone under South America's coast – pushing up the Andes while disappearing into the Peruvian/Chilean trench.

Six years after Darwin's famous visit on the *Beagle*, which was to influence his eventual Theory of Evolution, another young man destined to gain immortality through his writings visited, the author-to-be of *Moby Dick*:

> Herman Melville sailed on the *Acushnet* to the Enchanted Isles in 1841 as a young man. It was his first whaling voyage. It is unlikely that he ever saw these islands again, but he revisited them many times in his imagination, transforming them into something rich and strange.
>
> (Margaret Drabble's foreword to Melville 2002: vii)

What struck many of the early visitors was the seemingly desolate nature of them, weathered rock, fuming vents, little fresh water, strange creatures – a veritable hell, rather than the paradise we see it as today. Melville was not impressed at first, describing them as:

> A group rather of extinct volcanoes than of isles, looking much as the world at large might after a penal conflagration… It is to be doubted whether any spot on earth can, in desolateness, furnish a parallel to this group.

(Melville 2000: 5)

Strangely, there was a legend that 'to them change never comes – neither the change of seasons nor of sorrows', as Melville relates. If this were but so, we may not have to worry about their devastation.

But, alas, change came, in the form of the men Melville kept company with, decimating the islands' population of turtles, and any other natural riches they could plunder. Amazed at how docile the native fauna was, these first visitors availed themselves of this easy meat. And so it seems from its discovery the seeds of its destruction were sown it – and yet its doom goes back a lot further than that:

> A living museum of natural history, born from fire and ultimately destined to die beneath the waves, the islands of the Galapagos exist on an endless geological conveyor belt.

(Stewart 2006b)

Evidence of this can be found in the Carnegie Ridge, a chain of submerged ancestral islands, called 'seamounts', these sunken volcanoes lie to the east – and show what will one day happen to the Galápagos Islands. The oldest of the chain by geological standards is 'Española in the east… [is] soon to go the way of its vanished predecessors and disappear beneath the waves.' (Stewart 2006b: 6)

The Galápagos Islands seem to offer us, like Easter Island (explored in the next chapter), a parable of humanity, of the rise and fall of civilisation, and by the vast geological time scales, a perspective on time and history. By the forces of eruption, erosion and continental drift the actual islands themselves are fated to be lost:

> Millions of years from now every Galapagos island we see today will be drawn beneath the waves.

(Stewart 2006b: 22)

This is the fate of all islands – some sooner than others. It is a process that has been going on since the birth of the planet and will continue long since humankind has faded away or moved on in search of new planets to sustain itself, for new Easter Islands, which we will look at next in 'The Island That Ate Itself'.

Chapter seven

The island that ate itself

Oisín wandered about. He was pretty good at wandering. He was a poet after all. And there wasn't much else he could do. Niamh was occupied on 'official princess business' and so all Oisín could do was, well, wander.

'Don't look so downcast. I've got work to do, hun: fêtes to open, tournaments to judge, hearts to break,' his new wife explained. 'Go and enjoy yourself – you're in paradise! But not too much, those nymphs are little minxes! I have eyes and ears everywhere!'

So, Oisín found himself wandering over a perfect hilltop, amidst golden ranks of flowers, lonely as a … as a … buttercup? It was no use. The muse wasn't with him today. She was elsewhere. If everything was too perfect, there was nothing to write about, no grit in the oyster.

Oisín sighed, and set to exploring the island.

Anyone he bumped into seeming to be lolling about. In hammocks, in bowers, in pagodas of fabulous design. An eternal siesta of the soul.

Too much carousing more like. Party by night, sleep it off by day. Oisín had seen the pattern before. Back at Aengus's place, the palace of Brugh na Boyne – the god of love's shag-pad. Here, in the kingdom of the bone-idle, soft-furnishings were king. And snack-food.

Oisín's stomach rumbled. His body was telling him it was lunchtime when he hadn't actually exerted himself all morning. Wandering doesn't burn off many calories.

'The trouble with paradise,' brooded Oisín, wanting to feel disgruntled about something – although it was probably more to do with Niamh abandoning him, 'is there's nothing much to do.'

Except design endless leisure pursuits… Oisín groaned. More mirth! More hilarious carousing!

But every new idea was met with indolence, after the initial enthusiasm waned.

In a land where no one works, nothing gets done!

Sure, the inhabitants were free from want, from hunger, cold, disease, old age, death.

Everything except boredom.

And there's only so much ambrosia you can eat...

~~~~~~~~~~~~~~~~~~~~~~~~~~~~~~~~~~

Lost islands have been created and are being created by both manmade and natural forces: both are environmental facts in the broadest sense. The qualitative difference is the latter is usually slow and sustainable (even a volcanic eruption, however devastating, eventually gives rise to new life). Manmade forces seldom are, as we will look at below. The quantitative difference is the *rate* and *scale* at which these lost islands occur. Climates have always changed, but over millennia, not decades:

> The predicted rate of change of three degrees a century is
> probably faster than the global average temperature has changed
> at any time over the past ten thousand years.

> (Houghton 2004: 10)

Foremost climate change scientist, Robert May, says: 'the steadiness of the last 6000–5000 years is thought by many to be part of the reason why we have developed civilization.' (Price 2006b: 131) According to May, Thomas Lovejoy concurs that in a '10,000 year period of relative climate stability' the majority of human history is written – civilizations have risen and fallen. A period of climatic instability, and it will all be unwritten.

Climate change, or as it tends to be referred to now 'climate chaos', coupled with a vast human population and a rapidly altered landscape creates too many variables, an unpredictable outcome – a Mandelbrot set of potential futures. Nevertheless, climate modeling has become big business, the Hadley Centre for Climate Prediction has cornered the market in Britain – digital augurers for the New Roman (American) Century – and in 2006–7 the BBC/OU ran the world's largest climate model experiment with the help of thousands of personal PCs around the globe, all running slightly different variations on a model running from 1820 to 2080.

There was uncertainty for a while – perhaps perpetuated by the oil lobby (as suggested in the 2006 film/book/powerpoint presentation, *An Inconvenient Truth*, by Al Gore) – about first the existence of, and then the causes of global warming. Now there is a broad scientific consensus that it is a fact, (IPCC report 2006) and has been brought about by manmade factors – ones which are escalating it out of control, unless decisive action is taken now. As Robert May warns:

> ... seemingly small things today commit us to consequences that
> will unfold over several human lifetimes.

(May 2006: 132)

There are many sobering examples from history about the devastating impact of humans on their environment – it is a long and sad list of humanity's greed, short-sightedness, stupidity and arrogance. In this context we will focus on ecological lost islands that haunt humanity's conscience. We will begin with the 'classic' lost island, the one which more than any has come to represent man's folly and humanity's potential fate.

The loneliest place on Earth

Easter Island, more accurately known by its Polynesian name of Rapa Nui, is perhaps the ultimate eco-parable, and has been cited as such in books such as Clive Ponting's *The Green History of the World*, and Paul Bahn and John Flenley's *Easter Island, Earth Island.* The latter stating in their preface:

> ... if Easter Island is seen as a microcosm of our own world, then
> this is, indeed, a cautionary tale relevant for the future of all
> humankind.

(Bahn and Flenley 1992: 9)

Like any negative space Easter Island has become a blank canvas for each writer's predilections and pet theories. The myth-making that has accrued around it is perhaps as telling of modern mentalities as of the original inhabitants' actions. We make apocalypses, like gods, in our own image.

The 150 square mile island is: 'the most isolated piece of inhabited land on the globe' (Bahn and Flenley 1992: 22): lost in the vastness of the Pacific Ocean like a planet in the depths of space. It lies 2,000 miles off the coast of South America; 1,250 miles from the nearest inhabited island, Pitcairn. Its famous igneous giants, the Moai, overlook a denuded landscape, bereft of trees, livestock and people, and have become the ultimate symbol of ecological suicide. Its cataclysmic decline was perhaps hardwired into its imposed name. With its Christianised moniker, Easter Island, the Eden myth was exported to one of the most remotest places on Earth. If it was a paradise, and in its unsullied state – sun, lush forests, bountiful seas, pristine beaches – it fitted the cliché of one, then it was one man most definitely exiled himself from, as Ponting soberly suggests:

> The history of Easter Island is not one of lost civilisations and
> esoteric knowledge. Rather it is a striking example of the
> dependence of human societies on their environment and of the
> consequences of irreversibly damaging that environment.

(Ponting 1991: 2)

It remained undiscovered by Western Civilisation until 1722, when, on Easter Sunday, Admiral Jakob Roggeveen, with his three ships, *Eagles, Thienhoven* and the *African Galley*, hoved into view. Roggeveen had been in search of the legendary southern continent. On that auspicious day Roggeveen gave the unknown island its name.

It is sadly ironic that *Christmas* Island was the site of the first Atom Bomb test – these two Christianised islands seem to act as apocalyptic parentheses for Western civilisation, the alpha and omega of Project Progress.

Like some visitor to a post-apocalyptic Earth, the Dutch Admiral Roggeveen:

> … found a society in a primitive state with about 3000 people
> living in squalid reed huts, or caves, engaged in almost perpetual
> warfare and resorting to cannibalism in a desperate attempt to
> supplement the meagre food supplies available on the island.

(Ponting 1991)

Roggeveen moored off coast for a week and only made landfall once. The landing party warily replenished the ship's supplies and left the island soon after, but its existence had been registered to the wider world. Rapa Nui's solipsism had been shattered.

Easter Island was stumbled upon by a Captain Cook, weak with hunger, in 1774 – he too had been searching for the fabled southern continent – and by other speculators briefly, who soon lost interest in this unpromising outpost. The Spanish annexed it, but did not bother to colonise. An American ship shanghaied twenty-seven slaves from the dwindling populace. In 1877, Peruvians sailors all but removed the rest, leaving only 110 old people and children. It was eventually taken over by Chile – and turned into 'a giant ranch for 40,000 sheep, run by a British company, with the few remaining inhabitants confined to one small village' (Ponting 1991: 1).

It was a ruthless food chain. The islanders ate their own island, then each other, then were replaced by more efficient food for Europeans.

Thus, despite being found, by the late nineteenth century a small but significant island (created by volcanic activity in the third century CE, settled by Polynesians in the fifth, with 7,000 inhabitants at its peak) was effectively 'lost' – all that remains of its civilisation are the six hundred-plus Ozymandias-like stone heads, the Moai: symbols of monumental folly and a warning to the world. Sentinel-like, their dark-browed glare warns us of what could so easily happen to our own civilisation. Would one day the Statue of Liberty be gazing blankly out in the same way?

From the scant remains it has been possible to piece together the fragments of the story of Rapa Nui. The surviving islanders' oral tradition, recorded before their cultural extinction, provided a nominal creation myth:

> Settlers [were] said to have come from a large, warm, green island
> to the west called 'Maroe Renga', probably in the Marquesas. One

tale relates that they left because of a cataclysm, when most of
their land was submerged beneath the ocean.

(Bahn and Flenley 1992: 71)

This tantalising shred is enough to get Atlantis-anoraks' antennae twitching, but is entirely probable among volcanic islands on the Atlantic Ridge or Pacific Ring of Fire.

Looking out from the lonely rock, surrounded by the endlessness of the Pacific Ocean, it would be easy to see why the inhabitants saw themselves as the 'last people':

'The people there believed that they were the only survivors on
Earth, all other land having sunk beneath the sea.'

(Bahn and Flenley 1992: 213)

Another myth recounted by Bahn and Flenley talks of an exiled chief, who follows a prophetic dream of an island 'to the east', with volcanic craters and pleasant beaches. This could describe any number of the myriad islands of the various '-Nesias', (Poly-, Micro-, Mela-) and probably is a story echoed throughout the Pacific, as tribes moved east to look for new land, a natural migratory phenomenon as an expanding population needs more resources – a watery mirror image of the colonisation of America, with its Western frontier pushed back all the way to the Pacific.

The islanders subsisted on a limited diet – only able to grow sweet potato, fish and gather bananas and figs. However, this gave them plenty of time to channel into other activities. Archaeological evidence from the island suggests a clan-based social system, one that became destructively competitive. From ceremonial centres called Ahu – a stone platform – the stone heads were raised, fifteen in a row, like a Polynesian football team standing for the national anthem. From quarries the heavy-browed, top-knotted giants were transported on rollers, made from tree trunks – as there were no livestock such as oxen capable of doing this for them. New rollers had to be made for each journey, as they shattered under the weight of the stone gods…The inevitable was going to happen, like a man sawing a branch that he sits on. To the onlooker this seems absurdly foolish – but consider the self-destructive activities our 'enlightened' civilisation perpetuates. Are we any wiser, with our four-wheel-drives and short-haul habits? We may smugly chide such folly, but Western civilisation continue to raise their Maoi, as the planet's resources dwindle; for example, golf courses in the desert; snow resorts in the sun; millennium white elephants; the world's tallest, largest, longest, et cetera – monuments to hubris, the new Babels of Babylon.

Rapa Nui society collapsed at its peak, as suggested by the many stone heads left unfinished – between 500 and 1,000 of them – like a chain of dominoes flicked over. Positioned on clifftops, the Maoi always looked outwards, across the unbroken blue ring of ocean, ultimate threshold guardians of a solipsistic civilisation: a solipsism dramatically punctured. These eery icons greeted the Europeans, and many were toppled on their arrival by the natives: their gods had failed them.

Yet the actually cause of their downfall was far less mysterious:

> The cause of the collapse and the key to understanding the 'mysteries' of Easter Island was massive environmental degradation brought on by deforestation of the whole island.
>
> (Ponting 1991: 5)

With no trees, there was no protection for the soil. Rain leached away what good soil was left. With no livestock to replace nutrients the landscape quickly became denuded. Forest-less, there were no materials to build houses, nets, clothing, boats. The Rapa Nuins trapped and doomed themselves.

Aunt Sallys on Ratopia

In academe theories are set up and toppled like Maoi on a cyclical basis – so many Aunt Sallys at a fun fair – the ground-breaking theory turns to orthodoxy, then becomes the target for the young iconoclast academic keen to make a reputation. Bahn and Flenley's theory has been challenged, as will no doubt the theories that have replaced them in popularity since. Among the key 'received wisdoms' currently prevalent are that the decline in population was most likely the result of early eighteenth century Dutch traders who brought diseases and took slaves from the island. Research indicates that 'first contact diseases' – typhus, influenza and smallpox – carry extremely high mortality rates, often exceeding ninety percent. The first traders to reach the island were likely to have carried such diseases, which would have spread rapidly among the islanders and destroyed the native population, compounding the apocalypse already wrought from within. This calamity was the last straw – Rapa Nui imploded

According to Terry Hunt of the University of Hawaii the creation of the Maoi did not led to the denigration of the island's resources – although it is hard to deny that that timber and huge manpower would have been needed to construct them – but the blame lies with rats. Hunt's research discovered the impact of this alien species on the ecosystem. They arrived with the Polynesians and within a century had increased to twenty million – with no natural predators on the island except for humans, the rodents gorged on the seeds of the island's trees, preventing them from regrowing. After the trees were gone, the island's rat population dropped off to a mere one million. They had eaten themselves out of house and home. It was the end of rat-opia.

The hungry island

Whatever the causes, the parable of Rapa Nui shows a classic arc of over-exploitation of resources:

> They carried out for us the experiment of permitting unrestricted population growth, profligate use of resources, destruction of the

environment and boundless confidence in their religion to take
care of the future. The result was an ecological disaster leading to
a population crash.

(Bahn and Flenley 1992: 213)

This was the prediction of Malthus, and haunted Victorians and the early twentieth century. Two world wars took care of that. When humanity gets too abundant, those apocalyptic horsemen, war, famine, plague, or pestilence, (Ring-Wraiths to strike terror into our hobbit-hearts, finding no sanctuary even in our sleepy Shires) seem to come along to winnow out the excess: Mother Nature's good housekeeping, in the guise of Kali.

The Club of Rome, a group of businessmen and computer specialists, predicted in the seventies that Earth will follow the same Malthusian pattern as Easter Island: a rising population using up ever-decreasing natural resources, and creating increasingly more pollution, will result eventually in a devastating population crash, the same old:

Deforestation, famine, warfare, collapse of civilisation and
population decline.

(Bahn and Flenley 1992: 212)

This pattern is being echoed on a macrocosmic level. It could be the history of the twenty-first century. Already wars are being fought over dwindling resources – 'peak oil' being the main one at present – and as Kofi Anann, former Secretrary of the United Nations, and others have suggested, water will be the cause of war in the latter part of the century. According to the World Water Council by 2020 water use is expected to have increased by forty percent, and seventeen percent more water will be required for food production to meet the needs of growing populations.

On an overheating planet, fresh water will be the most valuable commodity. Finally, when it is too late, humanity will learn to value what it had for free all along – air, water, soil, trees, wildlife – as prophesised by Black Elk and his ilk

Ponting, and many others, see the fate of Easter Island as a salutary warning to humanity:

Like Easter Island the Earth has only limited resources to support
human society and all its demands. Like the islands, the human
population of the Earth has no practical means of escape.

(Ponting 1991: 7)

What excessive follies we fritter away the Earth's resources on: endless consumerism; built-in transience; a throwaway culture; fashion dictating we must buy 'this year's look' and jettison last year's; high-tech gadgets that get upgraded every season; new formats forcing us to buy our collections of films and music all over again, et cetera. The impasse of capitalism – infinite growth based on infinite resources in a finite world – until one day we will wake up discover we have nothing to eat and the cars do not run anymore. All those 'useful' electrical goods rendered useless as the grid goes down; all that plastic junk cluttering up the planet by our landfill lifestyle; all those bits of plastic in wallets and purses rendered useless as the economy collapses... Then people will discover what real wealth is, what real skills are – or face extinction.

> Would it not be sensible to learn from the lesson of Easter Island
> history and apply it to the Earth Island on which we lives?

(Bahn and Flenley 1992: 213)

From microcosm to macrocosm

Macrocosmically, these are issues we are all threatened by. Ironically what was the site of modern man's 'genesis' may herald his apocalypse. The Galápagos Islands are the place of origin of *The Origin of the Species* (1859). Darwin visited it as a twenty-six year old man on the historic voyage of the *Beagle*. It would be later in his life he would consolidate his findings, but here the seeds were sown for the paradigm-shifting discovery – through the collection of, among other specimens, the famous finches. Darwin did not preserve these properly and they were lost, but fortunately others were collected with which he could base his world-changing research on.

Darwin noted that there is a 'web of complex relations' among species, moving 'onwards in ever increasing circles of complexity'. We are all part of this web of life, though many of us forget it.

Unfortunately, many of Galápagos' visitors have not been so sensitive to its ecology. Whalers, pirates, military personnel, settlers, tourism... The islands have been exploited and colonised, and with cheaper air travel, the problem is getting worse.

Some 30,000 people already live on five islands of Galápagos and the population is rising at about 5.7 per cent a year.

They need fuel, electricity, food and materials in order to sustain themselves and the vast majority of these goods are shipped to the islands from the mainland. A direct result of this need is the introduction of alien species that severely threaten native flora and fauna. Every one of us who visits this fragile ecosystem may be contributing at least indirectly to its damage. (Stewart 2006b: 233)

Once again, this illustrates the depressingly familiar *fait accompli* that we destroy the paradises we seek. It is as if we cannot accept an Eden without wanting to bring about its Fall.

Even the diehard atheist and controversial geneticist Richard Dawkins, author of *The Selfish Gene* (1976), and *The God Delusion* (2006), uses evocative language in describing the Galápagos Islands in the foreword to Stewart's book, likening it to a scientific paradise: 'A geological and biological Eden, the evolutionary scientists Arcadia.'

Yet can we act like God and prevent this from happening? Gore and others now argue that it is now a *moral* choice. We cannot just stand by and let the world be destroyed. We are aware of the problems. We have the knowledge and technology to solve them. The responsibility is ours.

Yet when it comes to saving wildlife, this can become a difficult issue. Are polar bears better off in zoos than on melting ice? How much can we 'interfere'? Should we? Should we let evolution do its work? Do we risk destroying what we seek to preserve, for instance by turning wilderness into 'parks' of leisure resource? There is the case of the Galápagos penguins:

> We know that the population status of the Galapagos penguin depends on sea temperature, because of the food supply. But if the El Nino events are happening too often, the penguins can't repopulate – its numbers can't go up. Well, therefore it needs to move into waters that are cooler. But where will that be? It lives at the moment on a very isolated oceanic archipelago. There is no further land suitable, say, 1000 miles (1610 km] further north. So what are we going to do? Do we look for an equivalent place in the southern hemisphere – the same latitude, same currents – and release them there? Do we try to preserve what we see as natural, in our very narrow time perspective, or do we say we are actually interested in having functioning, self-sustaining populations in the 'wild'?

(Price 2006: 59)

Are we to become modern Noahs? Some would argue yes – what are needed are modern 'arks', so-called 'eco-refugiums' or areas in which a population of organisms can survive a period of unfavourable conditions.

Perhaps some nature reserves, wildlife sanctuaries, safari parks, even zoos, serve this purpose, though how 'natural' can an animal be in such an environment – and how it affects their behaviour – is a contentious issue. For instance, the Whale and Dolphin Conservation Society has amassed wide-ranging evidence against the detriments of keeping cetaceans in captivity: neurotic behaviour, illness, infertility, aggression, mortality, et cetera.

The Galápagos Islands sum up many issues concerning lost islands. Threats to the Galápagos Islands, and islands in general, as listed in the Summer 2006 issue of *BBC Wildlife* magazine are:

    i.   Loss of isolation
    ii.   Loss of focus
    iii. Population growth
    iv. Complacency

Another 'threat' comes from man's curiosity. Many of these sites bear the legacy of this – and archaeology can help us piece together the puzzle, factors we shall look at next in 'Stick in the Mud'.

Chapter eight
Stick in the mud

Oisín wandered the perfect shoreline, along the perfect beach on another perfect day. Things couldn't be better. Every day he woke up next to a vision of loveliness, his Niamh, and every night drank mead with his beautiful wife to consecrate their honey-moon. He'd been on Tír nan Og for nearly a month now. And he'd seen many wonders and had many adventures – fighting giants, riddling with dwarves, rescuing damsels – but one can even tire of those after a while. There was something troubling him and he couldn't quite put his finger on it, and so he decided a brisk walk along the coast was in order.

As the Fenian poet gazed out across the sea towards the rising sun he sighed. Over the horizon, back in the real world, was Erin… Suddenly Oisín stubbed his toe on something, sticking out of the sand. He cursed, but then it caught his eye. He bent down and pulled up what looked at first like a stick of driftwood from the sand. Then he gasped. In his hand he held the unmistakable stump of a gae bolg, a broken spear of the Fianna – his father's warband – stained with battle, washed up from his homeland…

Rolling the battered shaft in his hands, laden with time in the way nothing in Tír nan Og was, Oisín thought of his father, Fionn, of his companions, his hounds even. His homeland seemed as remote as the past… And he realised he was homesick. He was missing Erin. He was missing his family and friends. And what made it worse he hadn't been able to say goodbye properly. If only he could go back one last time…

~~~~~~~~~~~~~~~~~~~~~~~~~~~~~~~~~~

Archaeology has a lot to tell us about lost islands. Indeed, in a science which professes to be the 'study of human history and prehistory through the excavation of sites and the analysis of physical remains' (*Concise OED*) it could be argued that it dedicates itself to the rediscovery of the 'lost islands' of history – whether a 'lost' medieval village cleared for sheep farming; a cluster of Neolithic hut circles on a moor rendered uninhabitable by climate change; a 'lost' stone circle – such as

Poet's coast. Kilve, East Quantoxhead, where Coleridge wandered, close to his home in Nether Stowey.

Avebury, rediscovered by John Aubrey while foxhunting in January 1649; the lost city of the Incas, Machu Piccu – discovered by Yale archaeologist Hiram Bingham in July 1911; or indeed a lost underwater kingdom, as detailed below.

In a similar fashion to the spear found by Oisín, what has become known as Sea Henge was discovered by a Norfolk beachcomber…

Seahenge: a saw point

'In the Spring of 1998 a circle of prehistoric timbers exposed by the receding tide, was found projecting from sands at Holme-next-to-Sea in Norfolk', so the Flag Fen website summarises the beginning of this controversial saga. The Channel 4 Time Team microsite says of their broadcast in 1999 on Seahenge:

> Never before has a Time Team programme been the focus of so
> much public interest and controversy…

In late 1998 Norfolk Archaeology Unity undertook fieldwork, discovering the 'circle' was 'probably early Bronze Age'; and was in fact 'egg-shaped, made of 55 split oak timbers with a maximum diameter of 6.78 metres' (Flag Fen website). In the centre an inverted tree trunk had been placed in a pit.

In January 1999 *The Independent*, published an evocative front page photograph of what they dubbed 'Sea Henge', conjuring up the false impression of a Stonehenge-next-the Sea, which attracted hordes of visitors, many of them pagan. Modern druids claimed it as a ritual site of their ancestors.

Yet its exact purpose remains a mystery. Like many of such 'sacred' sites, each visitor seems to invest it with their own preconceptions or preoccupations. Those who claimed Seahenge as their own found it slip through their grasp in a flabbergasting act of archaeological vandalism – but perhaps this is the nature of the place, the Sea Henge site being an intertidal zone, a dangerously liminal place. It is located on a Victoria Sandwich of layers – Upper Chalk overlain by a series of Quaternary and Holocene deposits. Resting on the chalk are 'a sequence of sands and gravels of marine and glacial/periglacian origin' – which suggest the effects of the Ice Age – and most interestingly of all, these are overlain by forest bed deposits – overlain themselves by intertidal sand, but proving this site was once on land. It is highly unlikely it was constructed to be inundated. 'It was probably on the shore or inland when it was in use' (Wood 2000). Even Flag Fen staff agree that:

> ...even the smallest Bronze Age religious structures were constructed with enormous care and by large numbers of people.

> ... The trees were felled with bronze axes and then split with wooden wedges. Measurements of the axe-marks show that between 51 and 59 axes were used. If each person only owned one axe, it suggests how many people must have worked together to create Seahenge.

> ... Beyond the timber circle lay the North Sea, which was seen as the realm or dwelling place of the ancestors. Seahenge was deliberately placed between the ancestral world – the sea – and that of the living – the land, tying the two together.

This is a surprisingly confident supposition – since how can the archaeologists know that the sea was 'seen as the realm or dwelling place of the ancestors' by our Bronze Age ancestors? And yet, this chimes with my intuition on the subject, and seems to be echoed in the Anglo-Saxon ship burials at Sutton Hoo (just down the East Anglian coast) and the Viking Ship Burial on the Isle of Man – explored below – as well as the plethora of folkloric evidence and the cosmology handed down to us from myths and legends: that the soul of deceased went over or into the sea.

If the Flag Fen assumption is correct – that the Seahenge builders did think of the North Sea as the dwelling place of their ancestors – then the Seahenge builders were right, as the discoveries on the seabed have proved. During the last Ice Age, Britain was connected to Europe: the rich fishing area known as Doggerbank was inhabited by Mesolithic hunter-gatherers in a lost zone called Doggerland, a vast plain that stretched across from Britain's east coast to what is now Denmark, northern Germany, Holland, Belgium and France (also featured in a Time Team special, 'Britain's Drowned World', April 2007). Mammoth skulls, sabre-tooth tiger fangs and worked flint have been trawled up from this inundated world – a real lost land below the sea where the ancestors lived.

Seahenge seems to be a deliberate ritual dialogue with the sea. At the risk of reducing it all to Freudian 'phallus-see', is the inverted oak trunk housed within the shaft of the earth meant to represent the union of the sky-orientated god and earth-embodied goddess, resulting in a fecund harvest, either on land or sea? The symbolism seems blatant – to us, but who knows what it represented to the mind of the Bronze Age shore-dweller? Whatever ritual significance it had has now been rendered meaningless by the timbers removal inland, out of context. Preservation to some. Others would call it desecration.

What had remained undisturbed – and preserved – for millennia was, within weeks of being revealed, cut up and taken away. For the Archaeologist Trust decided the best course of action was to remove the exposed timbers from the shoreline for preservation. This was done with chainsaws and a certain degree of cloak-and-dagger surreptitiousness in the middle of the night. It seems those who removed it were aware of the strong reaction they would provoke. When the media got hold of this, the emotive reactions were almost unprecedented – only Stonehenge had been more of a bone of contention between pagans, the general public, English Heritage and archaeologists.

The Flag Fen feature on Sea Henge has a *nota bene,* perhaps to prevent the wrath of the pagan community being directed to their door: 'The Seahenge timbers are now being conserved in Portsmouth by the Mary Rose Trust to ensure that they will be preserved for the future.' Since then it has decided they will be housed in the Kings Lynn Museum in a specially-prepared room.

Seahenge offered us a tantalising and dramatic window into our nation's past – and like the fictional Brigadoon it was only there in the cold light of day for a brief while – before being whisked away, catalogued and stored, leaving a gaping hole, the intention and effort of its builders destroyed: a marker of our changing coastline gone for good.

The pub lunch of a lifetime

Flag Fen's discovery was a similar 'stick in the mud' scenario – the story goes that in 1982 archaeologist Francis Pryor, returning from a pub lunch, stubbed his toe on an interesting piece of timber sticking out of the ground (another version says a digger working on a drainage ditch displaced a piece of timber 'split in a very distinctive manner'). His archaeologist curiosity piqued, Pryor returned to take a sample. When it was carbon-dated, it turned out to be 6,000 years old. After being fully excavated, Flag Fen, as it became known, was revealed as a late Bronze Age ritual site consisting of an artificial island – rectangular huts on a huge timber platform the size of two football pitches, supported above the water.

This structures 'sacredness' is suggested by the surrounding water, which separates the platform from the mundane world. Unlike many crannogs – which it closely resembles in many other ways – this was not inhabited. Evidence of settlement was found nearby, but not on it; similarly suggesting its sacred usage. It seems every clan had its own ritual space on the platform, like plots in a cemetery. It was connected to the land by a kilometre-long alignment of 60,000 posts, arrayed in five rows and orientated towards the midwinter sunrise. Amazingly, these have been preserved in the fen peat and a section can be viewed in the Preservation Room, where jets of moisture regularly spray the exposed section to stop it decaying. Unlike Seahenge, this site has been preserved in situ. The damp room has the breath of a grave about it and gives the visitor a spine-tingling feeling, perhaps a sensation that could be called chrono-vertigo, as one gazes back through a window into the distant past.

Shinewater Blues

Flag Fen is an extraordinary site but by no means unique. Flag Fen seems ostensibly similar in set up to Glastonbury Lake Village, although the fact one site was habited and the other was not differentiates them: they served widely different functions. However, a more recent discovery unearthed a sister site in East Sussex, Shinewater, in 1995. Regarded as 'one of the most important prehistoric finds of recent years', ('Sussex 'Flag Fen' decays without record') an article laments how the Bronze Age settlement and ceremonial site is decaying because no money can be found to pay for an archaeological excavation: having been found, it seems certain that Shinewater will become another lost island.

How many other Shinewaters are out there? Who knows how many have been destroyed by time, or man's apathy? Yet others may await to be discovered – other sticks in the mud to be stumbled upon? Could the many folk tales, legends and myths of mysterious islands be ancestral or place memory of these early islands? Perhaps it is time archaeology took heed of these possible oral clues, linguistic treasure maps to lost islands: an holistic approach to the past.

Glastonbury Lake Village

Although the evidence is that Glastonbury has not been an island for thousands of years, if ever, it has certainly surrounded by easily-flooded plains since the last Ice Age, (9,000 BCE) and its earliest inhabitants adapted to these uncertain conditions very well, as the remarkable evidence of the 'Glastonbury Lake Village' and surrounding trackways prove.

The so-called 'Glastonbury Lake Village', more accurately a 'marsh-edge settlement' (Rahtz 1993: 22–3) was discovered in 1892 by Arthur Bulleid, and excavated with the help of H. St George Gray in the early part of the twentieth century. A pallisaded enclosure, built on stilts and platforms of thirteen major round houses, and two dozen or so minor ones, annexe huts, and smaller huts for baking, guards, workshops, plus granaries and probably enclosures for livestock. An enormous amount of effort would have been required to create such a settlement, but it would have afforded protection – it could only be approached by canoe through the reedy maze of marshes, if it could be found at all in the misty fastness, and one can see how such a place may have given rise to legends of 'strange islands', elusive brigadoons – for it would have been inundated at some points. It is very similar in construction to the crannogs of Ireland and Scotland.

The lake village's preservation and discovery was almost miraculous, but even more remarkable was the discovery of the Sweet Track in 1970, the oldest manmade trackway found in Europe – a raised walkway stretching four kilometres, tree-ring dated to be from the winter of 3,807–6 BCE, constructed of hewn planks of timber, two kilometres of heavy handrails and 6,000 pegs. For 5,776 years it had been preserved in the peat. Other trackways criss-crossed the treacherous marshes, including the erroneously titled Abbot's Way (when it was discovered in 1835 it was thought to have been the works of monks) but has now been dated to 2,500 BCE.

The Peat Moors Visitors Centre near Shapwick on the Levels recreates the lake village and Sweet Track, with Iron Age roundhouse reconstructions, craft demonstrations and special events, including the burning of a mini-whicker man at their annual Samhain Fair.

When I returned from Lyonesse

The Isles of Scilly, a cluster of two hundred odd rocks, islets and islands, lie twenty-eight miles of the south-west tip of Cornwall and form the most south-westerly point of Britain. Benefitting from the Gulf Stream, they are the only British islands to enjoy a genuinely sub-tropical climate – and anyone who has visited the five main islands of St Mary, Tresco, St Martins, St Agnes and Bryher with their pale inkdust beaches, warm clear seas and lush tropical gardens would easily see why the Isles of Scilly have long been associated with the Fortunate Isles. (The Fortunate Isle is mentioned in Classical mythology, and quoted in the chapter on mythology, 'Into the West', and 'Walking on Brigadoon'). Some would claim them to be a candidate for Avalon, as they lay towards the setting sun and the isles certainly seems paradisal on a summer's day. They boast an impressive array of prehistoric sites (more than a 1,000), many of them burial sites, so one can see why they were thought of as otherworldly 'isles of the dead' – their first inhabitants certainly did. The eastern Isles boast two graves to King Arthur: Great Arthur (actually three Neolithic entrance graves and two cairns) and Middle Arthur (two well-preserved entrance graves). Yet there is something even more distinctive about the Isles of Scilly which qualifies them as a strong candidate for a 'lost island'. Jeanette Ratcliffe and Charles Johns say in their introduction to the island's archaeological heritage:

> An unusual aspect of Scilly's archaeology is the presence of
> remains below high water, the result of low-lying land being
> submerged by a gradual rise in sea level.

(Ratcliffe and Johns 2003: 2)

Ratcliffe and Johns go onto say:

> Current thinking suggests that the archipelago may have consisted
> of a single land mass stretching from the Western Rocks to the
> Eastern Isles and from Peninnis to Shipman Head. As the ice

sheets melted the sea level rose, and by 3000 BC submergence of low lying areas had led to the formation of a number of separate islands… Throughout later prehistory the sea continued to rise, but it was probably not until the end of the Roman period that today's islands began to appear. Even as late as the eleventh century AD most of these would have been joined at low water.

(Ratcliffe and Johns 2003 :4)

The evidence for this sea level rise is actually based upon the archaeological remains themselves:

This model for the submergence of Scilly is based on a sea level rise of 2.1 to 2.6 millimetres per year, calculated by using the vertical position of dated submerged archaeological remains, and assuming that they were originally sited just above the shoreline.

(Ratcliffe and Johns 2003 :4)

Further evidence comes from the intertidal peat deposits exposed in recent winter storms – peat only forms in fresh water. Such carbon-rich material is a gift to the archaeologists: 'Dating of these can reveal when they were formed and when they were overwhelmed by the sea' and the pollen can give us a clue as to the type of vegetation present at the time.

In the Mesolithic Period, 8,000 to 4000 BCE, 'camps would probably have been concentrated around the coastline which is now submerged', hence little trace of them remains – even on higher dry land, finds are rare because the Mesolithic people mainly used organic materials easily decomposed.

Examples of submerged archaeology include Stone Row on Higher Town Beach, St Martin's, and submerged field walls and the foundations of Iron Age huts submerged at high tide on Samson Flats. Furthermore:

Scilly is first mentioned as insula sillina by classical Roman writers of the 1st–3rd centuries AD, but the name is of native pre-Roman origin and may incorporate that of a Celtic female deity, similar if not identical to the water goddess, Sulis [sic – Sul] worshipped at the hot springs of Bath.

(Ratcliffe and Johns 2003 :4)

Ratcliffe and Johns suggest the carved stone of Chapel Down, St Martin's, may be the effigy of a Celtic god and evidence of such activity.

There are legends of bells below the waves between Scilly and the mainland – Jennifer Westwood excellently lists and deconstructs these in her thorough gazetteer of British sites, *Albion*:

The tradition of a lost land between Land's End and the Scilly Isles is mentioned by Camden in his *Britannia* (trans. Holland, 1610).

St Mary' Bay, the Isles of Scilly.

> He points to a group of rocks about midway between Land's End and Scilly 'called in Cornish *Lethowsow*; by the English, *Sevenstones*' as evidence that Cornwall extended further west. The Cornish, he says, called the area bounded by the rocks *Trevga*, 'a dwelling', and there were reports of windows 'and other stuff' being fished up there, and of the tops of houses being glimpsed beneath the waves.
>
> (Westwood 1985: 27)

The faraway magic of the Isles of Scilly have fuelled countless speculation of a lost land – though the truth is it was connected to the mainland at least until the end of the last Ice Age. It seems to have been part-and-parcel of the legend-building of the Cornish/Breton legend known equally as Ys/Kêr Ys/Lyonesse, the shared ending redolent of another legendary sibilance, Atlantis, echoing the endless susurration of the sea. We will look at them and other tales of inundation, ancient and modern, in the chapter 'When the Levee Breaks'.

Viking ship burials

For islands of the dead to be reached, boats of the dead were needed:

> Since the ship was so strongly associated with the continuance of life, it was the proper antidote to death. Invoking the powers of fertility and rebirth gave men and women a way to defeat the grave by seeking the life that lies beyond it. In addition to the raw life energy symbolized by the Vanir and, by inference, the ship, there was the reasonable notion that a seagoing vessel could carry a soul on its journey across the waters of darkness to the Other World.
>
> (McNallen 1995)

Britain has a spate of annual re-enactments of Viking ship burials in York, Shetland and Peel. These are testimony of the Nordic influence to these isles. However populist they maybe (seeming to catch on after the Fifties film by Richard Fleischer, *The Vikings*, which portrayed the stereotypical horned raiders in glorious

Technicolor) there is evidence to substantiate such activity (chiefly from the account by the Arab traveller of the Early Middles Ages, Ibn Fadlan, of the cremation practices of the Rus along the Volga). Yet this describes the burning of a ship *on land*. If any ship burials did take place *out to sea* no physical evidence has been discovered (although it is mentioned in Norse myth and literature). For that we need to turn to land. I will look at two very different kinds of Viking ship burials here. First, in the Isle of Man.

Although currently surrounded by the Irish Sea, before the beginning of our present inter-glacial Man – or Ellen Vannin in the Manx language – was connected to mainland Britain by a landbridge. Giant (or Irish) Elk roamed its hills – the full skeleton of one can be seen in the Manx Museum, Douglas. Evidence of Mesolithic settlers has been found in sheltered dells like Glen Wyllin on the west coast. With the end of the Ice Age, Ellen Vannin was cut off completely and became an island. Situated strategically in the middle of an important waterway, it was much fought over by subsequent powers, including the Vikings who invaded, settled and gave their place-names to some areas, although their language did not live on through the tongues of their children. The Celtic language survived – Manx is a distinctive form of Gaelic. This could be an example of peaceful cohabitation and certainly the two races seemed to blend well, as seen in the physiognomy and surnames of contemporary Manx.

There is strong evidence of this peaceful coexistence at Balladoole, near Castletown in the South of the Island. This is the site of the famous Viking ship burial, on Chapel Hill (a.k.a. Fort Keeil – 'Keeil' being a Manx word for an early church, often sunken floored and low-roofed to survive the harsh weather, like the crofters' cottages). The visible part of the burial consists of a Viking long ship delineated by an outline of stones. The plaque states:

> The stones mark the position of a ship in which, beneath a low
> cairn of stones, the richly-adorned body of a Viking settler was
> buried with him were a woman, his horse and other livestock.
> This pagan burial of the late 9th century directly overlay Christian
> burials in stone-lined graves of the same period.

The ship is aligned north-north-east, towards Snaefell (the highest mountain on Mann) and south-south-west, towards the midwinter sunset. Its prow is marked by a white quartz stone. The location is breathtaking as it overlooks the dramatic coastline of the south, with the sea and its horizon dominating the view. The site must have been chosen with this in mind, as the hill is not particularly striking. However the Vikings were simply continuing the use of a location considered sacred by many previous generations of islanders, as the rampart of Celtic Iron Age hill fort (probably dating from first few centuries CE) encircles the hill-top, while near the ship burial is the sunken rectangle of a Christian keeil, and near that a Bronze Age cist burial. Each culture seemed to respect the one before it, different narratives overlapping, coexisting – until the twentieth century that is, when a modern quarry was started, cheek-by-jowl to the site and marring the view towards the coast.

Viking ship burial, Balladoole, Isle of Man.

Nevertheless it is a numinous site with a positive 'multi-faith' message of tolerance (like a Manx Hill of the Holies) and seems to provide the strongest evidence yet of a belief in an otherworldly afterlife towards the setting sun – one that could be journeyed there in a boat. Here the 'lost island' is Valhalla itself, the home of the valiant fallen – and could be reached by the Rainbow Bridge, Bifrost, guarded by that threshold guardian of the Aesir, Heimdal.

Margaret Killip, in her book, *The Folklore of the Isle of Man*, discusses the many superstitions of the island, notably the widespread fairy faith, mentioning a woman of Jurby who had seen a vision of the 'good people of the sunset land' (Killip 1986: 48). These were perceived to be the fairies, akin to the Irish *sidhe*, but like the Tuatha de Danaan – who seem to have been the aboriginal aristocracy of Ireland – could not these shining ones be the Norse ancestors who 'sailed' into the mythic west?

Man's Viking ship burial has an even more famous counterpart, in the Anglo-Saxon site of Sutton Hoo in Suffolk. The centre's introductory literature explains:

> In a field overlooking the River Deben at Sutton Hoo near
> Woodbridge, local archaeologist Basil Brown found a 90 foot long
> Anglo-Saxon burial ship in 1939. This led to the discovery of the
> most amazing collection of treasures that had lain undisturbed
> within the ship for over 1300 years.

One of the burial mounds at Sutton Hoo, Suffolk.

This high status burial is thought to belong to that of Raedwald, King of East Anglia, which took place in 625 CE. Again, like the anonymous voyager of Man, the dead chief is prepared for his voyage to the afterlife, and is incredibly well-equipped.

> At the centre of the chamber was presumably the body – though as the soil was so acid, it had not survived. Around the body were the most personal treasures. Above is the great 'purse lid' with elaborate gold decorations on the outside. The purse was probably attached to a wide leather belt by the three hinges at the top and fastened by the sliding catch at the bottom. The purse contained 37 gold coins, dated to around AD 625.
>
> (www.archaeology.co.uk)

The excavations in 1939 revealed a magnificent ship burial. The excavations took place under the shadow of war, and had to be hurriedly concluded. However the great barrow that covered the ship did not stand alone. It was merely the largest mound in a cemetery of nineteen mounds and numerous other burials, and in the Eighties, a new excavation was launched to reveal the rest of the cemetery.

Martin Carver directed the excavation on behalf of the British Museum and the Society of Antiquaries. Andrew Selkirk, the then editor of *Current Archaeology*, presented Carver's work as a drama in three acts in which we see the grand *Twilight of the Gods* of the pagan Saxons in face of the rising tide of Christianity that was to overwhelm them.

One of the most astonishing finds on the site was the burial of horse and rider, as recorded in *Current Archaeology*:

> The most spectacular of the recent discoveries was this double burial under a single mound, of a young man in the pit to the left, and his horse in the right hand grave.
>
> (Selkirk and Carver 1992)

Both horse and rider may have been fatalities in a conflict, or the horse may have been slain afterwards – the much-loved steed of its owner – but the symbolism echoes the ship burials: here the rider is given the means to journey to the afterlife like Oisín upon his fairy steed.

Both the Balladoole and Sutton Hoo burials seem to be symbolic psychopompic ships, loaded with essential items for the next life, seemed designed to send the high status passenger into the afterlife in style. This tradition is mirrored in many cultures. In the Batanes Province of the Northern Philippines I have ran the gauntlet of an underground river prone to flooding where stone coffin boats are placed in alcoves, moorings for the deceased on their night-journey along this Filipino Styx. In the Egyptian eschatological tradition, Osiris' boat of a million years – the inspiration for Han Solo's spaceship, the millennium falcon, in *Star Wars* – takes him through the twelves gates of night (Nut, the goddess of the underworld whose body is the starry firmament itself) to emerge at sunrise, resurrected.

Egyptian Atlantis

In 2001 an underwater archaeological site being excavated by a team led by Dr Franck Goddio in Aboukir Bay, off the coast of Egypt was discovered to be none other the great lost Egyptian city and port of Heracleion. According to the Greek historian Diodor Heracleion was named after the Greek culture hero, Herakles, in gratitude for saving the city from flooding by the Nile. A colossal statue of Hapi, the Nile god of flooding, was discovered amidst the inundated ruins. Neither Herakles or Hapi were able to save Heracleion from the ravages of the sea and other 'Acts of God':

> The scientists have concluded that the port was destroyed by a
> series of natural disasters, including at least one major earthquake.
> The harbour area appears to have been destroyed, and sunk
> beneath the rising sea, centuries before the suburb area of
> Canopus, and the 10 wrecked ships, bunched together, suggests a
> tidal wave. The entire city had probably gone, and disappeared
> almost without a reference from the historical record, over a 1,000
> year ago.'
>
> (Kennedy 2001)

The city, founded in 331 BCE, shared the fate of fabled Alexandria, also destroyed by earthquake and flooding. Not an island originally, it has been made a (submerged) one because the delta has changed so much the site is now more than ten miles from the modern coast.

The site is incredibly rich and has already yielded carvings from toppled buildings, drowned harbour walls and moorings, gold coins and jewellery plus a sphinx, a statue of Isis, and, critically, a *stelae* – an engraved black slab featuring an imperial edict on the taxes to be levied on Greek imports, stating the slab was to be sited at 'Heracleion Thonis'.

Discovery of further inscriptions reveal a shrine on the site to be dedicated to the Supreme God Amun, and Dr Goddio believes 'there is now enough evidence to

View from Clevedon, looking towards Steepholm and Flatholm.

show that the shrine was that of the famous temple of Herakles-Khonsu, which the Greek historian Herodotus says was visited by Helena and Paris, as they fled the fury of her husband Menelaus.' At the time of the article there was still a kilometre of ruins buried in silt, including the wreck of the ten ancient ships, remaining to be explored.

What other secrets of the past the sea will reveal? New evidence is always coming to light, pushing dates back, overturning the orthodoxy; for instance, evidence of human habitation in Britain has now been pushed back to 700,000 years (see Springer 2006). And there can be little doubt that other evidence has been washed away time and time again, forever leaving blank pages in the history of humanity. But perhaps our changing coastlines will give as much as they take, and new 'sticks in the mud' will be stumbled upon.

~~~~~~~~~~~~~~~~~~~~~~~~~~~~

Oisín is called home

Oisín gazed at the sea. He'd been gazing for days. Niamh was growing concerned. He'd been off his food. He'd stop coming to the banquets, mumbling his excuses. At first she thought it was something she'd said, something wrong with her. Then her thoughts turned harder – another woman…? She fumed and raged, but Oisín remained sad, placid, listless. Then she realised, it wasn't another woman – it was his father, his friends, his hounds. He was homesick.

When she came upon him standing on the eastern shore for the umpteenth time, holding the broken spear, her intuition was confirmed.

She came up to him, curled her arm through his, and rested her golden locks on his shoulder. For a while they just gazed at the translucent waters and listened to the sound of ths waves limpidly lapping at the pink sand. Then she turned to him and wrapped her hand around his, the one holding the broken spear.

'Go,' she said, a crack her voice . 'Go if you must.'

Oisín shook his head, went to protest. But his wife gripped his hand and held his gaze.

'I know your heart calls you home.'

'But I love you! I love this place!'

'Then promise, promise to return.'

'With, all my heart! This is paradise, you are perfect in every way – what more could a man want?'

'To see the green hills of his heartland one last time? To see his family, his friends…' Niamh's whispers were like sigh of the waves on the sand. 'To say goodbye.'

Oisín lowered his head. The sad look on his father's face when he rode off with his fairy bride-to-be haunted him. If he could have one last conversation with Fionn, to say what he needed to say, what he really felt about his might hero of a father, Fionn mac Cumhail, the greatest warrior Erin has ever produced, his heart would be soothed.

'Yes.'

Niamh turned, whistled into the wind. In an instant a white horse appeared; her fairy steed. She held the halter as he mounted without hesitation.

Oisín bent down to kiss his bride.

'This advice I give you. Listen well.' Her fey eyes pierced him. 'Stay on the horse. Do not set foot on Erin, or all will be lost. Visit the dùn of your father, spend as long as you need to, but do not dismount.'

It seemed like an odd request, but Oisín was all too eager to oblige her – after all, she had let him go, she had given him his freedom.

'Now go! Ride towards the sunrise. Do not stop until green Erin is beneath you. Go with my love, Oisín. May you find your way home, to where your heart belongs.'

Not knowing what to say to this, Oisín seized the reins and shook them. The horse galloped into the waves, swift as shadow, while Niamh watched from the shore of Tir nan Og, a single tear falling into the sand.

~~~~~~~~~~~~~~~~~~~~~~~~~~~~

Chapter nine

When the levee breaks

The crescent shoes of moonlight struck the surly brine, again and again, sounding sonic signatures to the deep, a booming base rhythm of speed, echoing the quickening heartbeat of Oisín, son of Fionn Mac Cumhail, poet of the Fianna, and husband of Niamh of the Golden Hair. He was on his way home, or at least his former home – for Tir nan Og, the Land of the Ever Young was now his adopted one, after he had yielded to the calls of its princess to join him, and what man could have resisted her fairy charms, her locks of sunlight, her eyes like the Well of Segais? And for a timeless time he had savoured her embrace, her kisses and caresses, his time with her had been a time in a paradise almost without flaw – but he had pined for the green hills of Erin and she had let him return for one last look and a final farewell to his father and friends, with the promise he would return, and with assurances he would not dismount the moon-white fairy steed she had leant him and step upon that good green earth…But how he had longed to cast one last look at the dûn of his father, of the deep green valleys of his childhood, the glens and groves of his youth, the mountains of his manhood. It was a love and it was a longing keener than even that which drew him to Niamh and her Otherworld. It was where he came from, it was what made him; it was in his bones and blood, his very soul.

And now he beheld, with a tug in his breast, the broken shores of his homeland: the wild Atlantic coast of Erin, pummelled by an inexhaustible cavalry of pale storm-horses – and joining their renewed charge was his fairy steed; riding over the surging foam as though they were frozen foothills, from wave to breaking wave the white horse leapt, from the ninth to the first, until its hooves of moonlight struck the hourglass sands of the beach with first a plash, then a thudding, as the waves sucked back themselves with an indignant hiss, leaving Oisín's steed on dry land at last.

He would have leapt down there and then but the poet remembered Niamh's warning, echoed in the sibilant song of the breakers, and so Oisín rode on – without stopping, carrying the energy of the wave inland where it would not break until he reached the dûn of Fionn, the greatest hero in the land.

Sand became dune, became grass, became forest. Foothills became mountains as onward he rode to the green hills of his blood. He rode like a whirlwind across Erin, a force of nature – a ghost horse glimpsed by those with the Sight, if there were any there to see it. But the hills were lonely.

And Oisín's heartland had changed beyond all recognition…

The shape of the land was wrong: it was as though all the hills and lakes had been moved about. And there were far more lakes than he remembered for that matter… The coastline had … moved. It had moved inland!

Everywhere, the effects of this inundation could be seen. The land was swamped. Dark swaying ranks of submerged forests could be glimpsed, the doleful toll of bells faint beneath the cold still water. As though he beheld Manannan's green land beneath the sea, Oisín gazed down at the Erin he knew below water. It was a view unfamiliar to him, a high view of a keen-eyed bird of prey, hovering over its hunting ground. The black eyes of chimneys looked up. Rows of cottages, whole villages, towns, roads running into lakes or emerging. He saw the map of the land as though through a glass, darkly. It was marred by more than the flood water. The good green soil suffocated beneath stone. All was walls, boxes for body and spirit. And ugly rusting hulks littered the new lake beds or lay abandoned by these broken metal roads.

With mounting panic Oisín soothed the long neck of his steed, which had become jittery as soon as they had made landfall. He whispered a sidhe spell into its ear, as much to reassure himself as his horse. Gripping the bell-strewn reins, the poet gave them a shake and they galloped onwards, hoping the next valley would break the nightmare, would show them Erin still lived.

But the wasteland of water did not end.

Steed and rider made their way with increasing difficulty to Oisín's heartland. If not for the horse's ability to run on water or land, it would have been nigh on impossible. But finally he was there. Oisín's heart leapt as he recognised the same familiar outline of Fionn's dún, as recognisable as the contour of a mother's bosom to a suckling child. The hills remained the same, but little else.

They were long abandoned and over-grown.

The glory of Fionn's hall had been reclaimed by the earth, so now it hardly seemed man-made at all, but an emanation of the green mother herself. Hard to believe these mounds had been raised by man, by his arms, and those of his fellow Fianna. Where were they now, those splendid warriors in the gleaming war gear? Where were the proud women, the fierce loyal hounds, the children full of life?

His throat dry, his chest tight, the poet called out, but his words fell dead in the air.

Erin was silent.

~~~~~~~~~~~~~~~~~~~~~~~~~~~~~~~~~~~~~~

In this chapter we will look at the different factors that cause islands to be lost by flooding: precipitation, flandrian transgression, tsunami, hurricane and global warming. Myth and history is overflowing with flood-tales – it is theme that runs through time from our earliest stories to the latest news reports. The lost islands of floods are certainly not a new thing, but there will be certainly more and more in the future. By heeding the lessons of the past, in legend or chronicle, folk tale and newspaper archive, we can prepare for what lies ahead: uncertain waters.

Mount Ararat and all that

Flood myths crop up around the world, in almost every culture, with such frequency one wonders whether they refer to the same event, several different ones, or if the devastating flood is a metaphor for something else, for instance, the waves of mass extinctions that have occurred periodically? Often it used as a 'Year Zero' excuse for a new regime, a *tabula rasa* upon which the survivors can build their 'purified' kingdom: an odious form of apocalyptic purging – divine genocide.

There are so many flood myths it would take up too much space to list them all – one would need an ark. Examples of floods myths include:

- Aboriginal Australian Great Flood (with a tradition stretching back 50,000 years, this can claim to be the oldest known myth).

- Babylonian: in the story of 'Gilgamesh' Utnapishtim is a proto-Noah.

- Greece: Zeus sent a flood to destroy the men of the Bronze Age.

This last one is worth looking at in more detail as it shows how such myths may have influenced the widely-known Biblical one:

> Prometheus advised his son Deucalion to build a chest. All other men perished except for a few who escaped to high mountains. The mountains in Thessaly were parted, and all the world beyond the Isthmus and Peloponnese was overwhelmed. Deucalion and his wife Pyrrha (daughter of Epimetheus and Pandora), after floating in the chest for nine days and nights, landed on Parnassus. When the rains ceased, he sacrificed to Zeus, the God of Escape. At the bidding of Zeus, he threw stones over his head;

they became men, and the stones which Pyrrha threw became women. That is why people are called *laoi*, from *laas*, "a stone."

(Apollodorus, 1.7.2; translation from www.talkorigins.org/faqs/flood-myths)

Even in this Greek myth there is a sense of judgement here on the 'bad people' before the flood:

> The first race of people was completely destroyed because they were exceedingly wicked. The fountains of the deep opened, the rain fell in torrents, and the rivers and seas rose to cover the earth, killing all of them. Deucalion survived due to his prudence and piety and linked the first and second race of men. Onto a great ark he loaded his wives and children and all animals. The animals came to him, and by God's help, remained friendly for the duration of the flood. The flood waters escaped down a chasm opened in Hierapolis.

And so this myth becomes very familiar – crystallising as the Old Testament Bible story. The Christian version is only one in a long line of such myths. Here the 'exceedingly wicked' early Greeks were hit on all sides, from above, below and all around: 'The fountains of the deep opened, the rain fell in torrents, and the rivers and seas rose to cover the earth'. This may describe tsunami or flandrian transgression, as we will look at below; but first let's focus on the 'torrents of rain'.

Deluge means 'A great flood or overflowing of water, a destructive innundation' and is 'Often used hyperbolically, e.g. of a heavy fall of rain' according to the *Concise Oxford English Dictionary* and we normally associate such a deluge with the start of The Flood: a sign of God's disapproval from above. We say the 'heavens opened' when it rains heavily, and sunshine on a day of special occasion (a wedding, garden fête, parade) is always seen as a 'blessing'. But what happens when it rains for forty days and forty nights? Noah found out, lucky enough to be given a tip off by God to start building his Ark, much to the mockery and amusement of his neighbours – but Noah, the ultimate boy scout, was the have the last laugh (a story drummed into the innocent victims of bible classes and recently retold in the 'hilarious' flood comedy, *Evan Almighty*; directed by Tom Shadyac and released 2007). Noah was prepared when the hard rain started to fall…

Mount Ararat, where Noah's Ark was said to have made landfall, has become a major archaeological site as Creationists try to prove the literal truth of the Bible. According to the Old Testament (Genesis 8:4), Noah's ark landed on the 'mountains of Ararat' (today known as Agri Mountain, Eastern Turkey) after the deluge. Great Ararat was first climbed in modern times in 1829. On 2 July 1840, large parts of the mountain were disturbed by an earthquake. The resulting avalanche buried a village and a convent on its lower slopes. An expedition from the United States ascended the mountains in 1949 in an unsuccessful search for evidence of Noah's Ark, although recent expeditions have reported finding timbers that some believe to have

British floods, Summer 2007.

come from the ark. It is still a zone of negotiation: in recent years the area around the mountain has been the scene of fighting between Turkish forces and Kurdish guerrillas.

Broken rainbows

If the Biblical deluge is to be believed, Ararat, for a while became a new island – one of the few visible landmasses in a drowned world. The olive branch found by the dove was meant to symbolise God's 'ceasefire' – a welcome sign of land, of new growth, and a symbol of peace ever since. The rainbow that rose 'the morning after' was meant to be God's promise that He wouldn't do it again, His covenant to the human race. The world's weather has proved otherwise.

Creationists have tried to use evidence of the proliferation of flood myths to prove that the Biblical scriptures are true. Fossils of seashells and other beasties all 'confirm' this belief. Creationist museums are even depicting this flawed view of history as fact: cavemen and dinosaurs together, *à la* Raquel Welch in *One Million Years BC.*

Finding evidence to fit the theory, or fitting evidence around a theory is not a new phenomenon. There is the story of the so-called Red Lady of Paviland. Revered William Buckland, then Dean of Oxford, was called to examine some human remains in a cave on the Gower Peninsula, South Wales in 1823. The skeleton was covered in red ochre and surrounded by jewellery and other ritual artefacts, so Buckland surmised it must be the burial of a woman, probably a prostitute servicing the local Roman garrison. Certainly no older than 8,000 years – the age of the Earth, according to his creed. Buckland, who went on to be Dean of Westminster, believed that no human remains could be dated earlier than the Great Flood that is recorded in the Bible.

This shows how we can be blinded by the myopia of our own belief systems. Buckland could not have been more wrong. The skeleton proved to be that of a young man from 24,000 BCE, buried in a cave created when the seas were eight metres higher than today. The Early Upper Palaeolithic male lived at a time when mammoth, mastodons and woolly rhinoceros roamed the tundra of the Severn Plain, before it was flooded at the end of the Würm Glacial around 13,000 BCE.

Buckland was only working within his own paradigm, as we all are wont to do. To his credit, he excavated the remains and preserved them in the Pitt Rivers museum, Oxford, where they remain to this day, a lost man from before the Flood.

Reasons to be fearful, Part One

If the prophets are to believed the world is always ending. Yet apocalypses have come and gone. The scaremongering that goes with them tells us to change our ways, to behave, to panic buy. Some, like the Millennium Bug, Y2K can be good for business.

Flood Myths seem to have in common these motifs or messages:

- Humans are guilty of transgression
- A God sends a flood as punishment
- Instructions are sent to an individual to build a craft
- The instructions include ensuring the survival of all species.
- The flood destroys the old race.
- After the flood, a new, less sinful race emerges to repopulate the earth.

It appeals to a deep-rooted desire in many of us to have the 'badness' washed away (either our own or others) and to start afresh. For the believer any Act of God is literally that. To some, even the Indian Ocean Tsunami was God's judgement: but on what it is not clear – thousands of innocent people? Even the latest floods to hit Britain have been taken by a few as a sign of God's disapproval: 'Some regard a disaster as an opportunity to score a moral point.' (Ferudi 2007). In the believer's mind floods on a large scale are a form of global oblation – and nothing at all to do

148

Borth beach, Cardigan Bay. Site of the legendary 'lowest hundred' of Cantre'r Gwaelod with its sixteen drowned cities. A fossilised forest, revealed at low tide, is nearby.

with global warming, lifestyle and all those flights. The blame is never on the believer's doorstep. It is always other people's fault. While they are the 'saved', the infidel/atheist/heretic/fanatic will drown.

Time and time again, floods are used to 'prove' God's vengeance upon the sinful, to wash clean the Earth – a harsh karma but one shared by many; a spurious sentiment expressed by psychopath loner Travis Bickle in Martin Scorese's 1976 film, *Taxi Driver*: 'Someday a real rain will come and wash all this scum off the streets.'

Flandrian Transgressions

When ice sheets melt, normally at the end of an Ice Age, large amounts of water are released back into the world's oceans, causing them to rise, with consequent inundation of coasts and deltas. This is called Flandrian Transgression.

The last Flandrian Transgression, from about 10,000 years ago, caused the separation of Ireland from the mainland of Great Britain, and of Great Britain from continental Europe. Tasmania was also separated from continental Australia during this period. Many river valleys were flooded, creating sea inlets knowns as 'rias' (common in Cornwall, Brittany and Spain). The same process flooded glaciated valleys, producing the fjords and fjards of Norway, Greenland and Chile.

Sarn Cynfelyn. Borth, Cardigan Bay. Gwyddno's weir – a man-made ridge exposed at low tide, possibly influencing the legend of Cantre'r Gwaelod.

The landbridges that once connected Britain to Ireland and Britain to Europe experienced a dramatic form of this kind of transgression – swift enough to be witnessed within a generation and to impact those living in the area known as Doggerland (*Time Team* special, 'Britain's Drowned World', April 2007). These experiences may have passed down through oral tradition. Although we are talking thousands of years here, consider how some Aboriginal traditions have survived for 50,000 years in Australia. Britain does not have an unbroken native tradition in the same way, but it has been occupied continuously during the 10,000 years since the last Ice Age and before, so who knows what fragments may have survived?

An area in Cardigan Bay known as Cantre'r Gwaelod in legend is a possible example of Flandrian Transgression, although the local folk tale offers a more prosaic explanation. The Cantre'r Gwaelod, or Bottom Hundred, was a great tract of fertile country extending from Ramsey Island north to Bardsey Island over what is now Cardigan Bay. It was forty miles long and twenty wide, low and level, highly populated and cultivated, with sixteen fortified towns 'better than all the towns of the Cymry except Caerleon-on-Usk.' it was said. The king was called Lord of Cantre'r Gwaelod in Dyfed (Pembrokeshire), although most of the land lay closest to what is now Cardigan-shire. It was defended from the sea by a strong embankment and sluices.

The Lord of the Cantre'r Gwaelod in 520 CE, so the legend tells us, was Gwyddno Garanhir; and the Keeper of the Embankment was Seithennin, 'one of the three immortal drunkards of Britain.' One evening there was a great banquet and Seithennin, in his usual state, left the sluices open. The sea came in remorse-lessly and the land was inundated. Those of the inhabitants who were not drowned escaped to Ardudwy, part of Caernarvon, and ascended the mountains of Snowdonia, the first time they had been populated.

Nowadays when the sea is very still and the water clear, the walls and buildings are said to be seen, and when the water below moves them, the church bells sound faintly.

The 'sigh of Seithennin' as he watched the Irish Sea cover the settlements – the costly results of his alcoholism – became a byword for thoughtlessness and regret in Wales.

Old salmon weirs, like the one below Borth – manmade ridges of stone that jut out into the sea, where whicker racks would have been placed, exposed and accessible at low-tide, may have been misinterpreted by some as the walls or roads of the lost 'cities'. However, the tidally submerged fossilised forest still visible on Borth beach does actually prove the bay *was* inundated at one time, probably during the end of the last Ice Age, a victim not of drunkenness but of Flandrian Transgression – a 'drink problem' on an altogether different scale.

Indian Ocean tsunami
Other causes of lost islands include the most devastating of all: tsunamis. Their power is etched into recent memory:

> At 0059 GMT on 26 December 2004, a magnitude 9.3 earthquake ripped apart the seafloor off the coast of northwest Sumatra.
>
> Over 100 years of accumulated stress was released in the second biggest earthquake in recorded history.
>
> It unleashed a devastating tsunami that travelled thousands of kilometres across the Indian Ocean, taking the lives of more than 200,000 people in countries as far apart as Indonesia, the Maldives, Sri Lanka and Somalia.
>
> (Lambourne 2005)

The Indian Ocean Tsunami prompted the largest relief fund in history, as people around the planet were touched with compassion – the impact reached many communities worldwide. Like 9/11 it was a global event, which seemed to touch everyone. Most people know of someone who 'was there'. The lucky ones survived.

The story that saved a people

Such events create their own mythos. Countless anecdotes from eye witnesses recorded by reporters, disseminated globally by massive media coverage, and virally by mobile phone, email, diary, blog and dinner party conversations have created a new canon of 'flood myths'. One of the most remarkable stories to come out of the Indian Ocean Tsunami is one that stands testimony to the efficacy of the oral tradition in preserving folk wisdom:

> The Onge tribe… have lived on Little Andaman for between 30,000 and 50,000 years and, though they are on the verge of extinction, almost all of the 100 or so people left seem to have survived the 26 December quake and the devastating waves which followed.
>
> Their folklore talks of 'huge shaking of ground followed by high wall of water', according to Manish Chandi, an environmental protection worker who has studied the tribes and spoke to some Onges after the disaster.
>
> 'When the earthquakes struck, the Onges moved to higher ground deep inside their forest and escaped the fury of the waves that entered the settlements,' he told the BBC News website after talking to some of the inhabitants who knew some Hindi as well as their own ancient languages.
>
> He said another aboriginal people - the Jarawa on South and Middle Andaman - also fled to higher ground before the waves.
>
> 'There's clear evidence that the aboriginals know about tsunamis and they know how to deal with them,' he said.
>
> (Bhaumik 2005)

It is said that there is a little bit of heaven in a disaster area. Many stories of human courage, compassion, selflessness, strength and faith attest to that. Disasters can bring out the best in people (what Professor of Sociology Frank Ferudi calls 'social capital'). It can also bring out the worst, as in our next cause of flooding, hurricane.

Katrina: America's wake up call to climate chaos

The word 'hurricane' is derived from *Hurican*, the god of evil of the Carib people of the Caribbean. Hurican was himself inspired by the Mayan god *Hurakan*, who destroyed humans with great storms and floods. His name could not be more appropriate for one of the most devastating forces of nature.

The most notorious one in the early twenty first century is Hurricane Katrina, which hit New Orleans on 29 July 2005, a day like 9/11 that Americans will never forget. Katrina highlighted significant failings in local and federal government in terms of inadequate response. It also revealed the faultlines of American society: endemic racism and an apparent caste system between rich and poor.

The aftermath of Katrina was devastating – specifically within the affected areas, with looting and violence, but also further afield, in the treatment of the 'underclass' refugees and the political fallout – the ripples of which will continue for some time.

152

Spike Lee's stirring 2006 documentary about the disaster, *When the Levees Broke: a requiem in four acts* (strapline: 'An American tragedy') charted the devastating events in soberly emotive detail.

> In the immediate aftermath of the storm, the reality of the third-
> world conditions in which many in the world's wealthiest nation
> live was literally washed up for the world to see.'
>
> ('New Orleans One Year On', *Guardian Weekend*, 29 July 2006)

The much-criticised director of the Federal Emergency Management Agency at the time, Michael Brown, said: 'We're seeing people that we didn't know exist.' (ibid.) Katrina revealed the seedy underbelly of American society, the disenfranchised underclass left to drown or die in a city abandoned by the rich. Scenes of a flooded New Orleans was a paradigm-shifting vision, turning America's view of itself on its head: a 'Third World disaster' on its doorstep.

A survivor of Katrina, Ernest 'Doc' Watson, a seventy-four year old jazz musician, describes the surreal devastation witnessed upon his return: 'Everything had floated and then just fell where it was… The refrigerator full of rotting meat, the furniture, the clothes…everything.' (ibid.)

More harrowing were the images of bodies floating in the toxic floodwaters, similarly left to rot. This was America reimagined by doomster J.G. Ballard. Fiction had become fact.

Cormac McCarthy's Pulitzer-prize-winning post-apocalyptic *The Road* (2006) described the journey of a nameless man and his son across a burnt America, capturing the concerns of a nation suddenly aware of its own vulnerability with austere beauty. In heartbreaking bleakness the author renders an America of rags and ashes, where 'The frailty of everything [is] revealed at last' (McCarthy 2006: 28)

Katrina became the costliest disaster in US history, and saw a sea-change in mainstream public opinion to the Bush administration, whose response was seen as woefully lacking and inept. Apart from the political fall-out there were more immediate consequences: oil spills, a city drowned in toxic sludge, the destruction of homes and New Orleans tourist economy, decimated industry and businesses, the damage to wetlands and marshes – important for coastal defence – and lost islands:

> 'The 40-mile long Chandeleur chain of barrier islands off the
> Louisiana coast which used to protect the delta from storm surges
> have pretty well gone,' said Laurence Rouse, of the oceanography
> department at Louisiana State University.
>
> (Vidal 2005)

If Hurricane Katrina was a one-off it would be bad enough, but hurricanes are going to be happening with increasing frequency:

> The global risk of hurricane disaster is increasing due to human
> activity. Populations are concentrating along the world's

coastlines—particularly in large urban areas. Improved forecasting
and emergency response have lowered hurricane casualty rates,
but as more people and infrastructure move into harm's way,
storms are likely to become more destructive.

(Handwerk 2005)

The next notch up from hurricanes are 'hypercanes' – wind speeds of over 500 miles
per hour, produced by superheated ocean waters in the wake of an asteroid's impact,
volcano eruption zone, or global warming, creating conditions for a storm the size of
North America, with a storm surge of sixty-plus feet and an eye nearly 200 miles
across. These unspeakably destructive weather patterns are predicted to ravage the
planet in the worst-case climate chaos scenarios.

Even if these apocalypses do not manifest at their extreme, the sobering fact remains
hurricanes look likely to become increasingly common. This means more displaced
populations, creating escalating numbers of 'climate refugees' – a seemingly new
phenomenon, but one as old as humanity. The difference is the scale and frequency
it will be happening on a planet of six billion plus. The citizens of New Orleans are
only the most publicised: those of low-lying islands like the doomed Tuvalu in the
Pacific are beginning to get noticed too.

Approximately a hundred million people live in areas below sea level. Could this
trigger a new 'Book of Invasions', echoing the Irish creation myth? One of the races
which were said to have invaded Ireland were apparently fleeing the impacts of a
flood. According to Sir Nicholas Stern, 200 million people will be permanently
displaced from their homes by rising sea levels if temperatures rise by two degrees.
(Stern 2006) Myth is about to become future history.

The world is hot enough

The final cause of lost islands is anthropogenic climate change – that is global
warming caused not by long-term natural processes, but by humans. There is broad
scientific consensus on the reality of this, as former UN Secretary General Kofi
Annan confirms: :

> The overwhelming majority of scientists now agree that human
> activity is having a significant impact on climate.

(Annan 2005)

Anthropogenic climate change is most likely to result in most devastation in the
future. The generic term for what we are considering here is Accelerated Sea Level
Rise (ASLR). The SURVAS (Synthesis and Upscaling of sea-level Rise Vulnerability
Assessment Studies) survey by Middlesex University lists the following:

Primary impacts of ASLR
Even small increases in sea-level rise could cause major primary impacts on the
world's coastal zones in terms of:

- Increased erosion

- Inundation and displacement of coastal wetlands and other coastal lowlands

- Increased risk of flooding and storm damage

- Salinisation of surface and ground waters

(SURVAS 2002)

Secondary impacts of Accelerated Sea Level Rise, according to SURVAS, include: detrimental effects on livelihoods and human health; direct threats to human life (via inundation, storm surge damages); threats to food production capacity including decline in irrigation water quality; decline in coastal crop yields, and degradation/disappearance of crucial ecosystems such as mangroves, coral reefs and coastal lagoons which act worldwide as fish and shellfish nurseries; decline in health/living standards as a result of decline in drinking water quality; threat to housing quality; associated increasing health hazards linked to relocation; and spreading of diseases.

Displacement of vulnerable populations is all too likely with the resulting 'relocation of impacted populations and associated political, economical, institutional, and cultural stress of both the displaced population and the host countries.'

Both SURVAS and the Stern Review predict that impacts on infrastructure and economic activity will be considerable: decline in land and housing property values; threats to major infrastructure (including strategic harbours, coastal roads, railways, health and school buildings); threats to major coastal industry and services (including oil/petrochemical plants and tourism); diversion of resources to adaptation responses to sea level rise impacts; increasing protection costs which may not be affordable to certain developing countries unless substantial aid is obtained; increasing insurance premiums; political and institutional instability, and social unrest.

Such economic concerns aside (it seems people only take notice when it will hurt their pockets or disrupt the status quo) a far more worrying consequence of Accelerated Sea Level Rise is threats to particular cultures and ways of life, such as atolls where retreat to higher inland areas is not feasible. Developing countries, as always, will feel the sharp edge of Accelerated Sea Level Rise most keenly. The rich will be able to retreat to their mountainous refugia, but it is the poor who will suffer the most.

Tuvalu

Sounding like one of the otherworldly islands of myth, Tuvalu in the Pacific may well become the stuff of legend as it faces a decidedly real threat:

> 'You have countries that are going to disappear – the small, island countries. You can have the best military equipment and the best technology, but what are you going to do? if your country is going

to disappear, the best technology will not prevent this. So, for example, Tuvalu, a small country in the Pacific, recently requested for the country as a whole, with a 10,000 population, the status of refugee – environmental refugee – because the people are realizing that the sea is rising and their country is disappearing.'

(Djoghlaf interviewed in May 2006: 126)

The BBC Weather Centre website: 'Climate Chaos', featured an article entitled 'Sea Level Rises' which mentions this eco-exodus:

> The islanders have already started to leave and the rest will have to do so in coming years if the trend continues.

Tuvalu is not the only one threatened, of course. The Marshall Islands are as equally doomed. Yet not just low-lying islands in the Pacific are endangered. 'It is estimated that 21 percent of the world's population already live within 30 km of a shoreline.' (SURVAS 2002). Virtually every major city is vulnerable, for most are founded on harbours or estuaries: New York, Los Angeles, London, Rio de Janeiro, Calcutta, Sydney... Say goodbye to romantic holidays in Venice; indeed say goodbye to Venice: name after the foam-born goddess of love, it seems doomed to return to the water... Say goodbye to the Arctic, to parts of the Antarctic, to the rainforest coastal zones of the Amazon... the list goes on.

Yet with the impact climate change, Britain is just as likely to become a 'lost island', and a taste of things to come was witnessed in the floods that hit Britain in the summer of 2007, when the Midlands were badly affected: parts of Gloucester, Tewkesbury and Oxford evacuated, thousands were without water, and there were looting, accidents, traffic jams and at least eight deaths:

> In the past two months, Britain has experienced the heaviest rainfall since records began in 1766, leading rivers to burst their banks and causing widespread, severe flooding, with up to 10,000 people forced from their homes.

> Up to 350,000 people remain without running water after the floods damaged power sub-stations and knocked out sewage systems. The country has not been so severely flooded since 1947, according to the Environment Agency.

> (London Reuters, accessed 26 July 2007)

The Environment Agency Sustainable Development Unit, said in June 2001:

> Major floods that have only happened before say, every 100 years on average, may now start to happen every 10 or 20 years. The flood season may become longer and there will be flooding in places where there has never been any before.

Author at Dunwich, site of a village lost to the sea. Suffolk.

This vision of a flooded Britain was prophesised by Richard Jeffries in his novel *After London, or Wild England* in 1885. It is a prophecy all too likely to come true: '… the risk of flooding looks greater than ever and not just in the UK, but throughout the whole world.' (BBC Weather Centre 2007)

With global warming resulting in climate chaos there will be increasing numbers of lost islands in the future – unless we act now, although some like maverick scientist James Lovelock argue we are already past the 'tipping point'. Even if we were to curtail our carbon habit now (ecologists are saying only a ninety per cent reduction will provide the necessary handbrake) the amount of CO_2 pumped into the atmosphere since the Industrial Revolution will have an impact on the planet for years to come, a deluge of our own creation. Dr Martin Luther King Jr. ominously once said:

> Over the bleached bones and jumbled residues of numerous
> civilisations are written the pathetic words: 'Too late.'

(King 1967)

~~~~~~~~~~~~~~~~~~~~~~~~~~~~~~~

The hills were empty. Oisín's green island of the heart, Erin of the Danaans, was not the land he knew. It had been changed beyond recognition.

With mounting panic, Oisín criss-crossed the Five Quarters in hope of seeing the familiar face of friend or foe – he would have kissed either with joy. He searched high and low for some living proof of the reality of his past, but there was no trace to be found. The land was flooded, the crops blighted, untilled.

Wildwood choked the fields and hills he knew.

The poet felt suffocated by this endless wilderness. It snatched at his fine elven clothes, made him feel a trespasser in his own country. The air was thick with decay, dank and cloying. After the rarefied air of Tir nan Og it felt stale and claustrophobic. The land he knew was drabber, darker, spiritless.

Then he caught a glimpse of some figures in the distance and Oisín's heart soared – but as he galloped towards them on his fairy steed, swift as the wind – it sank again. These were not the Tuatha de Danaan, the Lordly Ones, his people; these mud-stained mortals were shrunken somehow, diminished in stature and spirit.

The exhausted men had been struggling to overturn a large stone in a half-ploughed field, sweat dripping from their brows, faces contorted in effort, but cowered back as he approached, terror on their faces.

'Aaiieeee! A warrior of the Sidhe!' they cried, for that is what he appeared to them in his fine elven mantle, upon his white golden-maned horse. By his side his fine sword gleamed, as did his torc of nobility, his arm-rings over bulging sun-bronzed muscles, buckle and cloak-brooch glinting over elf-woven clothes. He dazzled them in his shining apparel.

They were hollow-cheeked, black-toothed, lank-haired, dressed in rags, and from the packs of junk upon their backs, scavengers.

At once, Oisín understood and took pity on them, whether they were his countrymen or not – they were human beings in need. He too had a burning hunger, for answers, but first, their need was greater.

Laughing, Oisín flipped the stone away with the swipe of his hand, as if it were no more than a pebble. The muddy, sweaty-browed workers cheered, their burden lifted away – but then they cried out in horror as Oisín's saddle strap snapped.

In a flash his fairy steed vanished, leaving a trace pattern of moonlight before that vanished too. With a sickening thump Oisín knew he was doomed. As soon his mighty frame touched the earth, the enchantment that protected him was broken and all the time held at bay in Tir nan Og flooded into him like a great wave.

A hideous transformation came upon the prince as soon as he fell to earth. His thick black locks thinned silver-white, his chest sunk, his hands were dappled with liver spots, teeth fell away, and clear eyes dimmed. His elven mantle seemed little more than beggar rags now, and his shining sword, a gnarled stick.

Before the eyes of the scavengers, this god-like figure withered away, from something out of legend to an ancient heart-broken man, weeping into his long white beard.

When they had recovered from their shock, the men drew near again and mocked the old man. The wizened husk of an old old man…They laughed nervously at first, then louder. How could they have mistaken him for a hero? Surely, a trick of the light, of hunger perhaps, or thirst? He seemed now no more than a bag of bones.

The future had caught up with him, and all that had befallen the land was revealed…

~~~~~~

We have looked at the actual causes of actual lost islands in the cold light of day. We have pursued both the lateral and logical paths, but what happens when the two clash? When the imaginary is applied to the actual, when belief systems are imposed or used to justify how we live our lives on this Earth? And what happens when the actual becomes imaginary, as in the depiction of First Nations people by Old World 'settlers'? What happens 'When Worlds Collide'?

PART THREE

When worlds collide

Chapter ten

Exiles from Eden

At first Oisín did not know what had befallen him. He seemed to be ranting, asking again and again about the mighty Fionn MacCumhail, about Oscar, Conan, Diarmuid and the other heroes of the Fianna... The scavengers shook their heads and laughed. Those were children's tales – legends of long ago. No one believed in them anymore. If they lived, they died a long, long time hence – if they lived at all.

Oisín grew angry at this, and tried to beat the impudent ignorant fools, but to his horror his strength failed him.

'What do you believe instead?' he finally asked them, his silver-haired head hung in despair.

'In the true Lord, Jesus Christ, and God, the father over all,' said one of them.

'Your God must be a mighty man to have defeated Finn and the Fianna,' sighed Oisín with abject weariness.

For a wind's breath he gazed at the ground, as if searching for meaning in all of this. 'How did they die?'

'In a battle, a warrior's death,' spoke the eldest, growing interested. 'But that was three hundred years ago, or so the seanachies say...'

' — But that'd be the poteen talking,' commented the youngest dryly, a cynical look in his eyes. The others grunted with laughter.

'Three hundred years!' The words struck Oisín like arrows. Suddenly he felt very, very old.

'And what, what of Oisín, poet of the Fianna?' he asked quietly, his voice as cracked as the Burren.

The oldest worker, who still had a gleam in his eye said, 'Oisín? We sing his songs still, but it is said he vanished with a fairy princess to Tir nan Og, and no one ever saw him again...'

' — If you believe in such nonsense,' interjected the youngest again, losing his patience. 'Enough! We have no time for fairy tales. We have mouths to feed if we can clear this field of stones. We need wheat not words. Out of our way, old man!'

Yet nothing would move him, for he wept inconsolably for all he had lost – all for three weeks in paradise. Yet he did not resent Niamh – he missed her now, more than ever, but doubted he would ever see her again.

Above Oisín's sobbing, bells tolled in the distance.

Suddenly remembering their Christian charity – or perhaps fear of divine punishment – the workers suddenly felt sorry for the broken figure. Between them they carried the wizened giant to the nearby monastery, presided over by the Patriarch himself, the 'serpent-banisher' the men called him in awed whispers. Heads bowed, they asked for the monks' help and returned to the fields.

The holy men received the devastated Oisín with gentleness and compassion. They made him as comfortable as they could; and the Patriarch was interested in hearing his story – Oisín, relieved to find someone willing to listen, related everything that happened to him: his life with the Fianna, his summoning by Niamh of the Golden-hair, his time in Tir nan Og, and his return to Erin. The Patriarch commanded monks to fetch vellum, ink and quills and to write down everything the ancient said, however strange…

Yet Oisín discovered their own story was just as strange. These robed, disciplined men followed a tortured man on a cross. They called him the 'one true lord'. According to them all other gods were false. And stranger still were their stories: a man and a woman had lived in a garden, in innocent and abundant bliss, just like Tir nan Og, until the woman had eaten a fruit from a forbidden tree, tempted by a talking snake! Then they had been cast out. Forced to work, to wear clothes, to suffer disease, old age and death – all for a bit of scrumping! 'If your god was so short of apples, he could have had seven cartloads of mine!' beamed Oisín.

The stern Patriarch looked at him with his flinty eyes. Sucking in cold breath, he said: 'Let me begin…'

~~~~~~~~~~~~~~~~~~~~~~~~~~~~~

Currach and courage

Imagine the scene – the austere cloisters of a monastery, quills scratching away in a scriptorium, the low murmur of matins, a young monk drawing water from a well on a chilly morning, cupped hands over a brazier in the one warm room, the silent but companionable breaking of fast, the steady round of the daily chores and prayers, a

Book of Hours undisrupted for decades... a Christian idyll of contemplative withdrawal from the world and its ways – shattered by the winding of a horn in the distance. Suddenly chaos reigned as panic sets in. The richest treasures are quickly hidden away, but there is no time to save themselves as the peaceful seclusion of the monastery is violently broken by massive figures in mail and leather armour, some bearing animal skins, furs, iron helmets over blonde manes lank with sea-mist, broth-stained beards and black grinning teeth, eyes flashing steel blue, thickly-muscled arms and necks bearing dragon tattoos, serpent-headed torcs. Ringed-hands gripping axes hungry to do their work ... Viking raiders!

Many of the monks would be murdered, the treasures of the monastery raided, the abbot tortured until he revealed the hiding place of the holiest holies – then left blood-eagled in the body-strewn yard, food for the raven-god. The long-ships would pull away, leaving the burning ruins behind them.

However stereotypical and possibly non-representative of Norse culture as a whole something like this would have happened during the first recorded Viking raid in 793 CE by Norwegian marauders on the holy island of Lindisfarne. This scene would have been repeated along the north-eastern coast of Britain throughout the Viking Age of expansion from 793 CE – the clash of worlds, Christian and pagan, monk and warrior, seclusion and aggression, study and action, research and plunder, peace and war – pushing the monks further and further west in search of less hazardous locations for their retreat from the world.

But the world kept catching up. The fear of attack and desire for safety drove monks all the way to Iceland, where it seems they settled in the Westman Islands as early as the sixth century – long before the official settlement of Iceland began.

These monks on the move in search of the quiet life, sailing in their hide-bound wooden-framed currach vessels were forced from one potential 'Eden' to another, created a wide diaspora of Celtic Christianity across the westerly isles off Britain's coast and beyond. Saint Brendan may have made the first transatlantic crossing in such a vessel to America in the sixth century. Tim Severin proved this could be done in 1978 by sailing in such a precarious craft from Ireland to Newfoundland. Often such voyages were an act of faith as the sailors put their fate in the lap of the gods or God.

Not all Viking migration was aggressive and it seems likely that trading, settling and inter-marrying took place, the latter evidenced by the widespread Nordic DNA still in evidence in Britain today (Richards 2001; Capelli *et al* 2003). .

Different factors to those that drove the monks west instigated the Vikings' search for new land. Pressures on land and resources back in Scandinavia and Denmark forced them to look for new 'Edens' to settle – fertile soil, fertile women, land won by strength of arms, the warrior's way. Britain and Ireland was 'appropriated' by the colonists – in a similar way that Old World settlers would do so in America in an act of ancestral 'bad karma'. Everyone searches for the garden.

Chalice Well Gardens. A Somerset 'paradise' – walled garden.

The garden

The idea of Eden has haunted mankind for at least two thousand years. There are analogues in almost every faith and tradition. The Persian word for 'walled garden' gave us the word 'paradise'. The Hebrew word *eden* means 'delight'. The Garden of Eden was a paradisical garden, the garden of original delight.

In the Judaeo-Christian creation myth, the Book of Genesis, God is reported to have said (though who was around to witness and record it?): 'Let us put him [Adam] in command of the fishes of the sea, and all that flies through the air, and the cattle, and the whole earth, and all the creeping things that move on earth' (Genesis 1:26).

God bid Adam to 'take command', and this has been taken as the mandate for man to exploit nature ever since, though some Christians have tried to live in harmony with nature and have not found it at odds with their faith, such as St Francis of Assisi and all the hermits and monks who have lived, or still live, close to nature on numerous 'lost islands', monasteries, hermitages and retreats. The fault lies not with these sacred texts but the misinterpretation and appropriation of them.

Adam's dereliction of duty was not his creator's fault. God had provided a beautiful frame for his pièce-de-résistance, a being that would incur the envy of angels: a human being: 'God had planted a garden of delight, in which he now placed the man he had formed.' (Genesis 2:8)

165

The garden Adam was given 'to cultivate and tend' had everything Adam needed, including a cloned companion, formed from his spare rib – Eve – plus plants to name, animals to talk to, naturism… What more could he want? Eden is not only an anagram of 'need': it is its opposite.

The tree

There was only one 'house rule' in God's garden – do not eat the fruit from the Tree of Knowledge of Good and Evil: 'Thou mayest eat thy fill of all the trees in the garden except the tree which brings knowledge of good and evil; if thou eatest of this, thy doom is death.' (Genesis 2:17)

Pretty clear instructions; and someone would be pretty stupid to disobey them – or would they? Basically, it is an order to remain in blissful ignorance instead of attaining self-awareness. Is not the eating of the apple, the path of wisdom rather than ignorance? Instead of blaming Eve for humanity's fall, should not we thank her for its emancipation? Philip Pullman takes this line in *His Dark Materials* trilogy, in which a new Eve brings about the destruction of 'the Authority'. In Pullman's story Original Sin is symbolised as 'dust', something adults attract from the moment of puberty: it is a metaphor for matured consciousness. We must leave the garden of childhood innocence to reach maturity. It is a healthy, if heart-breaking, sundering that many are scarred by and many yearn for during the rest of their lives. Such longing has been depicted in literature as diverse as Wordsworth's 'The Prelude', A.E. Housman's 'A Shropshire Lad', Laurie Lee's *Cider With Rosie*, Dylan Thomas's 'A Child's Christmas in Wales' and Dennis Potter's *Blue Remembered Hills*.

Like a Christmas tree, the tree featured in the Eden myth is burdened with baubles of iconographic meaning. On one level is symbolises fecundity, growth, natural order, shelter and stability. Its archetypal appeal may even descend from our own evolutionary 'family tree'. Once, our distant ancestors lived among them. The forest canopy was synonymous with safety and society: we could dash up into the trees if a deadly predator ventured near, or groom one another for tics in contented closeness during periods of peace. Gazing upon them we are looking back at our 'roots'. Trees appeal to the primal man in us, the oldest parts of our cerebral cortex. Their form echoes the bronchial passages of our lungs, and their function mirrors it also – converting our out-breaths into oxygen, as we breathe in their outbreaths, good clean air. Trees are the lungs of the world.

The 'world tree', the *axis mundi*, crops up in religions across the globe. With is roots deep below the earth and its highest branches way up in the sky, the world tree is often thought to enable shamanic-like spirit journeys to both the underworld and the heavens from the 'middle earth' on which we live. It is kin to the Qabalistic Tree of Life, with each of its ten *sephiroth* a sphere-like fruit containing a world, a level of consciousness to be attained. Between these are twenty-two paths, corresponding to the major arcana of the tarot – which can be navigated by the initiate back to the source.

'the tree of life also in the midst of the garden and the Tree of Knowledge of good and evil' (Genesis 2:9) The ancient oaks of Gog and Magog, Glastonbury.

In Norse mythology the world tree linking the nine worlds is called Yggdrasil, the World Ash, on which Odin hung Christ-like for nine days and nights – losing an eye, in sacrifice for the sacred knowledge of the runes he wins for humankind. In Welsh cosmology there are similarities with the three main worlds of the Norse: Annwn (underworld); Abred (middle earth); and Gwnyvyd (upper world) – also paralleled in many cultures – but with a fourth, Ceugant, the ineffable place of Hên Ddihenydd, the 'Ancient and Unoriginated One' – the residence of the Godhead that none can enter. Of concern to us here is the middle realm, Cylch y Abred, the middle world. The Barddas, the bardic body of lore, states: 'Here, good and evil are in equal measure, and hence there is free will, for in Abred every act is one of choice and consent'. This seems worlds apart from the Biblical Eden, yet some Christians would say without this choice the cosmic struggle between good and evil played out in us would be meaningless. We have to decide. We have to choose between right and wrong.

The fruit

We all know what happened in Eden. Eve was tempted by the Serpent (Satan in disguise) and ate of the fruit, and Adam manfully or foolishly chose to join her. The Serpent said: 'God knows well that as soon as you eat of this fruit your eyes will be opened, and you yourselves will be like gods, knowing good and evil.' (Genesis 3:2–5) Eve liked the sound of this, and the look of the fruit, for: 'it was pleasant to look at and charmed the eye' (the precursor to retail therapy perhaps) and, giving in to the desire of knowledge, plucked it, ate it, gave some to her husband, who 'ate with her' and so their doom was sealed. 'The eyes of both were opened' and they became aware of their nakedness and grew modest all of a sudden, covering their 'shame' with fig leaves. Yet for this sacrifice, like Odin losing his eye, they had a precious thing: self-awareness, consciousness, 'dust'.

In many shamanic cultures the eating of plants with psychotropic properties is a perilous path to knowledge – a way of communing with the spirits and ancestors. Currently such methods are seen as releasing 'entheogens': psychoactive substances that are thought to create mystical experiences. Not evil in themselves – they have just been made so by those who wish to control knowledge and stand as threshold guardians to the realms of spirit. 'They' do not want us going there under our own steam, only 'through Christ', in other words through *them*: the priesthood, the powers-that-be. That is not to say such things should be done willy-nilly, without due respect and guidance – best to let an experience guide initiate you and bring you back safely. Even better, seek enlightenment the healthier, more sustainable way – through study, meditation, and spiritual disciplines such as yoga or *Tai Chi Ch'uan*.

The taboo-laden fruit (it is never referred to as an apple in Genesis) in the biblical Garden of Eden is depicted radically differently in Celtic tradition, where otherworldly beings lure heroes to the 'Isle of Apples' with a branch from its orchard (see the chapter 'Into the West'). W.B. Yeats hauntingly alludes to this in his poem *The Song of Wandering Aengus* when he refers to the 'silver apples of the moon, the golden apples of the sun.' This is a far more positive depiction of such objects of ritual power. Yet, their effect can be just as devastating. The Greek beauty contest in which Aphrodite wins the golden apple causes the Trojan Wars – when Athena and Hera get their own back for not being selected by Paris. All hell breaks loose because of these goddesses scorned. The cuckolded King, Menalaus, is a mere pawn for their vengeance.

One of Herakles' twelve labours is to win the golden apples of the Hesperides. He asks Atlas to get them for him: offering to shoulder his burden for a while and hold the whole world up. When Atlas comes back, successful in his quest, Herakles tricks him into holding the globe again and off he goes with the Hesperidean fruit.

Avalon is connected to apple lore, being linked etymologically to *Afallon*, the Isle of Apples. Another island, Bardsey, has its own apple, the rarest in the world it is said (until recently only one grew – now more have been cultivated on the mainland from clippings) and is supposed to be a place where 'no one dies except of extreme old age,' and so is thought of by some as a candidate for Avalon. This connection between fruit and longevity is echoed in Genesis 3:22: '… now he has only to lift his hand and gather fruit to eat from the tree of life as well, and he will live endlessly.' Humankind has been deprived access to this Tree of Life ever since and as a result we have come to know disease, old age and death (all things a sojourn in the otherworld seem to remedy). This is the bitter harvest Adam and Eve reaped. For that taste of forbidden knowledge they had to face the consequences of their actions: they had to face judgement.

"And when the woman saw that the tree was good for food, and that it was pleasant to the eyes, and a tree to be desired to make one wise, she took of the fruit thereof, and did eat" (Genesis 3:6).

Exile

God 'discovers' their transgression, or at least feigns surprise – for is He not omniscient? He castigates them and casts them out like an angry landlord whose tenants have broken the terms of their agreement:

> So the Lord God drove him out from that garden of delight, to
> cultivate the ground from which he came; banished Adam, and
> posted his Cherubim before the garden of delight, with a sword of
> fire that turned this way and that, so that he could reach the tree
> of life no longer.

> (Genesis 3.23–24)

This scene is memorably rendered in the climactic stanza of Milton's poetic epic, *Paradise Lost*:

> Some natural tears they dropped, but wiped them soon.
> The world was all before them, where to choose
> Their place of rest, and Providence their guide.
> They, hand in hand, with wandering steps and slow,
> Through Eden took their solitary way.

> (Book XII: 644–9)

And so the first man and first woman were exiled from Eden; and their firstborn, Cain, was similarly banished after murdering his farmer brother, Abel: 'So Cain was banished from God's presence, and lived as a fugitive, East of Eden.' (Genesis 4.16)

And as descendants of Cain, 'East of Eden' is where we have been ever since – or is it?

If we imagine ourselves 'fallen', then we are – it becomes self-fulfilling prophecy. If we believe we have been exiled from Eden – that is God's garden, God's grace – then we exile ourselves. We are no more distant from the divine than our earliest ancestors. The 'Garden of Eden' is all around us, if we have but the eyes to see it and if we do not desecrate it. Unfortunately that is something humanity does all too well – it has destroyed the 'garden' since the first tools were invented. Many Edens have been destroyed over the millennia, as the ruins of civilisation from Egypt to Easter Island prove – usually when such societies become victims of their own success, grow too big, and, over-exploiting their resources, collapse in on themselves. Clive Ponting explores this in *The Green History of the World: The environment and collapse of great civilisations*, concluding:

> Instead of seeing the environment as the foundation of human
> history, settled societies, especially modern industrial societies,
> have acted under the illusion that they are somehow independent
> from the natural world, which they have generally preferred to see
> as something apart which they can exploit more or less with
> impunity.

(Ponting 1992: 406)

Many have attempts have been made to restore this balance, with tribal societies often looked to as role models in developing sustainable 'intentional communities', the modern term for communes or social utopias. If we cannot earn our place in paradise – if we cannot gain entry to the walled garden of God – then we have to create our 'heaven' here on Earth. Yet utopianism is a risky business, for one man's utopia is often another man's dystopia. Hitler's Germany illustrates this to the extreme, but let us take a hypothetical example closer to home. Picture a line of gardens on a council estate. In some people sit quietly reading a book, sunbathing with headphones on, do a bit of gardening, mow the lawn, play with the dog; while others blast out loud music, light smelly fires that ruin your washing, argue, do noisy DIY, have pets they do not look after properly or rubbish they rarely throw out. Each one of those gardens is a potential utopia, but not always to the person next door.

Eden is the Christian utopia, the good place that exists nowhere. No one has ever found it, but that does not stop people from trying. As with all utopias there is an inherent tension in such places – the real world is always trying to get in: what could be called 'reality transgressions'. This is a constant phenomenon (but not necessarily a problem) in all walks of life. Indeed it can be a healthy thing, a breath of fresh air, providing some much-needed clarity on the subject. And it can also provide the necessary frisson in the creative process. Sri Lankan author Romesh Gunesekera, writer of an alternative version of his homeland, *Reef*, in 1994 complains that:

'So the Lord God drove him out from that garden of delight...' (Genesis *3.23–24*)

'though I'm trying to make an imaginary space, the real world is constantly invading it.' (Jaggi 2007) ('Lost Horizons', Maya Jaggi, *Guardian* Review, 05.05.07)

Such discretist enclosures – polders – are destined to fail. It is difficult to maintain the integrity of inviolate borders indefinitely. The second law of thermodynamics – the non-availability of energy in a closed system – demands otherwise. An Eden with closed barriers may maintain its integrity, but will eventually wither away through lack of new life, like the forbidden garden in Oscar Wilde's fairy tale, 'The Selfish Giant'. We must let in others if the 'garden' is to find renewal. This act of boundary rupture can lead to its destruction but that is the risk that must be taken. To do otherwise is to ossify. An Eden without flowers, without laughter, without music, without love, is no Eden at all.

The biblical exile from womb-like Eden, where all our needs were catered for, was a form of divine caesarean, creating a birth trauma in the Western psyche ever since called The Fall – when basically we were 'pushed out of the nest'. Ever since it seems we have been trying to get back.

Return to Eden

Gardens offer a refugium from the world, a place of sanity, tranquil order, soothing to the eye and to the ear. They are a patch of order among the rude chaos of the world, against unruly nature and self-willed wilderness. In their own gardens, people

171

act as 'garden deities' and control their 'creation' and decides what lives, what dies, or at least what is welcome and what is unwelcome. And so the garden becomes a portrait of the gardener, a mirror of their mental health, or horticultural understanding. Monk-like, they endeavour to make their monastery gardens mini-versions of paradise, constantly seeking out 'the worm' in the fruit, pruning sinful weeds, helping everything to grow towards The Light.

Popular in the Victorian era, the time when collecting and categorising was at its fervent peak, botanical gardens tried to re-establish the divine order of things:

> Ideally, they reasoned, just as the affinities and relations between different species of herbs, flowers and trees would be clarified in the encyclopaedic garden, so the harmony that reigned between beasts in the original Eden might also be re-established.

(Schama 1995: 537)

The provision of public parks in the Victorian era and the rise in 'garden cities', which came about at the start of the twentieth century as an enlightened response to the repercussions of the Industrial Revolution, tried to redress this a little, providing breathing spaces in urban areas, places of leisure, relaxation, elemental healing – ponds, trees, grass, flowers, birds, sunshine, fresh air – a recreation of Eden in our 'fallen' cities, which we all can re-enter, for a while – until the gates are locked at dusk, anyway.

The continued popularity of gardens, both domestic and stately, is another mundane manifestation of this, as people recreate their own personal Arcadias – whether in their back garden or in the grounds of a country house – for display, status and pleasure. Like a bunch of 'Adams' commanded by their Creator to 'cultivate and tend it', we all seek a return to an Edenic state, albeit not normally naked! It is de-stressing, good exercise, productive (of fruit and veg) and often the only way people intimately connect with the land. Though a little patch of 'God's green Earth' we can all be stewards of the land.

The British cult of landscape gardening, led by Capability Brown, was an attempt to create a British Eden, an accessible Elysium, nature tamed, ordered, controlled – a statement of wealth, of a wealth able to afford such architectural fripperies as follies, grottoes and hermitages complete with resident hired hermit:

> Eden-behind-walls was, then, the very opposite of Pan's Arcadia

(Schama 1995: 538)

Walled gardens have their own, 'lost islands' feel to them. Frances Hodgson Burnett's 1909 fantasy *The Secret Garden* captures this well – the inkling that perhaps there are fairies at the bottom of the garden, or perhaps a gateway to another world.

The idea of lost Edens haunt us still – and there is little more appealing than a lost garden, hence the huge popularity of the Lost Gardens of Heligan, in Cornwall, and

Lost Arcadias. An overground British landscape garden.

the sister project, also created by Tim Smit, the Eden Project, in the old china clay pits of St Austell, an impressive healing of industrial wasteland, which has conjured up a tropical rainforest in Cornwall and created an accessible 'Eden' we can all return to. One almost expects to see the droids Huey, Dewey and Louie tending the biodomes, but unlike Douglas Trumbull's 1972 eco-SF classic, *Silent Running*, this story has a far happier ending.

Destroying Eden

Whenever we stumble upon some unspoilt piece of nature – a tropical island, a virgin rainforest, we often call it 'edenic' or paradisal, the commonest clichés which spring readily to our lips, often influenced by holiday brochure spiel. It seems we still have the blueprint of paradise in our cultural cortex. We seem to judge everything by its Platonic standard, by the 'Eden' mark. The myth of paradise is used to sell every 'unspoilt' resort, which are often anything but unspoilt by the time it has been developed to cater for the hordes of tourists who descend in their carbon-emitting jumbo jets. We destroy our planet-paradise in the race to these micro-paradises. We ruin them by our very presence – with litter, waste, pollution, imported culture, lifestyles – unless it is an exceptionally sensitive eco-tourist holiday. The lowest impact, ultimately, is no impact – not to go tthere at all.

Yet even one man going into the wilderness, for instance, wild camping, can have unexpected impact – he can bring disease to a tribe without the immune system to fight it, as happens in Peter Matthieson's 1966 parable against 'god-games', *At Play in the Fields of the Lord,* which in the wave of eco-awareness in the late Eighties and early Nineties was turned into a Hollywood movie – at a time when Amazonian Indians were perceived as living in an Edenic state from which Western man had fallen, the cult of the noble savage a hundred years on. Yet this time it was tinged with the realisation that 'their days were numbered' as habitat was destroyed and indigenous culture endangered. White Man's Guilt has given way to consumer guilt – 'buyer's remorse' – in the wake of the ultra-materialist Eighties. By our habits we destroy what we desire, for example hardwoods from the Amazon. This seems to be the *fait accompli* we are cursed with. To want something, to consume it, we inevitably destroy it, because the core truth is we cannot have our cake, and eat it.

This is the heart of the lost island mythos: their doom is seemingly hard-wired into them all. We desire them, yearn for them, seek them out or imagine them into being. But if and when we find them we inevitably destroy them by our presence, greed, stupidity, violence or sterilizing logic, rationalising and categorisation. Whatever mystery was present is plundered, tainted, marketed or destroyed.

Do we create Edens only to destroy them? Do we exile ourselves? Desiring the impossible, because it's *not* there, rather than appreciating what we have. Seeing salvation in 'the beyond', instead of the here and now? Heaven as elsewhere, but never at our feet?

The idea of a paradisal island is perhaps biologically programmed into us because we are all ejected from the paradisal womb, the embryonic first Eden, and from the nurturing of our mothers – perhaps symbolic of living in harmony with Mother Earth herself. The utopian ideal of a life free of care, hunger, cold and disease is perhaps the ragged fragment of this early life when we had all our needs tended to, when we did not have to toil, in utero and in infancy.

Of course, this Edenic state could not be sustained. Where the 'mother' nourished, the 'father' banished: the rise in the patriarchal phallic-power of the spear-wielding hunter subsuming that of the matrilinear foragers taking place over millennia, as what become humankind emerged from the pre-consciousness of the primal forest. We walked out of Eden on two feet, with a rumble in our bellies and weapons and tools in our hands – providing us with the means to conquer the world.

So, our island Earth could be 'lost' in another way, a paradise we have lost through if not Original Sin, then through continual 'sin' against the Earth: the flawed notion that we have dominion over all of creation, that we are apart from nature, not a part of it. We have exiled ourselves from Eden. We have lost what we had all along: the inheritance of our ancestors, squandered, and perhaps ruined for future generations: Planet Earth.

Could this self-imposed exile be a state of mind though? Is it indicative of the Descartean divide between spirit and matter, between *mythos* and *logos*: the two fundamental ways of seeing the world as defined by the Greeks – the mythic and the rational? The follower of *mythos* would ask 'Is the original 'island state' of bliss within the Source itself, the Godhead?' The follower of logos might ask ' Is it the ultimate lost island before the Big Bang – or whatever cataclysmic catalyst started the chain reaction of the universe? ' The *thing*ness of nothing, the emptiness before All-That-Is?

Maybe the very purpose of these lost islands is for us to be cast out of them – conceptual nests, which we *must* leave for our spiritual development – to learn, to grow, to rediscover the true value of, and perhaps to *earn* our place in once again.

Louis MacNeice affirmed our flawed humanity in his 'anti-edenic' poem, *Apple Blossom*:

> And when from Eden we take our way
> The morning after is the first day.

To be exiled from Eden implies a transition from one state to another: from the blessed to the cursed according to christian thinking, perhaps the opposite to the agnostic. One zone rejects the other – like a metabolism rejecting a virus, here by the ultimate antibody: Archangel Gabriel with his flaming sword. Ever since humankind has been trying to get back in, to recover the state of grace once experienced, and the results are often devastating.

> When a simple or primitive society comes into contact with
> civilisation it undergoes cultural change
>
> (Maclean 1972: ix)

And yet this is not a one-way thing. There is a continual 'conversation' between the inner and outer worlds, a conflict over dominant realities – which is stronger, which will win? Eden is constantly under a state of siege, but like Troy it is doomed to fall for it has let in its own Trojan horse – humanity. The world we carry in us brings out the downfall of the paradise we seek, as we see played out in so many stories. Perhaps the most heart-breaking that history can share with us is 'How the West Was Lost'.

Chapter eleven

How the West was lost

The Patriarch watched the Fenian prince like a hawk waiting to pounce on its prey. The serpent-banisher could see that the poet was still enamoured by his lost dreams, muttering about a princess with hair like the sun and a land where there was no old age: Devil's daydreams!

'You are still wrecked among heathen dreams*,' he would chide the old stubborn soul, though not without begrudging fondness – for once he had met someone more so than he!

It was a war of wills, but like a good chess game not without its appeal.

The flinty-eyed monk cracked his knuckes and set to work.

The Patriarch tried to instill in Oisín the urgency of the situation: his soul was in peril – it hung by a thread. Below it was the eternal abyss of damnation. All that would save him was baptism, and then constant fasting and prayer. To which the Fenian prince would reply sourly:

'The things that most of all I hate: fasting and prayers.'*

'Your old world has died. Your heathen kin roast in the fires of Hell. This is a new world now. We have no need for your foolish legends any more, except to instruct in folly. Admit defeat.'

* from 'The Wanderings of Oisín', W.B. Yeats

~~~~~~~~~~~~~~~~~~~~~~~~~~~~~

Concerning actual 'lost islands' the Americas are the biggest of them all and deserve a chapter all by itself. Never has so much been projected onto an undiscovered continent, expected of it and been lost by it. The discovery of the American continent is a salient case study of all the perils that lie in wait for those seeking real lost islands, and so is worth looking in full here.

When looking at the United States of America the lines between the myth and the reality often blur – not surprising when so much of its identity is defined by its own dream factories in Hollywood. It is a nation constantly creating its own myth. It created its own 'Genesis' – starting with the Pilgrim Fathers and culminating with the Gold Rush – a creation myth often depicted heroically as 'how the west was won', a Promised Land waiting to be claimed by the intrepid.

Spielberg's 2006 TV series, *Into the West*, evoked this search for the lost idyll, relating by its title right back to the Celtic immrama and obsession with a paradise in the west. This is echoed in native American belief, whose diverse peoples have a similarly orientated eschatology; as related in this passage by William W. Warren, the son of of an Ojibway mother and a white father descended from one of the Mayflower pilgrims:

> When an Ojibway dies, his body is placed in a grave, generally in
> a sitting posture, facing west. … The soul is supposed to start
> immediately after the death of the body, on a deep beaten path,
> which leads westward.

(cited in McLuhan 1971 (1986: 33))

The Ojibway's soul travels west, stopping for nourishment at a giant strawberry (!); travelling onto a fast-flowing body of water – the only way to cross being over 'the rolling bridge', which turns out to be a serpent ready to devour the unwary. For four nights the soul camps on prairie, moving westward all the time, until it arrives at the 'land of the spirits', the Happy Hunting Grounds.

Happy hunting grounds

Common amongst First Nations people is the belief in an afterlife in what are often referred to as 'the happy hunting grounds'. Warren goes onto describe this First Nations Eden, where the soul finds:

> … his relatives accumulated since mankind was first created; all is
> rejoicing, singing and dancing; they live in a beautiful country
> interspersed with clear lakes and streams, forests and prairies, and
> abounding fruit and game to repletion – in a word, abounding in
> all that the red man most covets in this life, and which conduces
> most to his happiness. It is that kind of paradise which he only by
> his manner of life on this earth, is fitted to enjoy.

(cited in McLuhan 1971 (1986: 33))

Although this posthumous land shares traits with many 'lost island' paradises, it also could describe America before its 'discovery' by European settlers: a virgin, unspoilt land, bountiful, with game and space enough for all the tribes – tribes living in harmony with the land and largely with each other, or at least so the myth goes. This equilibrium, if it existed, was only reached after millennia – the first Clovis People pretty much wiped out all the megafauna.

According the first description in English of the Americas written by Captain Arthur Barlow in 1584 after his first-hand experience of mapping the Virginian coast:

> We found the people most gentle, loving and faithful, void of all guile and treason, and such as lived after the manner of the golden age.

Whether this Golden Age was a reality or not, it was certainly a lot more sustainable compared to what was to come. North America is so vast it remained on whole unspoilt by these low-impact nomads. This pristine environment became the earthly analogue for their otherworldly Eden, the 'happy hunting grounds' a mere continuation of life on Earth:

> ... Our dead never forget this beautiful world that gave them being. They still love its verdant valleys, its murmuring rivers, its magnificent mountains, sequestered vales and verdant lined lakes and bays, and ever yearn in tender fond affection over the lonely hearted living, and often return from the happy hunting ground to visit, guide, console, and comfort them.
>
> (Chief Seattle, speech to the Govenor of Washington Territory, 1853, transcribed by Dr Henry Smith)

This 'pre-conscious' existence – at least preconscious to Old World minds, is captured hauntingly in Terence Malik's sublime film, *The New World* (2006), which shows the arrival of the European settlers from the perspective of the First Nation peoples, camouflaged among the forest like nature spirits, living in symbiosis with their environment the same as forest people around the world – until their paradigm is shattered by invaders from this altogether alien reality, seeking 'a new other Britain in this new other world' (from a sermon of 1622 by Samuel Purchass, quoted in O'Toole 2007).

Christopher Columbus discovered America in 1492 – yet behind that well-known 'fact' there is a plethora of dark detail and contradictions. Was it a good thing? Or a bad thing? Was he actually the first? How can you discover a 'new' land that has been inhabited for millennia? What happens when the Old World tries to create a New World? The answers to these questions chart an often tragic tale of genocide, extinction, slavery and shattered dreams.

The wrong Indian

The discovery of America (as is commonly accepted) came about because the North-West Passage to the East Indies was being sought, a Western way that would not be controlled by the Arab and Turkish ports, who levied taxes and monopolised the flow of spices and other sought-after goods to the west – charging what they liked. And so it was commercial reasons which provided the motivation for continent's accidental discovery, ironic considering how it turned out – the World's richest nation, the Atlantis of Capitalism, where dreams come true – at a price.

Bison were not the first mega-fauna to be nearly hunted to extinction. The Clovis People did a thorough job before the likes of Buffalo Bill came along with his Winchester rifle.

Columbus named the new land 'West Indies' because he believed it was the coast of China. He thought of the indigeonous people as 'Indians' – *Red* Indians that is – and so the incorrect appellation stuck. It is still used erroneously to describe native peoples in the Americas (for example Amazon Indians). Any aboriginal person was an 'Indian' to the settlers through their Old World cultural lens.

During the 1580s artist John White was commissioned to accompany Sir Walter Raleigh on his exploration of 'Virginia', the area of North Carolina named after the 'virgin queen', Elizabeth I. White's watercolours provided England's first view of this New World. The Algonquins they met were rendered in the same style as his collection of ethnic groups from around the world, including ancient Britons, which he depicted as similar 'painted savages' wandering naked – a pre-civilised state like the First Nations people. The message here was clear: look how far we have come. We are surely following God's will to do the same in the Americas. It was imperialist rhetoric used to justify the centuries of expansionism and exploitation that followed: these savages need civilising and then they can be just like us.

The clash of cultures was thunderous. The Old World settlers ironically hoping to escape religious persecution and oppressive governments, brought all their ideological baggage with them, and created their own brand of persecution and oppression – wiping out Native Americans by bringing them the 'gift' of civilisation, in the form of guns, alcohol, God and smallpox-ridden blankets. The settlers, on the whole, stole their land, killed their braves, raped their women, brainwashed their children and wiped out their buffalo. America was the Home of the Brave only until the White Man came along.

Yet there were exceptions – there was good and bad on both sides, there were aggressive 'Indians' as well as kind ones. Not all were 'noble savages'. The Pocahontas story exemplifies thus – whereby an 'Indian' princess helped save a colony from starvation. She became the iconic 'nice Indian', packaged and marketed and sent to England to have an audience with the Royal Family, only to die on the journey back. She is lauded to this day, with statues, films, books, and other merchandising, a cultural icon reduced to a Disney doll. Pocahontas' popularity can perhaps be best understood as a conscience-appeasing gesture.

The story illustrates how one cannot thrive in a new land unless one receives the goodwill of the locals, or even the tutelary spirit – Pocahontas is a kind of goddess of sovereignty, a Modron of America, who takes under her wing the Old World 'children'. She has become the consoling fiction of the West – justifying the seizure and exploitation of the land. She opened the gates for them and blessed them. So many tribes were tricked into signing over land rights because they could not conceive how anyone could own the land – and many are still fighting for the return of native lands, forced to live in poor reservations. Yet they are not a disempowered people – they have their own land, their own laws, their own income (albeit primarily through casinos). Alcoholism, drugs and gang culture are rife on the reservations – indicative of soul-loss, of a dispossessed people. But many have reclaimed their dignity. The Powwow movement has spread over the world, and Native American teachings and techniques (for instance, the vision quest and the *inipi* sweat lodge ceremony) have never been more popular. So much so that 'ownership' of these tales and teachings has become a controversial issue. Not content with taking their land, the White Man now wishes to steal their culture: 'cultural misappropriation' it is called. Some, such as First Nations storyteller Gayle Ross, argue that only Native Americans should be allowed to share Native American stories, yet when every other American seems to claim some Indian blood, where do you draw the line?

Terri Windling in her article 'Turtle Island: the mythology of North America' argues the validity of a native folk tradition:

> The very idea of "the American West" has a whole folklore
> tradition of its own: cowboys and Indians, *banditos*, pioneers and
> the stories that surrounded them. In the West, Anglo, Hispanic
> and Native American folkways have collided and merged.

(Windling 1997)

Gone to Croatan

When the first settlers of Virginia moved off into the wild, lost in the Dreaming of the New World, they left an enigmatic carved message: 'Croatan', referring to an island itself now lost in the sands of time. Croatan, also Croatoan, is a former island off the coast of North Carolina, south of Roanoke Island. The island existed at the time of the first English attempt at colonization in 1585. It has since been obliterated by the shifting of the sands and is now probably a part of either Hatteras Island or Ocracoke Island. The colony of 121 people was established there at the direction of the English explorer Sir Walter Raleigh. The ultimate fate of the colonists is a mystery; some of them are supposed to have taken refuge with friendly native Americans on Croatan Island and to have eventually become absorbed into the tribe. The only trace of the colony was the word 'Croatoan' found carved on a tree.

Interest in the fate of the so-called 'lost colony' was renewed in the latter part of the nineteenth century, when a large group of mixed-blood native Americans of Robeson County in south-eastern North Carolina claimed that they were descendants of the vanished colonists and the Croatan tribe. Although this claim of ancestry cannot be substantiated, the group has been officially recognized by the state government as the Croatan Indians.

Since then 'Croatan [has] remained embedded in its collective psyche' (Bey 1985). These were only the first to succumb, to hear the 'call of the wild':

> Antinomians, Familists, rogue Quakers, Levellers, Diggers, and
> Ranters were now introduced to the occult shadow of wildness,
> and rushed to embrace it.
>
> (Bey 1985)

And this has stayed with Americans ever since – the pioneering spirit and its dream of self-sufficiency, of hacking your own land out of the wilderness, building your own log-cabin, hunting, fishing, living by your will and wits, at the behest of no man: what could be called the 'Walden ethic', after Henry David Thoreau's famous experiment in low-impact lifestyle and self-sufficiency, published in 1854 – subsequently becoming an environmental classic.

> From the Mountain Men to the Boy Scouts, the dream of
> "becoming an Indian" flows beneath myriad strands of American
> history, culture and consciousness.
>
> (Bey 1985)

'Becoming "wild" is always an erotic act, an act of nakedness' says Bey. It is almost a wish to enter an Edenic state – 'before the fig leaf', as it were. Those 'gone to Croatan' vanish into the wilderness, like the character at the end of J.G. Ballard's *The Drowned World* (1962) disappearing into the neo-primal jungle.

> During the next thirty years the pole-ward migration of
> populations continued. A few fortified cities defied the rising
> water-levels and the encroaching jungles, building elaborate sea-
> walls around their perimeters, but one by one these were
> breached. Only within the former Arctic and Antarctic Circles was
> life tolerable. The oblique incidence of the sun's rays provided a
> shield against the more powerful radiation. Cities on higher

ground in mountainous areas nearer the Equator had been
abandoned, despite their cooler temperatures, because of the
diminished atmospheric protection.

It was this last factor which provided its own solution to the
problem of resettling the migrant populations of the new Earth.
The steady decline in mammalian fertility, and the growing
ascendancy of amphibian and reptile forms best adapted to an
aquatic life in the lagoons and swamps, inverted the ecological
balances, and by the time of Kerans' birth at Camp Byrd, a city of
ten thousand in Northern Greenland, it was estimated that fewer
than five million people were still living on the polar caps.

The birth of a child had become a comparative rarity, and only
one marriage in ten yielded any offspring. As Kerans sometimes
reminded himself, the genealogical tree of mankind was
systematically pruning itself, apparently moving backwards in
time, and a point might ultimately be reached where a second
Adam and Eve found themselves alone in a new Eden.

(Ballard 1962: 24)

The Drowned World depicts a world after 'climate chaos' – the polar icecaps have
melted and temperatures have soared (although in 1962 the cause was 'scientific' –
the imagined consequence of an increase in solar radiation – rather than
anthropogenic climate change). The cities of northern Europe and America have
been submerged and transformed into beautiful tropical lagoons. However, more
than just a prescient prediction of global warming, Ballard attempts to show that
humans create their environment according to their unconscious drives. The
environmental catastrophe depicts in *The Drowned World* causes the characters to
regress mentally while simultaneously the real world transforms into a dream
landscape. More than forty years on from Ballard's sci-fi portent, climate change is
beginning to force humans to recreate their environment. However contemporary
unconscious drives seem hell-bent on creating a nightmare landscape rather than
Ballard's more benign dream zones of Croatanism.

A change of worlds

Chief Seattle, in his famous 1854 speech to the 'Big Chief in Washington', said: 'Let
him be just and deal kindly with my people, for the dead are not powerless. Dead,
did I say? There is no death, only a change of worlds.' This is an astonishing
perspective on death, and one that speaks volumes of the First Nation attitude to this
greatest of mysteries.

First Nations people have many legends of 'lost islands' – from Grandmother Turtle's
back upon which the world, Pratchett-like, is built; to the blessed land of the dead
beyond the mist – an analogue not only of the Land of Youth from the Celtic
tradition, but of the tale of Oisín and Niamh of the Golden Hair. One tale is worth
summarising here as it shows the overlap in the geography of the afterlife and
eschatological belief. It is from the Algonquin people, the first to be contacted.

The tale of the spirit bride

An Algonquin brave weds but his beautiful wife dies. He mourns for too long, until he hears of a medicine man who knows the way to the lands of the dead. He journeys over the mountain, and arrives at the old man's lodge where he is taken on a spirit-journey. He flies to a river-bank where he boards a bone-white boat and joins other ghost-canoeists who sail towards the misty coast – amongst them his wife. He chases after her, but is swept by the stormy seas like so much driftwood, until the Great Creator takes pity on them and blows them ashore the Island of the Blessed. There the young newlyweds are finally reunited. But the brave hears the chanting of the medicine man – he must return. He sails back to the river-bank and finds himself back in the old man's lodge. Thanking the shaman, the brave returns to his tribe, becoming a great chief – until his time to die, when he rejoins his wife on the Island of the Blessed. (Based on Taylor 1992)

Turtle Island

Turtle Island is a traditional name for North America. The name comes from a common indigenous creation story: The first human, a woman, tumbled from the sky to the earth below. At the time the earth was completely water. Birds caught the woman in their wings, but they needed land for her to live on. Several animals tried to dive to the bottom of the ocean to retrieve some dirt with which to build land. Finally, the muskrat succeeded. Placing the dirt on the turtle's back, the woman blew and sent the dirt expanding across the ocean, making land for her to live on and a place for her to give birth to the first. Another version says the turtle offered its back for the animals of the world to live on. This creation myth shows insight – for the turtle's shell could be seen as a metaphor for the American continental plate, floating on the magma and supporting all that lives upon it. Of course, the first storytellers were not to know this, but it is an interesting coincidence showing how such myths can be 'wise lies'. On another level, the the story teaches the importance of stewardship and the web of life.

The notion of Turtle Island has flourished in popular culture. Gary Snyder's Pulitzer prize-winning collection of poetry from 1974 was named after it. Terry Pratchett's Discworld novels steal the notion, revelling in its apparent absurdity. Turtle Island crops up as a name for several different islands across America and further afield, including two Fijiain islands and as an alternative name for the Haitian island Tortuga, the basis for the pirate utopia in the *Pirates of the Caribbean* films. Turtle Island is used by a number of First Nation organisations to promote cultural identity (for example the Turtle Island Native Network) where issues such as cultural sensitivity are discussed. Like 'Avalon' it is used by many companies wanting to appear native, environmentally-aware and deep-rooted.

Kilroy was 'ere

For centuries there have been legends of lost islands in the west. Some of these were reported in the early voyages of Celtic saints, the immrama of Bran Mac Febal, Brendan and Maelduin – indeed it is thought these could be accounts of actual voyages across the North Atlantic even to the shores of America. These intrepid holy men in their frail currachs may have been the first visitors to America since the Bering land bridge disappeared.

The Irish claim to America rests primarily on a mediæval work named *The Voyage of Saint Brendan*. This text describes Atlantic trips made by Brendan, an Irish saint from Munster, in the sixth century, in which Brendan lands on several different islands, some of which can be identified. After years of such landfalls, Brendan finally comes to 'The Land of Saints' somewhere in the Western Ocean:

> Then getting down from the boat they saw a spacious land with
> apple trees bearing fruit. While they were there it was never night.
> They took as many of the apples as they wanted and they drank
> from springs, and then for forty days they wandered over the land
> but they could not find an end to it. On a certain day they came
> to a great river flowing through the middle of the island. Then
> Saint Brendan told his companions 'We cannot cross this river,
> and we will never know how big this island is.'
>
> (Selmer 1959: 79, cited in Young 2001)

Brendan turns back, and America is spared the White Man for another thousand years, although others have claimed to have also reached there before Columbus.

Runestone cowboys

The Vikings have also been given the credit for the discovery of America – with the recording of the discovery in 1000 CE by Leif Eriksson and Thorfinn Karlsveni of somewhere called 'Vinland', the land of wine. According to the 'Vinland Saga' this was beyond Iceland, beyond Greenland – possibly Newfoundland, which, as the name suggests was one of the first parts of North America to be discovered in 1497. The Vinland Saga relates how the Vikings launched ambitious expeditions from Greenland to settle on the eastern seaboard of North America, but these attempts to colonize the New World five hundred years before Columbus were soon abandoned in the face of hostility from the indigenous peoples: an early case of sour grapes.

Stories of the abortive American venture are recorded in the medieval Icelandic sagas; but little authentic evidence of the Viking presence has been found, apart from substantial traces of a Viking Age settlement at L'Anse-aux-Meadows, in the north of the island of Newfoundland. All other Viking 'finds', such as the Kensington Stone, have been exposed as forgeries or hoaxes, or merely wishful thinking.

The 2006 film about the Viking discovery of America, *Pathfinder*, is based on the graphic novel by its director Marcus Nispel. This film is a typical Hollywood's comic book version of history. But Nispel was not the first to wish to rewrite history to suit prior agendas or tastes. A Viking America is a satisfying myth for white supremacists that prefer a past not tainted by anything other than Aryan blood. It has been imported into the 'warrior code' of the new Vikings of America, the Hell's Angels and their ilk, the latest in a long line of 'wild ones'.

Welshmen and Eskimos

The general consensus is that the Clovis People, known to have been mammoth-hunters, were the first settlers of America, coming over the Bering land bridge from Eurasia and sweeping down through the unpeopled continent between 11,500 and 11,000 BCE. They left behind distinctive leaf-shaped spears, first excavated in 1932 at Clovis, New Mexico: the site that gave them their name.

Yet other evidence has come to light that suggests otherwise: the Clovis migration theory was challenged from the Seventies, particularly after the excavation of Monte Verde, a site in south-central Chile, which was dated to at least 12,500 years ago. Further pre-Clovis evidence was revealed in 2000 at Cactus Hill, Virginia, where a 15,070 year-old hearth was excavated. This assemblage is taken to be evidence of the presence of some of the first human beings to have crossed the frozen land bridge of the Bering Strait and settled in the American continent.

Other evidence suggests Eskimos may have reached the continent long before Columbus. 5,000 year old remains have recently been discovered that appear Caucasian. And there is a prehistoric French connection. Some flint points about 40,000 years old are identical to those manufactured in southern France about the same time. These people travelled to the Americas via the polar ice inshore waters in their *kayaks* – perhaps slowly moving west over generations – and likely to be the ancient ancestors of the Inuit peoples.

Even the Welsh joined in on this 'who got there first' game, with a claim that a Prince Madoc made it there in 1170, setting sail from Porthmadog, although no firm evidence has come to light. Madoc was reputed to have been the son of the historical culture hero, Owain Glendower: Upon Owain's death in 1170, fighting broke out among the possible successors. Madoc was disheartened, says the story, and he and Rhirid set sail from Rhos-on-Sea to explore the western ocean with a small fleet of boats. They discovered a distant and abundant land where one hundred men disembarked to form a colony, and Madoc and the others returned to Wales to recruit settlers. After gathering ten ships of men and women the prince sailed west a second time, never to return. It is claimed he arrived somewhere in west Florida and even settled, producing a line of Welsh-speaking Indians – although the only account of that is from a Welshman, Rev Morgan Jones in 1669, who recorded his account after being captured by a tribe of Tuscaroras called the Doeg. Some would claim a linguistic connection but Madog, as the folk hero is spelled in Welsh, is pronounced with a 'c' ('Madoc'), as in Porthmadog.

Behind the Madoc myth may have been a political motive. Such stories served to bolster British claims in the New World to counter those of Spain. John Dee went so far as to assert that Brutus of Britain and King Arthur as well as Madoc had conquered lands in the Americas and therefore their heir, Elizabeth I of England, had a priority claim there.

This link, real or mythopoeic, and the subjugation of both 'red men' (the Welsh and First Nation) by the Sais, the English, is brooded upon by John Cowper Powis in his collection of essays *Obstinate Cymric*, published in 1973.

To this day the myth is nurtured on both sides of the Atlantic and, like the invented tale of the 'loyal hound' Beddgelert, it provides a patriotic fantasy that people want to believe.

Black rabbits and Brazilians

The discovery of the Americas provided fuel for every idle speculator. From the beginning America was a fabrication – a supposedly 'blank canvas' upon which a new country could be invented. This mass effort of imagineering lent itself readily to similar acts of mythological 'terra-forming':

> Interest in Atlantis revived with the discovery of the Americas, and since then has grown to the proportions of neurosis.

(De Camp 1970: 28)

Yet America itself was seen as that very land, in the legends of El Dorado and Hy-Brasil, the phantom island of many Irish myths that has 'manifested' in a variety of recent contemporary fantasy novels and computer games..

According to Celtic myth, Hy Brasil is said to be the home of the Fomorians and Fir Bolgs:

> The ghostly Isle of Brazil, which haunted the maps for many years was not finally exorcised until the Nineteenth Century. It was usually located a few hundred miles west of southern Ireland and described as circular – in one case as a ring of islands. This phantom land was kept alive by reports like that of a Captain Nisbet who in 1674 arrived in Scotland with some "castaways" he claimed to have rescued from the Isle of Brazil. He said that the island was inhabited by huge black rabbits and by a magician who had been keeping the castaways captive in his castle until the gallant captain broke the spell that bound them.

(De Camp 1970: 25)

Hy-Brasil is one of many such far-fetched travellers' tales lampooned by Swift in *Gulliver's Travels* (a pun on 'gullible'). It crops up in Terry Jones' 1989 film *Erik the Viking*. Fellow Python-turned-film-director, Terry Gilliam, makes reference to it in *Brazil*, his nightmarish mid-eighties re-imagining of Orwell's *Nineteen Eighty Four*, making a dystopia out of the utopia of Hy-Brasil. Another no-where somewhere in the west:

> 'Alas for romance! There never was such an island.'

(De Camp 1970: 25)

Hy-Brasil was never found, but ironically the South American country of Brazil was founded with its myth in mind; and a 'brazilian' denotes the full removal of female pubic hair, like a denuded rainforest delta – which is exactly what is happening to the Amazonian coast.

Invisible vssels

When the ships of the Old World first appeared on the shores of America it is reported that the native inhabitants were unable to see them because the pattern recognition part of their brain did not have anything to relate to – the ships belonged to a different paradigm altogether and may as well have been space ships from another world. Which in a way they were.

There are mentions of 'air-ships' in Irish literature and in the ancient Vedic literature of India, with its *vimanas*, or 'air-boats' (Devereux 2002: 16). This is not to argue for Von Daniken-esque early alien incursions into the ancient world, but whenever an 'advanced' paradigm collides with a 'primitive' one, it can trigger this cultural myopia – on both sides.

This is analogous to Edwin Abbot's 1884 parable of *Flatland,* where a two-dimensional world is visited by a three-dimensional shape, which the natives cannot comprehend, except the narrator Square. In the book, the three-dimensional sphere has the ability to stand inches away from a Flatlander and observe them without being seen. This is a powerful analogy for all forms of cultural myopia – some people just cannot see what is in front of their noses. In Abbot's view the Flatlanders lacked 'The Art of Sight Recognition' – objective vision once attained by Flatland's upper classes – and were limited to the subjective 'The Art of Feeling' innate in the lower classes. This elitist and dualistic notion was challenged by Square and a few fellow Flatlanders.

After all, what is objective when the scientist can affect the experiment, as in Schrodinger's Cat? But it is not intended to draw comparisons to First Nations people, who had their own civilisation before the Settlers came. If anything, the settlers were arriving in the wrong way, with inappropriate ceremony, the wrong cultural lenses or sensitivities. They saw only 'savages' and a rich land ripe for exploitation, much to their detriment – to explore a pre-conquest America would be a dream for any modern anthropologist, botanist, writer or photographer.

The betrayal of Motecuhzoma and the tears of Cortes

In the sad and sobering tale of the conquest of the Aztecs all the themes of the American cycle are played out in microcosm – as though it set the blueprint for both the Old and New Worlds' interaction – a blueprint based on greed, bloodshed and betrayal. It was one of the world's most spectacular culture clashes. History tells us – and this is one certainly written by the victors – that when the Spanish adventurer Hernán Cortés arrived in Mexico in 1519, Motecuhzoma (erroneously referred to as Montezuma) believed that he was the Aztec god-king Quetzalcoatl. Accordingly, Cortés was presented with offerings of gold and silver gifts. Instead of appeasing this visiting god, Motecuhzoma's act inflamed the Conquistador's lust for gold (the 'tears of the sun').

Later, fearful that the Aztecs would attack the outnumbered Spanish troops, Cortés held Motecuhzoma hostage. In June 1520 the Aztecs, growing restive under Spanish control, revolted. Cortés called on Montezuma to quell the revolt, but the Aztec ruler was stoned while addressing his subjects. He reportedly died three days later. In his subjects' eyes Motecuhzoma had failed, losing his sacred kingship and even the right to live. The public often savage those they adulate, swiftly turning heroes into hate-figures if they are perceived to have 'failed'.

Half the world's population would argue that the real gold brought back from the Mayan jungles was the humble cacao bean, from which chocolate is made. The New World got their revenge – by giving the Old World toothache. Recent research suggests chocolate is good for you – drinking a mug of cocoa before bedtime reduces heart disease. Perhaps this is the real elixir of life? Motecuhzoma drank fifty cupfuls of it a day! Maybe he was just high on chocolate – in a cocoa coma – allowing Cortes to obliterate his world: the ultimate death by chocolate.

God's golden shore

The legend of a lost city of gold fuelled the fervour of the plundering conquistadors and many treasure-hunters since:

> Before the Victorian steamboats pushed their way through the scummy waterweed of the Upper Nile and the Gambia, there had been Spanish, Elizabethan, and even German craft, adrift up the Orinoco basin, pulled by the tantalizing mirage of El Dorado, the golden paradise around the next bend.
>
> (Schama 1995: 5)

Yet, like many self-fulfilling prophecies it came true, with the blood-soaked splendour of Mayan and Inca gold, and the actual 'lost city' in the Peruvian Andes, Machu Piccu, which the Spaniards never found. These 'carrots' have lured the curious or acquisitive further and further into the land and its past ever since:

> … the treasure-cities of the Brazilian wilds have been one of the leading will-o'-the-wisps of speculative palaeology ever since the conquistadors wandered the length and breadth of this vast land seeking in vain for El Dorado.
>
> (De Camp 1970: 78)

The imperialist fantasies of Victorian adventure stories, such as Arthur Conan Doyle's 1912 story, *The Lost World*, perhaps fuelled the imagination of the 'lost islander'. In such vast untamed wilderness it is possible to imagine any thing the mind or its subconscious can conjure, and indeed, even to this day new species are being discovered in remote habitats (mainly insects and plants, but sometimes even mammals). Alas, many are becoming extinct faster than they are being discovered, as swathes of primal rainforest is destroyed for the logging industry, the rearing of cattle for the world's fast food restaurants, or the growing of soya bean. Yet lost cities are still being discovered – for instance, in the rainforest of Peru in the last decade (see Parsell 2002) – even as this tragic decimation takes place .

The real gold it seems are the rare medicines hidden in the rainforest – possible cures for cancer, for AIDS and other western ills. But in their greed, the 'treasure hunters' (the loggers and the multinationals who fund them) destroy this very horde, unable to see the wood for the trees; just as 'blind', perhaps, as those natives who could not see the ships, or the settlers who could not see their common humanity in the First Nations people.

Lost nation

After centuries of exploitation and increasing xenophobia of the outside world (the descendants of the settlers ironically fearing the 'outsider' themselves – as evidenced in America's increasingly isolationist policies in the latter twentieth century) something had to give. And it did in 2001, on the 11th September – known forever afterwards as 9/11, rather neatly echoing the 911 emergency number: the most devastating mnemonic in modern history (Armistice Day, the eleventh hour of the eleventh day of eleventh month, is an earlier equivalent – but at the other end of the cycle of war). This was the day North America was dealt the 'lightning struck tower' from the tarot of life. Nearly three thousand people lost their lives in this tragedy, whose consequences we are still experiencing, as wars continue, like forest fires, across the world, started from these towering infernos.

In the wake of this, the USA, a nation in shock and mourning, did indeed become a lost island – withdrawn, in shock, *in communicado* (email and cell systems jammed as people tried to contact loved ones), Some would say what happened was *because* of an insular mentality and arrogance in the world arena, as became clear all too quickly in the weeks after as the hawks of Washington invented a 'War on Terror' as a convenient excuse to railroad draconian legislation and ramp up the arms budget. The USA's response to 9/11 was convenient 'justification' for invading the oil-rich countries, which the New American Century plan had deemed was essential for securing the nation's energy needs.

Rather than plunge into the murky waters of politics I want to look at the psychological impact of 9/11 on America. It became a 'lost nation' in the sense of a nation sharing a sense of loss. This manifested in a raft of introspective sentiments, often maudlin movies which would not have been given the green light before 9/11. Americans needed their consoling fictions, turning to core myths, such as the TV series *Into the West*, revealing how at times of national crisis a nation recourses to its national (creation) myths; like Finland with the Kalevala.

Some may have even seen Peter Jackson's film trilogy of *The Lord of the Rings* (2001–4) as a metaphor of US against Them, the West against the Eastern Hordes. However the film could easily be turned around: Bush as Sauron, Blair as Saruman... as a Greenpeace film cleverly did, shown at Glastonbury Festival in the early 2000s, recutting the footage with subtitles to cheers from the festival-goers: the feisty hobbits recast as eco-protesters (diminutive Davids against the Goliath of the Multinationals!).

The ultimate post 9/11 show is the hit TV show *Lost* (created by J.J. Abrams and Damon Lindelof). Survivors of a plane crash somewhere in the Pacific find themselves on an unnamed tropical island. Over the 26 episodes of the first series we get introduced to each of the main characters, Jack, a doctor with a dark past; Sawyer, a reformed crook; Locke a disabled box salesman who can now walk; Michael, a black architect with a dysfunctional relationship with his son; Sun and Jin, a hot and cold Korean couple; Charley, an English addict rock star; Claire, an Australian pregnant single mum and a token 'mad French woman'...

As we discover elements of their back story our perceptions of each is recalibrated. No one is wholly good or bad, there is an interesting blurring of morality. On one level Jack is the good guy, Sawyer, the devil to his Christ, and the love interest is the 'Eve' figure in this lost paradise, torn between temptation and salvation. Yet she is not the only one fighting for her soul it seems in this lost Eden. They all are, it appears, as they must come to terms with their past, dealing with some 'issue' before being allowed to move on: as much as the protracted plot allows.

The characters seem struck in purgatory, and the interpretation that most intrigues me is that they are all dead – but do not know it. For forty-plus people to survive a plane crash with only minor injuries is highly unlikely. Maybe they all died, and have not come to terms with it, as supposedly happens to those souls who pass over suddenly. This is kept implicit, but there is enough Lynch-esque weirdness to suggest things are not what they seem: polar bears; black mist; dead characters from their past; a mysterious hatch; no search and rescue (passenger jets do not just go missing). Things are 'explained' in subsequent series, but taken on its own, the first series is Prisoner-esque in its obfuscation.

Everything is kept maddeningly ambiguous, and spun out over a long season but the fascinating thing here is that the whole thing could be seen as a consoling fiction for post 9/11 America. Four aircraft went down that day, with the passengers of Flight 93 putting up a good fight, it seems – being the only plane to miss its target. In a way, *Lost* could be seen as an indirect tribute to them – to the lost on those four flights, perfectly capturing the zeitgeist of the time, in the American hearts the victims of 9/11 still live on, and it is indeed consoling to imagine they still do, in a paradise somewhere.

They have gone onto a 'lost island' – an island paradise of plenty, though far from trouble free, not a million miles from the 'happy hunting grounds' of Tir nan Og, and their ilk. Here the beautiful dead can remain forever beautiful.

Traumatised America continues to brood on its now found vulnerability in post-apocalyptic musings like Cormac McCarthy's Pulitzer prize-winning novel, *The Road* (2006) and the films *The Day After Tomorrow* (2004), *Right at Your Door*

(2006), *I am Legend* (2007) and *Cloverfield* (2007). The cultural consensus is that the status quo is fragile and nowhere is safe. Furthermore, everything is connected and thus equally at threat (McCarthy calls this 'the fragility of everything'). The fractured narrative structure of post-post-modern movies such as *21 Grams*, *Crash*, *Babel* and *Syriana* also mirrors this cracked paradigm. Ragnarok is the new rock 'n' roll, and gloomy is the new black.

Cuba: close but no cigar

In Cuba we have another kind of lost island – one that is intentionally 'lost' to American citizens, who are banned from going there, because of the long-term trade embargo set up in 1960. This seems to have the opposite effect and makes it an even more alluring destination, adding a certain Che Guevara chic. To visit it is an act of rebellion, or a long distance one for the T-shirt anarchist: ideology rendered meaningless as a fashion icon. Cuba has a certain romantic appeal, as fully evoked in Wim Wender and Ry Cooder's 1999 film *Buena Vista Social Club*.

Michael Moore's 2007 film *Sicko* – about the state of the US health service – encountered hot waters, because a section of it was filmed there without the director obtaining permission from the US Government. The country, despite the inevitable difficulties faced by a developing country has an excellent health and education system. Its leader for half a century, Fidel Castro teeters on the brink of death, (being replaced by his younger brother Raul in 2008) but his iconic cigar has been cocking-a-snook to North America, like the Russian missiles in the Sixties crisis since 1959. Cuba is an embarrassing refugium of communism besieged by capitalist tides: ones that lures refugees to attempt the perilous crossing in makeshift rafts. Others barely escaped from Cuba with their lives during the revolution, such as the poet Reinaldo Arenas, who wrote about his experiences in *Before Night Falls* (1992 – made into a film in 2000 by Julian Schnabel) which illustrated the persecution homosexuals faced. Cuba may have many positive qualities but it is not a paradise for all.

Island of the lost

Perhaps the most harrowing 'lost island' of all is the notorious gulags of Guantanamo Bay off Cuba: Camp Delta. Guantanamo is the endgame of the American dream. Here democracy ends. A Channel 4 reporter called it 'an island with no law' (*C4 News* 12 Sept 2006). The so-called Land of the Free is imprisoning people without trial. Typical of the dehumanising process the prisoners are refered to as 'enemy combatants' (like 'gooks', the US name for Vietnamese insurgents; 'reds' for communists; or 'huns', 'krauts', 'the bosch' – British names for Germans in the two World Wars. Camp Delta detainees are commonly bound, hooded and incarcerated like Africans on slave ships bound for America. These slaves wear orange. Loud 'death metal' is played to them as a form of psychological torture. If they behave themselves they are given 'freedom fries'.

This same cultural imposition is taking place on a grander scale in Iraq where Western democracy is being imposed on a culture which does not share the same traditions. John Gray in his book *Black Mass: Apocalyptic religion and the death of utopia* comments bitterly 'The world has become more dystopian because the Americans sought to impose their version of utopia on Iraq.' (Gray 2007)

There have been calls to shut down Guantanamo Bay across the world, not least from American civil rights campaigners, of which the nation has a long and noble tradition, along with that of crusading liberal journalism and the Protest movement. America may yet sing its songs of freedom.

'... a world of little men'

Europe once fell in love with America. In the Fifties anything American was considered the epitome of cool (the much-loved *Eagle* comic adopting the American icon as its emblem; and even Tolkien's characters cried out in joy: 'The eagles are coming! The eagles are coming!'). This continued for the bulk of the second half of the twentieth century. As well as chewing gum, chocolate, nylons and comic books that GIs brought over during the Second World War, post-war American has had a huge cultural footprint on the world – rock 'n' roll, movies, motorbikes, Woodstock, McDonald's, the Simpsons, Ben and Jerry's, Calvin Klein, Starbucks – some aspects undoubtedly more welcome than others.

Today's so-called 'war on terror' is a clash of cultures every bit as distorted by the mis-perceptions of underlying cultural myths as was the conquest of the New World and the taming of the 'Wild West'. However this time the New World is imparting its neo-con imperialist mythos onto the some of the oldest cultural strata of the Old World, the Islamic states. America's attempts to resolve its peak oil crisis by imposing political control over key oil production countries such as Iraq and Afghanistan has made many in Western countries want to distance themselves from the American-led aggression.

Yet to see 'America' as the problem is taking a rather Cyclopean-view of things. There are many Americas. To those who burn the Stars and Stripes and chant 'Death to America!', which one do they wish to destroy: First Nations America? Hispanic America? Black America? To castigate a country because of its government is not doing justice to its diverse peoples. What percentage of the United Kingdom did Tony Blair fairly represent when he was in power? How many British citizens did *not* want to go to war in Afghanistan and Iraq, and how many were ignored?

In the US, signs are the tide is turning against the hawks. America wearies of an expensive war abroad – perhaps starting to recover from 'Vietnamnesia' – and the 2008 elections may provide the paradigm-shift in American politics. Many articulated and committed individuals – local activists, campaigners, film stars, writers, politicians – are providing voices of reason, voices of hope. They are no longer in the wildnerness.

Almost everyone loves America when it gets it right – although hard to remember in this current climate they, along with the pressure from Russia, undoubtedly saved the day in the Second World War. Perhaps like that amoral intergalactic gunslinger, Han

Solo (a waist-coated, shooting-from-the hip Gary Cooper in space) it will come good in the end. It will find its moral compass once more. It will no longer be lost.

> Once there were islands all a-sprout with palms: and coral reefs
> and sands as white as milk. What is there now but a vast shambles
> of the heart? Filth, squalor, and a world of little men.

Mervyn Peake *Titus Alone*

Chapter twelve

This island Earth

The young scribe placed his quill down and rubbed his wrist. Oisín's low-burning narrative had flickered out altogether. All that could be heard was the Danaan prince's death-rattle now, coming with increasing frequency between prolonged periods of anxious silence. The scribe squinted into the gloom of the cell. There was barely enough light coming through the small high window to illuminate the figure of the black-robed Patriarch, bent over the bed of the Fenian like Death himself, and yet there was a look of compassion in his sharp profile as he scrutinised the papery-thin skull of the prince, firm hand placed gently on the dying man's brow.

'There you go. That's it,' Oisín rasped, coughing violently. 'You've sucked my life out of my head. Happy now, you old carrion crow!'

The scribe held his breath, expecting the riposte. The Patriarch would normally not tolerate being spoken to like that, but he just smiled sadly.

Oisín's coughing subsided. 'Ah, look at me. A creeping old man, full of sleep, with the spittle of his beard never dry*,' he lamented.

The Patriarch looked at the Fenian prince with a wry smile. It would not be many winters before *he* was in the same state.

Oisín was unspeakably weary. His burden shed, alone of his kind, last of the Fenians: he no longer wished to be in this world. With a last sigh he gasped: 'Ah, me! to be shaken with coughing and broken with old age and pain, without laughter, a show unto children, alone with remembrance and fear; all emptied of purple hours as a beggar's cloak in the rain, as a hay-cock out on the flood, or a wolf sucked under a weir*.'

'Think of the past no more, my son. Nor the suffering of the present. Turn what time you have left to the future.'

Oisín met the Patriarch's urgent gaze: 'Your future, it kills me.'

  *'The Wanderings of Oisín', WB Yeats

Earth rise

The first 'public' view of planet Earth from space – the first time humanity had seen its home – was the famous 'earth-rise' photograph taken on Christmas Eve 1968 by the crew of Apollo 8, on a reconnaissance mission for future lunar landing sites. The iconic image should have shocked humanity into realising how unique and fragile our planet is – an oasis of life in a vast cold lightless desert. It was not until 1972, on the last trip to the moon, that the iconic 'blue marble' photograph was taken – the full hemisphere of the Earth lit by the sun, for once directly behind the Apollo space-craft. This has become the most-reproduced holiday snap in history, as Al Gore points out in *An Inconvenient Truth* (Gore 2006). Only then did humanity literally get the full picture. This was a paradigmatic moment in human history.

Edgar Mitchell, an Apollo 14 astronaut, said on observing this awesome sight, the home planet, in 1971:

> It was a beautiful, harmonious, peaceful looking planet – blue
> with white clouds, and it gave one a sense of... home, of being, of
> identity. It is what I prefer to call instant global consciousness.

Other astronauts have experience similar epiphanies. When Neil Armstrong and Edwin 'Buzz' Aldrin landed on the moon on 20 July 1969 to take those 'giant steps for mankind' a similar moment occurred as the astronauts beheld the first earth-rise seen from the moon's surface. The suitably named Armstrong lifted up his thickly insulated appendage and placed his thumb over the planet, a blue two-pence piece set on an infinite expanse of black velvet. In an instant six billion lives were blotted out. He said afterwards this did not make him feel big – it made him feel very, very small.

In such iconic moments the solipsism of humanity is shattered. The Earth, which is everything to us, is merely a small island in the vastness of space, one of countless billions – although, as far as we know, unique in sustaining life. The existence of life on Earth is highly unlikely – an act of evolutionary improbability. This makes our planet not only incredible precious but incredible fragile as well. It could be the only chance we have.

Ark mentality

Feelings of planetary mortality have been with us for millennia, as the various apocalyptic traditions around the world attest, but things took an altogether more realistic edge with the invention of the atom bomb – which, if not able to blow up the world completely, would certainly make it uninhabitable to most forms of life. With the escalation of the arms race against the backdrop of the Cold War this doom-laden scenario became increasingly probable, as the Doomsday Clock moved closer and closer to midnight. This created a wave of 'atomic nightmare' movies, most garishly sensationalist – humanity attacked by monster animals, mutants, aliens and hybrid humans. These played on our fears – fuelled by McCarthyism – and sold popcorn. Martians from the 'red planet' were none other than communists from outer space. The world was caught up in an ideological clash between two grand narratives, stereotyped as Ivan and Uncle Sam: the East and the West.

The 1951 science fiction film *When Worlds Collide* by George Pal (in which 'space arks' are rapidly constructed to save the lucky few from the immanent collision of two runaway planets) foreshadowed the ark mentality worryingly prevalent in contemporary space scientist circles – who seem to be looking 'anywhere but here' to save humanity. This Noahic attitude – 'God's given us the nod and the wink, so let's get out of here' – is perhaps the inevitable result of Western Christian hard-wiring. God-fearing Americans especially are brainwashed from their first day at state-funded 'faith schools' that the end is nigh, and only the chosen few will be saved, whether in an infidel-free paradise or WASP heaven. Salvation is elsewhere – the grass is greener on Uranus. It would be Douglas-Adams-funny, if it was not so deadly serious. The Vogon fleet is on its way, and they are practising their poetry.

Between Venus and Mars

As Douglas Adams once said,'Space is big. Very big.' It's a lonely universe out there, as far as we know. We are lucky to live on the third rock from the sun: not too hot, not too cold. Our number came up in the 'Thunderball' of creation. An incredible chain of 'happy accidents' led to life on Earth being here. We have not found any anywhere else, yet, with life – however high the possibility. In an infinite universe all things are possible. But until we find other life-sustaining planets, planets with the essential criteria for life (water being the main one), we live in a perilously narrow band of life, between Venus and Mars: 'On dead planets such as Venus and Mars, CO_2 makes up most of the atmosphere, and it would do so here if living things and Earth's processes did not keep it within bounds' (Flannery 2006: 5) but this delicate balance is in danger of becoming undone by humankind's carbon habit.

This dialectic is summed up by Aristotle, referring to Plato's Atlantis: 'He who invented it, also destroyed it.' This epitomises the story-arc of all lost islands, from their creation to their demise. It could be called the 'Atlantis *fait accompli*'. Alluring island paradises have 'doomed' written all over them, especially when they appear in myth or fiction, but increasingly so in reality – with climate change threatening all low-lying islands. Like the super-villain's underground base in a Seventies' James Bond flick, you know they are going to 'blow up' at the end. But could this fate say something about the human condition? Is this tendency to invent and destroy actually the impulse of Eros and Thanatos, of procreation and death?

We need to find a balance between the two extremes symbolised by Venus and Mars – the feminine and the masculine; compassion and focussed energy, – to solve this fix we are in: a chymical wedding on a grand scale. Psychologically it is telling that men are obsessed about going to Mars: named after the Roman god of war. Venus is too hot and toxic of course, but no one talks of missions to the planet of love – which, as the song goes, is what the world needs now: not more aggressive male energy, which the world has suffered under for too long.

The space between

To predispose towards Venusian or Martian paradigms, to create new matriarchies or patriarchies, is just continuing the conflicts that have blighted humanity throughout history as we swing from one state to another, each regime a reaction to the one before. One extreme creates another. The current state of the world offers many examples of this. What is needed is *balance*, between the actual and imaginary, the left and right-brained, the masculine and feminine. Both are needed. Two hemispheres, two worlds, both essential – and where they overlap, that is where new worlds are created and lost islands are found… in the interstices; what poet David Jones called 'the space between'.

Nature abhors a vacuum, and I think the human imagination does also. The Atlantic Ocean (and the Pacific to those along its rim) has become a mirror of whatever we project onto it, a cauldron-like repository for whatever we fear and desire. This seems to occur wherever there is a space too large to be observed in its entirety, wherever information is withheld, so our brains, like our eyes, fill in the gaps. The 'wet deserts' of Dartmoor, Exmoor, Bodmin, the Brecon Beacons, the Pennines, the Burren or the Scottish Highlands, for instance, provide a dreaming space for those who live within them on or their borders – their massive presence pervades the lives of those who live on their perimeters, under the shadow of giants. Yet perhaps this has been happening since the dawn of consciousness – when there became a distinction between what is known and unknown. What is unknown becomes mysterious and possibly sinister. This is made great capital of today. And at the dawn of mankind it was whatever was outside the frail circle of firelight, whatever lurked at the back of the cave, or whatever made the sky rumble with thunder, flash with lightning, blaze with comets or eclipses. Thus mythology and the imagination were born at the same time.

Yet fear and desire are closely linked. And as well as accommodating our shadow, the unknown can also embrace everything we desire. And so lost islands become hoards of everything the harsh realities of life deny us: abundance without toil, freedom from hunger, disease, ageing, enemies, loneliness and despair. It is no wonder then that many would go 'over the hills and far away' at the drop of a hat in these tales – as in life. As tourists we are continually looking for the next 'unspoilt' paradise, only to spoil it by our very presence. Even if we 'take nothing but photographs, leave nothing but footprints' our clumsy traipsing through the undergrowth can destroy orchids, insects and disturb birds. We are always the fly in the ointment – this is the Catch 22 of lost islands.

No doubt humanity will keep searching for and creating lost islands. Yet if we do not curtail our carbon habit, among other things, we may well find ourselves struggling to survive on a lost island called Planet Earth.

Archibald Macleish, responding to the first photograph of the planet in 1968 said:

> To see the Earth as it truly is, small and blue and beautiful in that
> eternal silence where it floats, is to see ourselves as riders on the

The most reproduced holiday snap in history. NASA

Earth together, brothers on that bright loveliness in the eternal
cold – brothers who know that they are truly brothers.

(Quoted in Gore 2006)

Klaatu's warning to humanity from *The Day the Earth Stood Still* (directed by Robert
Wise in 1951) to rings true today: 'Join us and live in peace, or pursue your present
course and face obliteration... the decision is yours.'

However it is always wise to remember that however dismal the prospect: 'No one
can absolutely know the future.' (Flannery 2006:7)

~~~~~~~~~~~~~~~~~~~~~~~~~~~~~~

And so we come to the end of our immram around the western lost islands of myth, literature, geology, ecology, alternative culture and history. I hope it has been an illuminating and entertaining immram, an odyssey of folly and wisdom. If it has inspired you to wander and dream, to visit lost islands in your imagination or in reality, then it would have succeeded. Bon Voyage.

> 'Delightful is the land beyond all dreams.'
> And the dreams of the islands were gone,
> And I knew how men sorrow and pass.
>
> W.B. Yeats , 'The Wanderings of Oisín'

~~~~~~~~~~~~~~~~~~~~~~~~~~~~~~

Oisín's Legacy

The ink dried on the vellum, black runes of blood.

The frail form of the ancient prince seemed to wither like a leaf in the autumn. A chill wind whistled through the cracks of the monastery, echoing and amplifying the last breaths of the dying man.

Yet he had gone beyond pain now. A look of serene peace came over Oisín.

The Patriarch asked the Fenian if he wanted to be baptised and accept the word of Christ, to save his soul – there was still a chance that he could make the gates of Heaven.

But Oisín, with a weak smile, shook his head, and then was still, as though distracted by something in the distance.

The serpent-banisher sighed. This one had slipped through his hands. Leaning closer he thought he caught a gleam in the old man's eyes – and strange, it looked like a white horse – but perhaps it was a trick of the light.

And with his dying breath Oisín whispered from far away, as though remembering something from long ago:

> 'Delightful is the land beyond all dreams.'

Bibliography

Ackroyd, Peter, 2002, *Albion: The origin of the English imagination,* Chatto and Windus.

Adair, John, 1976, *The Pilgrim's Way: Shrines and saints in Britain and Ireland,* Thames and Hudson.

Adam, David, 2007, 'US answer to global warming: smoke and giant space mirrors', *Guardian,* 27 Jan.

Adams, Douglas and Mark Carwardine, 1990, *Last Chance to See,* Heinemann.

'A.E.', 1990, *The Candle of Vision: Inner worlds of the imagination,* Prism Press.

Aldington, Richard and Delano Ames (trans), 1982, *New Larousse Encyclopaedia of Mythology,* Hamlyn.

Allen, Benedict, 2006, 'Where's heaven? Oh, there it is' *Independent on Sunday,* Review section, 23 July; http://findarticles.com/p/articles/mi_qn4159/is_20060723/ai_n16667864

Annan, Kofi, 2005, *In Larger Freedom: Towards development, security and human rights for all,* United Nations.

Ashe, Geoffrey, 1990, *Mythology of the British Isles,* Metheun.

Attenborough, David, 2000, 'State of the Planet' broadcast by BBC and released on DVD by 2 Entertain Video.

Bahn, Paul and John Flenley, 1992, *Easter Island, Earth Island,* Thames and Hudson.

Baker, Ian, 2006, *The Heart of the World,* Souvenir.

Ballard, J.G., 1962, *The Drowned World,* Gollancz.

Ballard, J.G., 1987, *The Day of Creation,* Gollancz.

Ballard, J.G., 2000, *Super-Cannes,* Flamingo.

Ballard, J.G., 2006, *Kingdom Come,* Fourth Estate.

Barker, Clive, 2002, *Abarat,* Harper Collins.

Barrie, J.M., 1911, *Peter Pan,* reprinted Penguin Popular Classics, 1995.

Benham, Patrick, 1993, *The Avalonians,* Gothic Image.

Bey, Hakim, 1985, *TAZ: The temporary autonomous zone, ontological anarchy, poetic terrorism,* Autonomedia; www.hermetic.com/bey/taz3.html

Bhaumik, S., 2005, 'Tsunami folklore "saved islanders"', http://news.bbc.co.uk/1/hi/world/south_asia/4181855.stm

Bord, Janet and Colin, 1972, *Mysterious Britain,* Garnstone Press.

Borges, Jorge Luis, 1967, *The Book of Imaginary Beasts,* Penguin.

Bradley, Marion Zimmer, 1984, *The Mists of Avalon,* Sphere, London.

Bradley, Marion Zimmer and Diana Paxson, 2004, *The Ancestors of Avalon,* Voyager.

Brown, Jonathan, 2007, 'Father Ted fans invade as fight for real Craggy Island is settled', *Independent*, 24 Feb.

Burkeman, Oliver, 2007 'Second Life: exploding pigs and volleys of gunfire as Le Pen opens HQ in virtual world', *Guardian*, 20 Jan; www.guardian.co.uk/technology/2007/jan/20/news.france

Burnett, Frances Hodgson, 1911, *The Secret Garden*, Heinemann.

Burroughs, William S, 1988, *The Western Lands*, Picador.

Campbell, Duncan, 2006, 'Landmark moment: artist claims sovereignty of new Arctic island', *The Guardian* 13 May; http://arts.guardian.co.uk/news/story/ 0,,1774082,00.html

Campbell, Joseph, 1949, *The Hero with a Thousand Faces,* Pantheon.

Capelli, Cristian *et al*, 2003, 'A Y chromosome census of the British Isles', *Current Biology*, 13:11, 979–84; www.sciencedirect.com/science

Carey, John,1999, *The Faber Book of Utopias*, Faber.

Carey, Julian, 2007, 'Hippies: tipi valley', BBC R4, broadcast 08 May.

Clarke, Hilary, 2005, 'Archaeologists find Western world's oldest map', *Daily Telegraph*, 18 Nov; www.telegraph.co.uk/news/main.jhtml?xml=/news/ 2005/11/18/wmap18.xml

Clarke, Lindsay, 1990, *The Chymical Wedding*, Picador.

King, Angela and Sue Clifford, 2006, *England in Particular: A celebration of the commonplace, the local, the vernacular, and the distinctive,* Hodder and Stoughton.

Clute, John, 1997, 'Godgame', in J. Clute and J. Grant (eds), *Encyclopedia of Fantasy*, Orbit.

Coates, Chris, 2001, *British Utopian Experiments 1325 to 1945,* Diggers and Dreamers Publications.

Colley, Linda, 2007, 'Brave New World', *Guardian Review*, 21 April; http://books.guardian.co.uk/review/story/0,,2061332,00.html

Collins, Cecil, 1981, *The Vision of the Fool,* Kedros; reprinted Golgonooza 1994.

Connor, Steve, 2007, 'The temperature is rising – and humans are to blame', *The Independent*, 03 Feb; http://findarticles.com/p/articles/mi_qn4158/ is_20070203/ai_n17204291

Cope, Julian, 1998, interview in *Kindred Spirit* 45.

Cope, Julian, 1998, *The Modern Antiquarian*, Thorsons.

Crowley, John, 2000, *Little, Big,* Millennium, Gollancz.

Curtin, Jeremiah, 1975, *Myths and Folk Tales of Ireland,* Dover.

Dames, Michael, 1976, *The Silbury Treasure* Thames and Hudson.

Dames, Michael, 1977, *The Avebury Cycle,* Thames and Hudson; 2nd edn 1996.

Dames, Michael, 2006, *Taliesin's Travels*, Heart of Albion.

Dames, Michael, 2007, *Roman Silbury and the Corn Goddess*, Heart of Albion.

Dawson, Ian, 1996, 'Manannan's Island', *Albion*, 23, 11–17.

De Camp, L. Sprague, 1970, *Lost Continents: The Atlantis theme in history, science, and literature,* Dover.

De Camp, L. Sprague, and Catherine C. de Camp, 1972, *Citadels of Mystery*, Fontana.

Denning, Kathryn, 1999, 'Apocalypse past/future: archaeology and folklore, writ large', in C. Holtorf and A. Gazin-Schwartz (eds), *Archaeology and Folklore*, Routledge.

Devereux, Paul, 1992, *Symbolic Landscapes,* Gothic Image.

Devereux, Paul, 2002, *Mysterious Ancient America: an investigation into the enigmas of america's pre-history*, Vega.

Diamond, Jared, 2006, *Collapse: How societies choose to fail or survive*, Penguin.

Dom, David, 2005, 'The origins of Avalon'; www.druidcircle.net

Dowling, Tim, 2006, 'The beach, the sequel', *Guardian Travel*, 23 Sept; www.guardian.co.uk/travel/2006/sep/23/ecotourism.fiji.tribewanted

Drabble, Margaret, 2006, 'The English degenerate', *Guardian Review,* 12 Aug; http://books.guardian.co.uk/review/story/0,,1842437,00.html

Dunbavin, Paul, 2003, *Atlantis of the West,* Robinson.

Edwards, Malcolm and Robert Holdstock, 1983, *Realms of Fantasy,* Paper Tiger.

Evans, Kate, 2006, *Funny Weather: Everything you didn't want to know about climate change but probably should find out,* Myriad Editions.

Ferudi, Frank, 2007, When the waters clear', BBC website; http://news.bbc.co.uk/1/hi/magazine/6913404.stm

Flannery, Tim, 2006, *The Weather Makers: The history and future impact of climate change*, Allen Lane.

Fontaine, P.F.M., 1998, *Mythical Eyes: History, counter-history and myth,* Avon Books.

Fortune, Dion, 2003, *Glastonbury: Avalon of the heart,* Red Wheel; originally published under the name Violet Mary Firth as *Avalon of the Heart,* Muller, 1934. .

Fowles, John, 1965, *The Magus,*Cape.

Frazer, James George, 1922, *The Golden Bough: A study in magic and religion.* Abridged edition.

Gaiman, Neil, 1998, S*tardust,* Titan.

Gantz, Jeffrey (trans.), 1976, *Mabinogion,* Penguin Classics.

Garner, Alan, 1997, *The Voice that Thunders,* Harvill Press.

Gilchrist, Cherry, 2007, *Explore Alchemy*, Heart of Albion.

Golding, William, 1954, *Lord of the Flies,* Faber.

Gore, Al, *An Inconvenient Truth*, 2006, Bloomsbury.

Grahame, Kenneth, 1908, *Winds in the Willows,* Methuen; reprinted Penguin London 2007.

Graves, Robert, 1975, *The White Goddess,* Faber.

Graves, Robert, 1990, *Greek Myths: Vols 1 and 2,* Faber.

Gray, Alasdair, 1981, *Lanark,* Canongate..

Gray, John, 2007, *Black Mass: Apocalyptic religion and the death of utopia,* Allen Lane.

Hancock, Graham, 2002, *Underworld: The mysterious origins of civilisation,* Michael Joseph.

Handwerk, Brian, 2005, 'Eye on the storm: Hurricane Katrina fast facts', *National Geographic*, 6 Sept; http://news.nationalgeographic.com/news/2005/09/0906_050906_katrina_facts.html

Hawthorne, Nathaniel, 1850, *The Scarlet Letter: A romance,* reprinted 2003 Penguin Classics.

Heaney, Seamus and Ted Hughes (eds), 1982, *The Rattle Bag*, Faber.

Heath, Robin and John Michell, 2004, *The Measure of Albion: The lost science of prehistoric Britain,* Bluestone Press.

Hesse, Herman,1973, *The Journey to the East,* Panther; translation by H. Rosner of *Die Morgenlandfahrt,* 1945.

Hesse, Herman, 1975, *Wandering,* Picador, London; translation by J.A. Arlington of *Wanderung: Aufzeichnungen,* 1920.

Hill, Selima, (ed) 1998, *Paradise for Sale*, Poetry Library.

Holdstock, Robert, 1984, *Mythago Wood,* Gollancz.

Holdstock, Robert, 2007, *The Broken Kings,* Orion.

Homer-Dixon, 2007, *The Upside of Down: Catastrophe, creativity and the renewal of civilization*, Souvenir Press.

Hope, Murry, 1991, *Atlantis: Myth or reality* Arkana.

Houghton, John, 2004, *Global Warming: The complete briefing,* 3rd edn. Cambridge UP.

Hurlstone Jackson, Kenneth, (trans), 1971, *A Celtic Miscellany*, Penguin Classics.

Huxley, Aldous, 1932, *Brave New World,* Chatto and Windus.

Huxley, Aldous, 1960, *The Doors of Perception and Heaven and Hell,* Chatto and Windus.

Huxley, Aldous, 1962, *Island,* Chatto and Windus.

Irving, Washington, 1832, *Tales of the Alhambra*, Ediciones Miguel Sánchez.

Jaggi, Maya, 2007, 'Lost horizons', *Guardian Review*, 5 May; http://books.guardian.co.uk/review/story/0,,2072451,00.html

Jameson, Fredric, 2007, *Archaeologies of the Future*: *The desire called utopia and other science fictions*, Verso.

Jeffries, Richard, 1885, *After London, or Wild England.*

Jeffries, Stuart, 2007, 'Apocalypse now', *Guardian Review*, 7 July; http://books.guardian.co.uk/review/story/0,,2120367,00.html

Jha, Alok, 2007, 'Call for wildlife reserve to cover 30% of oceans', *The Guardian*, 09 July; www.guardian.co.uk/environment/2007/jun/09/conservation.wildlife

Jones, David, 1937, *In Parentheses*, Faber.

Jones, Tobias, 2007, *Utopian Dreams,* Faber.

Jung, Carl, 1964 *Man and his Symbols*, Aldus

Kavenna, Joanna, 2005, *The Ice Museum: In search of the lost land of Thule,* Viking.

Kennedy, Maev, 2001, 'Great lost city of ancient Egypt revealed', *Guardian*, 8 June; www.guardian.co.uk/international/story/0,3604,503588,00.html.

Keynes, Geoffrey (ed), 1957, *Blake*: *Complete writings*, Nonesuch.

Killip, Margaret, 1986, *The Folklore of the Isle of Man,* Batsford.

King, Angela and Sue Clifford (eds), 1998, *Trees, Rivers and Fields*, Green Books.

King, Martin Luther Jr., 1967, 'Beyond Vietnam' speech, April 4, 1967, Riverside Church, New York.

Kirby, W.F. (trans), 1985, *Kalevala: The land of the heroes,* Athlone Press.

Lamb, G.F., 1995, *The Wordsworth Dictionary of Shakespeare Quotations,* Wordsworth.

Lambourne, Helen, 2005, 'Tsunami: anatomy of a disaster' BBC News;
http://news.bbc.co.uk/1/hi/sci/tech/4381395.stm

Lanchester, John, 2007, 'It's a steal' *Guardian Review*, 7 April;
http://books.guardian.co.uk/review/story/0,,2051671,00.html

Lean, Geoffrey, 2006, 'Amazon rainforest 'could become a desert'', *Independent
on Sunday*, 23 July;
http://findarticles.com/p/articles/mi_qn4159/is_20060723/ai_n16667898

Lean, Geoffrey, 2006, 'Dying forest: one year to save the Amazon', *Independent on
Sunday*, 23 July; www.independent.co.uk/environment/dying-forest-one-year-
to-save-the-amazon-408926.html

Livingstone, Dinah, 2000, *The Poetry of Earth*, Katabasis.

Llosa, Mario Vargas, 1991, *The Storyteller,* Faber.

Lovelock, James, 1979, *Gaia: A new look at life on Earth*, Oxford UP.

Luna, Luis, Eduardo, 1999, *Ayahuasca Visions: The religious iconography of a
Peruvian Shaman,* North Atlantic Books.

Lynas, Mark, 2007, *Six Degrees: Our future on a hotter planet,* Fourth Estate.

McCarthy, Cormac, 2006, *The Road,* Picador.

Macfarlane, Robert, 2005, 'The burning question', *Guardian Review*, 24 Sept;
http://books.guardian.co.uk/departments/scienceandnature/story/0,6000,15770
93,00.html

Macfarlane, Robert, 2007, 'Go wild in the country', *Guardian Review*, 14 July;
http://books.guardian.co.uk/review/story/0,,2125607,00.html

McIntosh, Alastair, 2004, *Soil and Soul*: *People versus corporate power,* 3rd edn,
Aurum.

McKay, George, 2000, *Glastonbury: A very English fair,* Gollancz.

Mackenzie, Donald, 1996, *Mythology of the Babylonian People*, Bracken.

Maclean, Charles, 1972, *Island on the Edge of the World*, Canongate.

McLuhan, Terry, 1971, *Touch the Earth: A self-portrait of Indian existence,*
Outerbridge and Dienstfrey; reprinted Abacus 1986.

McNallen, Stephen A, 1995, 'Fire on the water: the myth and history of Viking
funerals', *Runestone* 13.

McNally, D.R., 1981, *Irish Wonders,* Gramercy.

Manguel, Alberto, and Gianni Guadalupi, 1999, *The Dictionary of Imaginary
Places* Bloomsbury.

Manwaring, Kevan, 2004, *The Long Woman,* Awen.

Manwaring, Kevan, 2008, *The Well Under the Sea,* R.J. Stewart Books.

Martel, Yann, 2002, *Life of Pi,* Canongate.

Matthews, Caitlín, 2001, *Celtic Book of the Dead*, Grange Books.

Matthews, John, (ed) 1993, *From Isles of Dream:* Visionary stories and poems of the
Celtic renaissance, Lindisfarne Books.

Matthews, John, 2002, *Taliesin*, Inner Traditions.

Matthiessen, Peter, 1965, *At Play in the Fields of the Lord*, Random House.

May, Robert, 2006, 2006, in *Planet Earth*: *The future*, BBC Books.

Melville, Hermann, 2002, *The Enchanted Isles,* Hesperus; first published as 'The
Encantadas or Enchanted Isles', 1854.

Michell, John, 1983, *The New View Over Atlantis*, Thames and Hudson.

Michell, John, 1994, *At the Centre of the World: Polar symbolism discovered in Celtic, Norse and other ritualised landscapes,* Thames and Hudson.

Milton, John, 2005, *Paradise Lost,* Arcturus, London.

Mirrlees, Hope, 1926, *Lud-in-the-Mist,* Collins.

Monbiot, George, 2006, *Heat: How we can stop the planet burning,* Allen Lane.

Moorcock, Michael, 1987, *Wizardry and Wild Romance: A study of epic fantasy,* VGSF.

Moore, Alan, 1993, foreword to Steve Wilson, *Robin Hood: The spirit of the forest,* Neptune.

Moore, Helen, 2006, *Changing Nature: Digital notes of an eco-poet,* Green Seer Books.

More, Thomas, Francis Bacon and Henry Neville, 1999, *Three Early Modern Utopias,* Oxford UP.

Morrison, Sophia, 1929, *Manx Fairy Tales* (2nd edn); reprinted The Manx Experience 2002.

Mosley, Ivo, 1994, *The Green Book of Poetry,* Frontier.

Moss, Stephen, 2007, 'Kings of all we survey', *Guardian,* 24 March; www.guardian.co.uk/saturday/story/0,,2041775,00.html

Nanson, Anthony, *2005, Storytelling and Ecology,* University of Glamorgan Press.

Nelson, Resa, 2007, 'Pathfinder blends oral history with fantasy in the tradition of a Norse saga', *Realms of Fantasy,* Vol 13: 5, 10–16.

Nicolson, Adam, 2007, 'Our island paradise', *The Guardian* 14 July; www.guardian.co.uk/travel/2007/jul/14/beach.scotland

O'Toole, Fintan, 2007, 'Virgin territories', *Guardian Review,* 10 March; http://books.guardian.co.uk/review/story/0,,2030463,00.html

Okri, Ben, 1995, *Astonishing the Gods,* Phoenix.

Ondaatje, Michael, 1992, *The English Patient,* Bloomsbury.

Orwell, George, 1949, *1984,* Secker and Warburg.

Ovid, 2004, *The Metamorphoses* (trans. D. Raeburn), Penguin.

Palmer, Mary, 2008, *Iona,* Awen.

Parsell, D.L., 2002, 'City occupied by Inca discovered on Andean peak in Peru', *National Geographic News,* http://news.nationalgeographic.com/news/ 2002/03/0314_0318_vilcabamba_2.html

Paulin, Tom, 2007, 'The invisible worm', *Guardian Review,* 3 March; http://books.guardian.co.uk/review/story/0,,2025117,00.html

Paz, Octavio, 1985, *One Earth, Four or Five Worlds: Reflections on contemporary history,* Cacarnet.

Peake, Mervyn, 1950, *Gormenghast,* Eyre and Spotiswoode; reprinted 1999 as *The Gormenghast Trilogy,* Vintage Classics.

Pearce, Phillipa, 1958, *Tom's Midnight Garden,* OUP.

Pemberton, Cintia, 1999, *Soulfaring: Celtic pilgrimage, then and now,* SPCK.

Pennick, Nigel, 1996, *Celtic Sacred Landscapes,* Thames and Hudson.

Pepper, David, 1991, *Communes and the Green Vision: Counter culture, lifestyle and the New Age,* Green Print.

Pirsig, Robert M, 1974, *Zen and the Art of Motorcycle Maintenance,* Bodley Head; reprinted 1999 Vintage Classics.

Ponting, Clive, 1991, *A Green History of the World: The environment and the collapse of great civilisations*, Sinclair Stevenson.
Powys, John Cowper, 1932, *A Glastonbury Romance*, Simon and Schuster.
Powys, John Cowper, 1934, *Weymouth Sands*, Simon and Schuster; reprinted 2000 Penguin.
Price, Mark Stanley, 2006, in *Planet Earth: The future*, BBC Books.
Pullman, Philip, 1995, *Northern Lights*, Scholastic Press, London.
Pullman, Philip, 1997, *The Subtle Knife*, Scholastic Press, London.
Pullman, Philip, 2000, *The Amber Spyglass*, Scholastic Press, London.
Pullman, Philip, 2003, *Lyra's Oxford*, David Fickling.
Quiller-Couch, Arthur (ed.), 1906. *The Oxford Book of English Verse*, Oxford UP.
Radford, Paul, 2004, 'The drowned world', *Guardian 2020*, 11 Sept; www.guardian.co.uk/science/2004/sep/11/ meteorology.scienceofclimatechange
Rahtz, Philip, 1993, *English Heritage Book of Glastonbury*, Batsford.
Raine, Kathleen, 1967, *Defending Ancient Springs*, Oxford UP.
Ramsay, Jay, 2004, *The Crucible of Love*, O Books.
Ransome, Arthur, 1930, *Swallows and Amazons*, Cape.
Ratcliffe, Jeanette and Charles Johns, 2003, *Scilly's Archaeological Heritage* (2nd edn), Twelveheads Press.
Rees, Alwyn and Brinley Rees, 1961, *Celtic Heritage: Ancient tradition in Ireland and Wales*, Thames and Hudson.
Richards, Julian, 2001, *Blood of the Vikings*, Hodder and Stoughton.
Roberts, Tony, 1974, *Myths and Legends of Pembrokeshire*, Abercastle.
Robertson, Kim Stanley, 2004, *Forty Signs of Rain*, HarperCollins.
Rogers, Pat (ed.),1993, *Johnson and Boswell in Scotland*, Yale UP.
Rolleston, T.W., 1994, *Celtic Myths and Legends*, Senate; reprint of *Myths and Legends of the Celtic Race*, 1911.
Rowe, Jonathan, 2007, 'The man who said nothing', *Ecologist*, 37:4.
Schama, Simon, 1995, *Landscape and Memory*, Harper Collins.
Schama, Simon, 2007, 'The lost art of great speechmaking' (introduction to reprint of Winston Churchill's 'We shall fight on the beaches' speech), *Guardian*, 21 April; www.guardian.co.uk/greatspeeches/story/0,,2062012,00.html
Selkirk, Andrew and Martin Carver, 1992, 'Sutton Hoo: A drama in three acts', *Current Archaeology*, 28, 324–30.
Selmer, Carl, 1959, 'Navigatio Sancti Brendani Abbatis' from *Early Latin Manuscripts*, Notre Dame.
Shippey, T.A., 1982, *The Road to Middle Earth*, Allen and Unwin.
Sinclair, Iain, 2001, *Landor's Tower*, Granta.
Sinclair, Iain, 2005, *Edge of the Orison: In the traces of John Clare's 'Journey out of Essex'*, Hamish Hamilton; reprinted Penguin 2006.
Solnit, Rebecca, 2000, *Wanderlust: A history of walking*, Viking.
Somerville, Christopher, *Coast*, 2005, BBC Books.
Springer, Chris, 2006, *Homo Britannicus: The incredible story of human life in Britain*, Allen Lane.
Spufford, Francis, 2002, *The Child that Books Built: A memoir of childhood and reading*, Faber.

Stern, Nicholas, 2006, *Stern Review on the Economics of Climate Change,* Cambridge UP; http://www.hm-treasury.gov.uk/independent_reviews/ stern_review_economics_climate_change/stern_review_report.cfm

Stewart, Paul D., 2006a, 'Galapagos', *BBC Wildlife* magazine, Autumn, 50–7.

Stewart, Paul D, 2006b, *Galápagos: The islands that changed the world,* BBC Books.

Stewart, R.J., 1990, *Magical Tales: the story-telling tradition,* Mercury.

St Exupéry, Antoine De, 1939, *Wind, Sand and Stars,* Heinemann; reprinted Penguin 1995.

St Exupéry, Antoine De, 1945, *The Little Prince,* Heinemann.

SURVAS, 2002, Synthesis and Upscaling of sea-level Rise Vulnerability Assessment Studies; www.survas.mdx.ac.uk/content.htm

Taylor, Colin, 1992, *Native American Myths and Legends,* Senate.

Tennyson, Alfred, 1842–85, *The Idylls of the King* (12 volumes).

Theroux, Paul, 2005, 'Rumble in the jungle', *Guardian,* 14 May.

Thomas, Pat, 2006, 'How to beat denial: a 12 steps plan', *The Ecologist,* 26; www.theecologist.org/archive_detail.asp?content_id=683

Thomas, R.S., 2002, *Residues,* Bloodaxe Books.

Tolkien, J.R.R., 1954–5, *The Lord of the Rings,* Allen and Unwin.

Tolkien, J.R.R., 1983, *The Monsters and the Critics: And other essays,* Allen and Unwin.

Troyes, Chretien de, 1991, *Arthurian Romances,* Penguin Classics.

Trubshaw, Bob, 2005, *Sacred Places: Prehistory and popular imagination* Heart of Albion.

Vagg, Robert and Helene Hepworth (eds), 2006, *Migratory Species and Climate Change: Impacts of a changing environment on wild animals,* UNEP/CMS/DEFRA; www.cms.int/publications/pdf/CMS_CimateChange.pdf

Vidal, John, 2005, 'Oil spills, ravaged industry and lost islands add to the hurricane's toll', *The Guardian,* 9 Sept; www.guardian.co.uk/international/story/0,,1566007,00.html

Vogler, Christopher, 1992, *The Writer's Journey,* M. Wiese.

Westwood, Jennifer, 1985, *Albion: A guide to legendary Britain,* Granada.

Westwood, Jennifer, 1997, *Sacred Journeys,* Henry Holt.

Westwood, Jennifer and Jacqueline Simpson, 2005, *The Lore of the Land,* Penguin.

Whitaker, Raymond, 2006, 'The monkey that could save the world', *Independent on Sunday,* 20 Aug; www.independent.co.uk/environment/the-monkey-that-could-save-the-world-412641.html

Warner, Marina, 1994, *From the Beast to the Blonde,* Chatto and Windus.

White, T.H., 1958, *The Once and Future King,* Collins.

Williams, Merryn and Raymond Williams (eds), 1986, *John Clare: Selected poetry and prose,* Methuen.

Windling, Terri, 1997, 'Turtle Island: the mythology of North America', *Realms of Fantasy*; www.endicott-studio.com/rdrm/forturtl.html

Wood, Chris, 2000, '"Seahenge": the Holme tree ring, online at http://norwichmoot.paganearth.com/seahenge.htm

Wooding, Jonathan (ed), 1998, *The Otherworld Voyage in Irish Literature,* Four Courts.

Worthington, Andy, 2004, *Stonehenge: Celebration and subversion*, Alternative Albion.

Wynne-Jones, Diane, 1996, *Tough Guide to Fantasy Land,* Vista.

Young, Simon, 2001, 'The voyage of beyond the sea', *Fortean Times* 151, 40–4; www.forteantimes.com/features/articles/262/ the_voyage_of_beyond_the_sea.html

Younge, Gary, 2006, 'Gone with the wind', *Guardian Weekend,* 29 July; www.guardian.co.uk/katrina/story/0,,1831459,00.html

Index

1984 186
2001: A Space Odyssey 57, 86, 90
2012 106
21 Grams 191
9/11 189

Abbot, E. 187
Aber Gwenwen y Maych 91
Abersoch 78
About Schmidt 88
Accelerated Sea Leevel Rise 154–6
Ackroyd, P. 38
Adair, J. 90
Adams, D. 196
Adonais 40
'A.E.' 43
After London 40–1, 58, 157
Albion (Ackroyd) 38
Albion (Westwood) 134–5
alchemy 11
Alice's Adventures in Wonderland 37
Amaringo, P. 23
Ancestors of Avalon 35
Anderson, H.C. 86
Anglesey 67–8, 78
Annan, K. 154
Antic Hay 55
Apocalypse Now 48
Apollo space missions 195, 198
apples 23, 95–7, 167–8
Arastaois 5–6
Aronofsky, D. 90
Arran islands 78, 81
Arthur, King 15
Arthurian myth 15, 19, 44, 92, 101–2;
        see also Morte d'Arthur, Le
At Play in the Fields of the Lord 174
Atlantis 1, 3, 32–5, 60, 94, 113–14,
        139–40, 196
Atlantis 46

Atlantology 32–3, 46
atolls 114
Astonishing the Gods 59
Aubrey, J. 129
Australian myth 145
Avalon 1, 15, 19, 23, 28, 35, 94–107,
        113
Avalon 94
Avalon Landing 94
Avalon Sunset 94
Avebury 90–1, 129
axis mundi 166
Aztecs 187–8

Babel 191
Bahn, P. 121–6
Baker, I. 1
Ballard, J.G. 56, 153, 181–2
Bardsey Island 1, 15, 23–4, 65, 68–71,
        88
Barrie, J.M. 50–1
Barry Island 78
Bates, P.R. 79
Bath (*Aquae Sulis*) 20, 97, 100
Beach, The 59
Beatles 55
Bevis 41
Bey, H. 181
beyuls 1
Bifrost 19, 137
Big Fish 58
Bikini Atoll 114
Binsey Poplars 40
Blackwood, A. 54
Blake, W. 23, 38–40, 104
Blavatsky, Madame 88
Blue Remembered Hills 166
Book of Imaginary Beasts, The 32
Books of the Dead 15
Bold as Love 58

Book of Lost Things, The 60
Borges, J.L. 32
Borroughs, W. 55
Borrow, G. 42
Borth 149–50
Boswell, J. 42
Brave New World 55
Bradbury, R. 45, 57
Bradley, M.Z. 35, 95
Bran mac Ferbal – *see* Voyage of Bran
    mac Ferbal
Bran the Blessed 20, 72
Branwen 20
Brazil 186
Brecht, B. 46
Brendan – *see* Voyage of St Brendan,
    The
Bridge of Leaps 19
Brigadoon 1, 66, 80, 106, 131
Brigadoon 66
Brittany 80
Browning, E.B. 54
Brownsea Island 71
Bryson, B. 60
Buckland, W. 148
Buddha 19
buddhism 1, 18, 87
Buena Vista Social Club 191
Bulleid, A. 126
Bunyan, J. 85, 91
Burnett, F.H. 47
Burning World, The 55
Burroughs E.R. 45
Burrrowbridge Mump 101
Burton, T. 58
Butler, S. 38
Byron, Lord 41

Cailleach 16
caldera 113–14
Caldey Island 71
Cambridgeshire 131–2
Campbell, F. 89
Campbell, J. 27
Camus, A. 55
Canterbury Tales, The 84

Cantre'r Gwaelod 20, 150–1
Carmichael., A. 43
Carmina Gadelica 43
Carroll, L. 37, 52
Carver, M. 138
Cauldron of Plenty 3, 15
Celtic Book of the Dead, The 15
Celtic Twilight 42–3
Chalice Well, Glastonbury 105–6,
    165–6
Charon 19
Chaucer 84
Child That Books Built, The 54, 60
Child, F.J. 43
Christmas Island 122
Churchill, A.105
Churchill, W. 65
Cider With Rosie 166
Clarke, A.C. 57, 86
Clevedon 3
Clifford, S. 82, 93, 95, 101, 103
climate change 120–1, 125, 127,
    153–6
Cloud Atlas 60
Cloverfield 191
Clovis People 185
Clute, J. 58
Cobbett, W. 42
Coelho, P. 85
Coleridge, S.T. 14, 21, 41–2, 100, 129
Collins, Cecil 86
Coming of the Fairies, The 50
Common Ground 82
Connolly, J. 60
Conrad, J. 48–9
continental plates 111–14
Cooder, R. 191
Cook, Captain 122
Cooper, S. 54
Cope, J. 21
Coppola, F.F. 49
*Cormac's Adventures in the Land of
    Promise* 25
Cornwall 80, 90, 173
Cramond Island 80
crannogs 71–2, 131

Crash 56, 191
Croatan 180–2
Crome Yellow 55
Cronenberg, D. 56, 191
Cronus 26
Crucible, The 55
Cuba 191
Cuchullain 19
currachs 163–4
Cusa, Nicolas of 4

Dames, M. 10, 90–1
Dark is Rising, The 54
Darwin, C. 49, 126
Davidson, F. 16
Dawkins, R. 126
Day After Tomorrow, The 190
Day of Creation, The 55
Day the Earth Stood Still, The 198
De Camp, L.S. 32–3, 186, 188
Devereux, P. 187
Diana, Princess 72
Dictionary of Imaginary Places 5
Divided Kingdom 60
DNA 164
Dom, D. 95, 100
Doomwatch 58
Doyle, A.C. 45, 50, 117, 188
Drabble, M. 46–7, 117
Drowned World, The 56, 181–2
Dr Who 56

Earthsea trilogy 57
Easter Island 118–27
Eavis, M. 99
Eco, U. 59
Eden 165, 169–75
Eden Project 173
Egyptian myth 15
El Dorado 186, 188, 189
Eliot, T.S. 6, 46
Empire of the Sun 56
Encantadas or Enchanted Isles, The 49
Encyclopaedia of Fantasy 58
England in Particular 82
English Patient, The 10

Erewhon 38, 50
Erik the Viking 186
Essex 80
Etain 13
eustasy 115
exile 169–71

Faroe Isles 81
Father Ted 78
Ferry, B. 94
Ferudi, F. 152
Finding Forester 94
Fisher King 92
Flag Fen 131–2
Flandrian transgression 149–51
Flannery, T. 196, 198
Flatland 187
Flenley, J. 121–3, 125–6
flood myths 145, 148–9
Folklore of the Isle of Man, The 77, 137
Fortune Isles, The 1, 24
Fortune, D. 76, 104
Fountain, The 90
Four Quartets, The 6
Fowles, J. 49–50
Francis, J. 86–7
Frankenstein 57
Frazer, J.G., 43
Future Primitive 58

Galápagos Islands 1, 49, 116–18, 126–7
gardens 165–6
Garland, A. 59
Garman, N. 47
Garner, A. 4
Gebbie, M. 51
Geoffrey of Monmouth 96
Gerald of Wales 78, 96
Gilgamesh 32, 47–8, 145
Ginsberg, A. 55
Glastonbury 1, 23, 92, 95–107, 132–3, 167; *see also* Chalice Well
Glastonbury Festivals 105–6, 189
Glastonbury Lake Village 133–4

Glastonbury Romance, A, 46
Glastonbury Zodiac 104, 107
God Delusion, The 126
God games 49–50, 56, 59, 174
Goddio, F. 139–40
Golden Bough 43
Golding, W. 49
Gondwana 112
Gore, A. 120, 195, 197–8
Gower Peninsula 81, 82, 148
Gozo 9
Grahame, K. 47, 52–4
Grant, J. 58
Grapes of Wrath, The 24
Grassholm 72–3
Greece 5–6, 9, 139
Greek myth 19, 26, 145–6
Green History of the World, The 170
Gregory, Lady 43; *see also*
    Mabinogion
Gruinard Island 63
Guadalupi, G. 5, 95
Guantanamo Bay 191–2
Guest, C. – *see* Gregory, Lady
Guinevere 19
Gulliver's Travels 37–8, 50, 186
Gunbesekera, R. 170–1

Handwerk, C. 153–4
'happy hunting grounds' 177–8
Hardy, T. 45
Harry Potter 61
Hawaii 113
Hawthorne, N. 4
Heart of Darkness 48–9
Heart of the World, The 1
Heath, R. 75
Heimdall 19
Hemingway, E. 46
Hesse, H. 87–9
Hilton, J. 45
His Dark Materials 52, 166
Holmes, Sherlock 45
Hooker, J., 46
Hopkins, G.M. 40
Holdstock, R. 58

Homer 57
Houghton, J. 120
Housman, A.E. 166
Hunt, T. 124
Hurricane Katrina 152–4
Hutton, R. 53
Huxley, A. 46, 55, 57
Hy-Brazil 186–7

I am Legend 191
Iceland 1, 115–16
immram 1
In Arcadia 59
In Memoriam: Idylls of the King 40
Inconvenient Truth, An 120, 195
Indian Ocean tsunami 151–2
Into the West 177
Iona 1, 73
Ireland 78
Irving, W. 93
Island 55
Island of Dr Moreau, The 49–50
Island of the Day Before, The, 59
Isle of Eigg 80
Isle of Man 1, 19, 20, 73–4, 87, 180,
    135–7, 139
Isle of the Blessed, The 1
Isles of Scilly 1, 20, 24, 69–70, 75, 94,
    127–9
isostatic rebound 114–15
Israel 145
Itinerarium Cambriae 78

Japan 115
Jeffries, R. 40–1, 58, 157
Johns, C. 133–4
Johnson, S. 42
Jones, D. 23
Jones, G. 59
Joseph of Arimathea 104
Journal of a Tour to the Hebrides, A 42
Journey to the East, The 88
Journey to the West 88
Journey to the Western Isles of
    Scotland 42
Joyce, J. 46
Jurassic Park 45

Kama Sutra 88
Kekova 2
Kennedy, M. 139
Kerouac, J. 55
Kerr, A. 105
Kêr-Ys 1, 20, 75, 135
Kilda 37
Killip, M. 72, 137
Kilve 112, 129
Kimber 75
King Kong 45
King, A. 82, 93, 95, 101, 103
King, M.L. 157
Kingdom Come 56
Kipling, R. 56
Kubla Kahn 14, 41

L'Anse-aux-Meadows 184
Lady of Shalott, The 104
Lake Bala 78, 79, 91
Lake Isle of Innisfree, The 43–4
Lancelot 19
Land That Time Forgot, The 45
Landscape and Memory 63
Lang, F. 57
Last and First Men 57
Last Men in London 57
Lavondyss 58–9
Lee, L. 166
Le Guin, U. 57
Lemuria 113
Levy, A. 60
Lewis, C.S. 47, 106
Life of Pi 60
liminal places and times 10, 11, 19
Lindisfarne 80, 81, 164
Lindsay, D. 57
Little Andaman 152
Little Britain 60
Little Prince, The, 2
Lleu Llaw Gyffes 97
Llyn Peninsula 90
Llyn Tegid – *see* Lake Bala
Llyr Llediaith 10
Lonely Valley 16
Long Woman, The 46

Longfellow, H.W. 42
Look Back in Anger 55
Lord of the Flies 49
Lord of the Rings, The 47, 55, 57, 184
Lost 50, 184
Lost Girls 51
Lost Horizons 46
Lost World, The 45, 182
Lovejoy, T. 114
Lud in the Mist 47, 55
Lundy 70–1
Lyke Wake Dirge, The 16, 18
Lyonesse 45, 69, 127–9

Mabinogion 11, 20, 67, 91
McArthur, E. 83
McCarthy, C. 147, 185
Macculloch, J. 37
Macdonald, G. 43
Macfarlane, R. 60, 76, 77
McIntosh, A. 74–5
Maclean, C. 37, 169
Macleish, A. 191–2
Macleod, F. 43
McNallen, S.A. 129
McNally, D.R. 72
MacNeice, L. 169
Magis, The 49–50
Maiden Castle 46
Maldon, Battle of 75
Malik, T. 172
Malta 9
Maltwood, K. 98, 101
Manannan Mac Lir 19, 20
Manguel, A. 5, 89
Man Who Would Be King, The 56
Martel. Y. 60
Martian Chronicles, The 57
Master of the World 50
Matrix, The 27
Matthews, C. 15
Matthieson, P. 168
Maugham, W.S. 48
May, R. 114–15
Mayan prophecies 100
mazes 70

Measure of Albion, The 75
Mecca 86
Méliès, G. 57
Melville, H. 49, 117–18
Merlin 19, 56, 97
Metropolis 57
Michell, J. 75
Mieville, C. 57
Miller, A. 55
Miller, H. 46
Milton, J. 32
Mirrless, H. 47
Mists of Avalon 35
Mitchell, D. 60
Moby Dick 49, 117
Monkey 88
Mont St Michel 80, 100
Moon and Sixpence, The 48
Moore, A. 51
Moore, M. 191
Moraroa Atoll 114
Morgan le Fay 19, 96
Morgannwg, I. 97
Morre, T. 36
Morris, W. 38
Morrison, V. 94
Morte d'Arthur, Le 40, 101, 102, 106
Motecuhzoma 187–8
Mount Ararat 146–7
Mount Rushmore 86
Mu 113
Murdoch, I. 46
Mysterious Island, The 50
Mythago wood 58

Narnia series 47, 54
Nation, T. 58
Nepal 1
New World, The 178
Newfoundland 184
News from Nowhere 38, 50
Niamh – *see* Oisín
Nicolson, A. 65, 79
Nineteen Eighty Four 186
Noah 146, 196
Norfolk 129–31

Northey 80
Northumberland 80
Notes from a Small Island 60

O Brother, Where Art Thou? 24
Obstinate Cymric 186
Odysseus 9, 89
Odyssey 24, 25
Ogygia 9
Oisín and Niamh 3–4, 8–9, 10, 11, 14,
    29–31, 43, 62, 84, 94, 110,
    119–20, 128, 139, 140–2, 143–5,
    158–9, 176, 194, 199
Okri, B. 59
Ondaatje, M. 10
One Million Years BC 147
Onge tribe 152
Orkney 78, 81
Orwell, G. 185
Osbourne, J. 55
Osiris 15
Our Lady's Island 78
Owen Glendower 46

Pabbay 78
Palmer, M. 89
Pan 59
Pangaea 111
Papa Stronsay 78
Paradise Lost 32
Pathfinder 184
Pavane 57
Paxspn, D.L. 35
Peake, M. 193
Pearce, P. 47
Pennick, N. 65
Perdido Street Station 57
Peter Pan 50–1
phantom islands 77–8
Pharos 5
Pilgrim of Love, The 93
Pilgrim's Progress The 85, 91
pilgrimage 85–93, 104
Pilgrimage, The 85
Pink Floyd 55
Pirates of the Caribbean 183

Pirsig, R.M. 5, 88
Planetwalker 87
Plato 60, 32–7, 196
Point Counter Point 55
polders 58–9
Pole, W.T. 104
Ponting, C. 121–2, 124, 125, 170
Porius 46
Potter, D. 166
Potter, Harry 27
Powis, J.C. 186
Powys, J.C. 46–7
Pratchett, T. 183
Preiddu Annwn 3, 15
Preistholm 78
Price, M.S. 127
Priest Island 78
priest islands 78
private islands 79–80
Proverbs of Hell 39
Pryor, F. 131
Puck of Pook's Hill 56
Pullman, P. 51–2, 166
Pwyll, Lord of Dyfed 11

Rahtz, P. 99–100, 102–3, 107, 132
Rainbow Bridge 19, 137
Ransome, A. 47
Ratcliffe, J. 133–4
Red Lady of Paviland 148
Red Riding Hood 59
Reed, C. 55
Reef 170–1
Renaissance 94
Right at Your Door 90
Rime of the Ancient Mariner, The 21, 22
Road, The 153, 190

Roberts, K. 57
Roberts, T. 77
Robertson, K.S. 58
Robin Hood 58
Roggeveen, J. 122
Rowliong, J.K. 61
Rubiyat 88

Rumi 88
Rural Rides 42

Sacred Journeys 85, 89
Sacred Places 26
St Cybbi's Well 90
St Exupéry, A. de 2
St Michael's Mount 80
St Modron's Well 90
St Patrick's Island 78
St Patrick's Purgatory 78
St Paul 19
Sarte, J. 55
Scarlet Letter, The 4
Schama, S. 63, 82, 172, 188–9
Schellenberg, K. 80
Scilly Isles – *see* Isles of Scilly
Scotland 11, 12, 16, 42, 68, 71–2, 73, 78, 80, 81
Scott, W. 42
Sea Priestess, The 76
Seahenge 129–32
Sealand 79
Seattle, Chief 178, 184
Secret Garden, The 47
Selfish Gene, The 126
Severin, T. 164
Shakespeare, W. 15, 20, 22, 49, 53
shamanism 9–10, 23
Shangri-La 1, 44–7, 54–5
Sharp, C. 43
Shylaman, M.N. 58
Shelley, P.B. 35, 40
Shelley, M. 57
Shetlands 78, 82, 135
Shinewater 132
ship burials 135–9
Sicko 191
Sinclair, I. 40
Small Island 60
Snyder, G. 183
Soil and Soul 80
Solnit, R. 89
Somerset 3, 22, 96–7, 1007, 112, 129; *see also* Avalon; Bath; Glastonbury

Song of Hiawatha 42
Song of Wandering Aengus 18, 27–8, 43
Southern Mail 2
Southey, R. 42
Soylent Green 58
Springer, C. 140
Spufford, F. 54, 60–1
Stafford, W. 63–4
Stapledon, O. 57
Star Trek 25, 57
Star Wars 27, 133
Stardust 47
Starmaker, The 57
starseed people 106
Steinbeck, J. 24
Steiner, G. 46
Stern Review 154–5
Stevenson, R.L. 41–2
Stewart, P.D. 116–18, 126
Stewart, R.J. 11
Stukeley, W. 94
Super-Cannes 56
SURVAS 154–5
Survivors 58
Sussex 132
Sutton Hoo 130, 137–9
Swallows and Amazons 47
Sweet Track 133
Swift, J. 37, 57, 186
Swindon 91
Syriana 191

Tales of the Uncanny and Supernatural 54
Taliesin 3, 15, 19, 20, 28, 79
Taliesin (1988 film) 35
Tam Lin 10, 12, 16, 17–18
Tammuz 16
tectonic acivity – *see* continental plates
Tennyson, A. 40, 105–6
Things to Come 57
Third Man, The 55
Thomas the Rhymer 10–14, 16, 17
Thomas, D. 41, 43, 166
Thomson, R. 60

Thoreau, H.D. 37
Thousand and One Nights, A 88
Thule 1, 3
tidal islands 80–1
Time Machine, The 100
Time Team 129. 150
Tir nan Og 1, 13
Titus Alone 193
Tolkien, J.R.R. 44, 47, 55
Tom's Midnight Garden 47
Tortuga 183
Travels with a Donkey in the Cévennes 41
Treasure Island 41
trees 166–7
Troy Towns 75
Trubshaw, B. 26
Truman Show, The 58
tsunami, Indian Ocean 151–2
Turkey 2
Turtle Island 182
tutelary spirits 20
Tuvalu 155–6
Twenty Thousand Leagues Under the Sea 50
Two Brothers, The 17–18

USA 152, 176–86, 189–93
Utopia 36

Verne, J. 50
Vidal, G. 153
Vikings 135–9164, 184
Vikings, The 135–6
Village, The 58
Vision of the Fool, The 86
Vita Merlini 19, 100
Vladi, F. 79–80
Vogler, C. 27
Voice That Thunders, The, 4
volcanoes 113–14
Voyage dans la Lune, Le, 57
Voyage of Bran mac Ferbal 1, 10, 15, 27, 183
Voyage of St Brendan, The 185
Voyage of the Argo 25
Voyage to Arcturus 57

Walden 37
Wales 11, 42, 67–71, 72, 75–6, 78–9, 81, 82, 90, 95, 149–51; *see also* Bardsey Island; Gower Peninsula
Wandering 89
Wanderlust 88
War in the Air, The 50
Washer at the Ford 16
Watchet 22
Weir, P. 58
Wells, H.G. 49, 50, 100
Wender, W. 191
Western Isles 42, 81
Westwood, J. 85, 91, 134–5
Weymouth Sands 46–7
When I Set Out for Lyonesse 45
When Worlds Collide 57, 196
White, J. 179
Wild Wales 42
Wilde, O. 171
William of Malmesbury 96
Willows, The 54

Wilson, A. 46
Wiltshire 90–1, 97, 129
Wind in the Willows, 47, 52–4
Wind, Sand and Stars 2
Windling, T. 180
Witness 58
Wizard of Oz 60, 89
Wolf Solent 46
Wood Magic 41
Woolf, V., 46
Wordsworth, W. 40–1, 166
world tree 166
Worms Head 81
Writer's Journey, The 27

Xanadu – *see Kubla Kahn*
Yeats, W.B. 18, 27, 42–4, 199
Ynys Enlli – *see* Bardsey island
York 135
Ys – *see* Kêr-Ys
Zen and the Art of Motorcycle Maintenance 5, 88

Also from Heart of Albion Press

Myths of Reality

Simon Danser

'This liberal author's knowledge of contemporary society is amazingly broad. He exposits the mythic depths (and appearances) of everything from 'the myth of science' to superhero attitudes of contemporary American nationalism.

'Along the way he challenges many superficial trivialities about myths functioning in culture. He regards the mythic as a primary, highly effective agent of social ideology, and is never hesitant about demanding that the garments of our truly mythological capitalism are ill-fitting and socially harmful.

'This is the best book I know in terms of disclosing the pragmatic functioning of myth in society.'

William Doty, Professor Emeritus, The University of Alabama and author of *Mythography: The study of myths and rituals*

Simon Danser asks us to think of myths as like the lenses in spectacles – we see the world through them, but rarely see them in their own right. He then systematically focuses on the myths at the core of the belief systems which create every aspect of what we take to be reality: religion, politics, commerce, science, knowledge, consciousness, self-identity, and much else that we take as 'given'.

This book reveals how reality is culturally constructed in an ever-continuing process from mythic fragments transmitted by the mass media and adapted through face-to-face and Internet conversations.

> 'And now, in 2005, there is a powerful new voice from outside American culture to motivate the old symbol and myth chasing posse. This time it comes from England and author Simon Danser in his short but brilliant book *Myths of Reality.'* John Fraim *Jung Pages*

Published by Alternative Albion, an imprint of Heart of Albion Press.
ISBN 1 872883 80 X. 2004. 215 x 175 mm, 205 + xiv pages, paperback. **£12.95**

Stonehenge:
Celebration and Subversion

Andy Worthington

This innovative social history looks in detail at how the summer solstice celebrations at Stonehenge have brought together different aspects of British counter-culture to make the monument a 'living temple' and an icon of alternative Britain. The history of the celebrants and counter-cultural leaders is interwoven with the viewpoints of the land-owners, custodians and archaeologists who have generally attempted to impose order on the shifting patterns of these modern-day mythologies.

The story of the Stonehenge summer solstice celebrations begins with the Druid revival of the 18th century and the earliest public gatherings of the 19th and early 20th centuries. In the social upheavals of the 1960s and early 70s, these trailblazers were superseded by the Stonehenge Free Festival. This evolved from a small gathering to an anarchic free state the size of a small city, before its brutal suppression at the Battle of the Beanfield in 1985.

In the aftermath of the Beanfield, the author examines how the political and spiritual aspirations of the free festivals evolved into both the rave scene and the road protest movement, and how the prevailing trends in the counter-culture provided a fertile breeding ground for the development of new Druid groups, the growth of paganism in general, and the adoption of other sacred sites, in particular Stonehenge's gargantuan neighbour at Avebury.

The account is brought up to date with the reopening of Stonehenge on the summer solstice in 2000, the unprecedented crowds drawn by the new access arrangements, and the latest source of conflict, centred on a bitterly-contested road improvement scheme.

> *'Stonehenge Celebration and Subversion* contains an extraordinary story. Anyone who imagines Stonehenge to be nothing but an old fossil should read this and worry. [This book is] ... the most complete, well-illustrated analysis of Stonehenge's mysterious world of Druids, travellers, pagans and party-goers'. Mike Pitts *History Today*

ISBN 1 872883 76 1. 2004. Perfect bound, 245 x 175 mm, 281 + xviii pages, 147 b&w photos, **£14.95**

Sacred Places
Prehistory and popular imagination
Bob Trubshaw

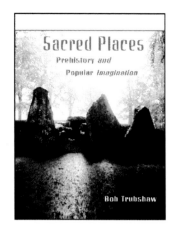

Sacred Places asks why certain types of prehistoric places are thought of as sacred, and explores how the physical presence of such sacred sites is less important than what these places signify. So this is not another guide book to sacred places but instead provides a unique and thought-provoking guide to the mental worlds – the mindscapes – in which we have created the idea of prehistoric sacred places.

Recurring throughout this book is the idea that we continually create and re-create our ideas about the past, about landscapes, and the places within those landscapes that we regard as sacred. For example, although such concepts as 'nature', 'landscape', 'countryside', 'rural' and the contrast between profane and sacred are all part of our everyday thinking, in this book Bob Trubshaw shows they are all modern cultural constructions which act as the 'unseen' foundations on which we construct more complex myths about places.

Key chapters look at how earth mysteries, modern paganism and other alternative approaches to sacred places developed in recent decades, and also outline the recent dramatic changes within academic archaeology. Is there now a 'middle way' between academic and alternative approaches which recognises that what we know about the past is far less significant than what we believe about the past?

Bob Trubshaw has been actively involved with academic and alternative approaches to archaeology for most of the last twenty years. In 1996 he founded *At the Edge* magazine to popularise new interpretations of past and place.

> '*Sacred Places*... is a very valuable addition to the small body of thoughtful work on the spiritual landscapes of Great Britain and therefore recommended reading.' Nigel Pennick *Silver Wheel*

> 'One of the best books in the field I have ever read.'
> D J Tyrer *Monomyth Supplement*

ISBN 1 872883 67 2. 2005. 245 x 175 mm, 203 + xiv pages, 43 b&w illustrations and 7 line drawings, paperback. **£16.95**

The Princess Who Ate People

The psychology of Celtic myths

Brendan McMahon

Childhood, adolescence, courtship and death. Personal identity and madness. These are the key themes of many myths in traditional Celtic literatures. Although written many centuries ago, their narratives still reflect and define our essential humanity.

Many Celtic tales of exile and loss anticipate modem dilemmas of alienation but offer ways of understanding such difficulties without pathologising them. Individuals are seen in their social context and, in contrast, madness is identified with loneliness and isolation. The traditional stories describe how appropriate narratives help restore integrity and identity. These life-cycle narratives and concepts of identity are more complex and less fixed than psychoanalytic narratives which, by comparison, seem contrived or impoverished.

Psychotherapy assists people to construct a narrative which makes sense of their lives. However psychoanalysis too often relies on outdated and limited assumptions. By learning from the poets who created the Celtic myths, therapists can help their patients develop more appropriate personal narratives.

However this is not a book written only for psychotherapists. The stories considered here speak to all of us. McMahon helps us to fully understand these life cycle narratives and thereby helps us to understand ourselves. We need these myths now more than ever before.

Brendan McMahon is a practicing psychotherapist in Derbyshire who has written many articles and papers on therapy and Celtic myth. He is also a poet and university teacher.

ISBN 1 872883 88 5. January 2006. Demy 8vo (215 x 138 mm), 102 + viii pages, 5 specially commissioned illustrations from Ian Brown, paperback **£9.95**

Taliesin's Travels

A demi-god at large

Michael Dames

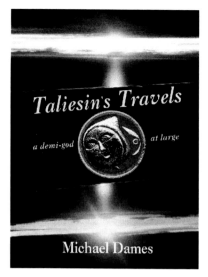

Taliesin's Travels brings fresh significance to one of Britain's best-loved tales.

For over a thousand years the impish Taliesin has enthralled and enlightened people. As a farmer's son, he is grounded in the land. Yet, because his mother is the goddess Nature, he can travel, free as a demi-god, throughout time and space.

Thanks to his intimate contact with spirits of place, sun and underworld, Taliesin reveals and portrays the interconnecting, ever-transforming essence of life. His often painful and sometimes ludicrous adventures engage with creation in its entirety. Transcending history, he invites us to see our own millennium as a cyclical, mythic journey so that, like him, each individual comes to identify with the whole of creation.

With a keen sense of enjoyment, Michael Dames provides a deep and imaginative account of the tales and poetry associated with Taliesin. Prehistoric, Romano-British and Christian aspects of Taliesin's persona are brought together in a magical synthesis.

Michael Dames is well-known for his pioneering studies of the myths and legends of the British Isles. His previous books include *The Silbury Treasure, The Avebury Cycle, Mythic Ireland* and *Merlin and Wales*.

EAN 978 1872 883 892. ISBN 1 872883 89 3. February 2006.
245 x 175 mm, over 200 illustrations, paperback
£16.95

Footprints in Stone

The significance of foot- and hand-prints and other imprints left by early men, giants, heroes, devils, saints, animals, ghosts, witches, fairies and monsters

Janet Bord

'A delightful exploration of a truly mysterious subject. 9 out of 10'
Bob Rickard *Fortean Times*

'Fascinating stuff and highly recommended.' Mike Howard *The Cauldron*

'... a good and wide-ranging first step into investigating the significance of the foot imprint.' John Billingsley *Northern Earth*

From the earliest humans to the present day, there has always been a compulsion to 'leave one's mark': early cave art includes thousands of hand outlines, while many churches in Britain have foot outlines inscribed in lead and stone. These two extremes span almost 30,000 years during which time all kinds of persons, real and legendary, have left visible traces of themselves. But 30,000 years ago seems almost recent, when compared with the finding of some (admittedly controversial) fossilized human footprints in rocks apparently contemporary with dinosaur footprints that are tens of millions of years old.

Most of the footprints – and hand-prints, knee-prints, and impressions of other body parts – are clearly not real, having allegedly been impressed into rocks around the world by such high-profile figures as the Buddha, Vishnu, Jesus Christ, and the Virgin Mary, as well as a vast panoply of saints, whose footprint traces and associated stories occupy two chapters. Their horses also left hoof-prints, and other animals are represented too. Not surprisingly, the ubiquitous Devil has a whole chapter to himself – but giants, villains and heroes, such as King Arthur, also feature strongly. Witches, fairies, ghosts and assorted spirits have made their mark: there are many modern instances of phantom hand- and foot-prints, the latter often bloodstained and indelible.

Hundreds of imprints are described in this book, which concludes with location details for more than 100 imprint sites all around the world.

ISBN 1 872883 73 7. 2004. 245 x 175 mm, 263 + x pages, 112 b&w photos, 26 line drawings, paperback. **£14.95**

Also from Heart of Albion Press

Howls of Imagination

Wolves of England

Paul Williams

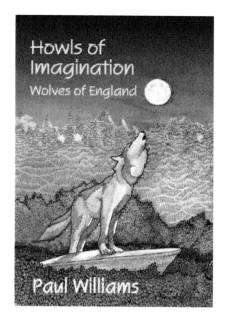

Wolves have been despised and persecuted by humans for centuries. They were eradicated completely in England by about 1509 and in Scotland and Ireland in the mid-eighteenth century. Yet superstitions and folklore continue to fuel a fear of wolves in modern day Britain – even though many of these popular beliefs are inaccurate. In *Howls of Imagination* Dr Paul Williams describes how these beliefs have arisen, and contrasts them with known information about wolves – and the relatively rare number of wolf attacks on humans.

Why did Christian allegories give wolves a 'bad press'? How did popular literature breed a hybrid lore by mixing legends about real wolves with myths about werewolves? Have children really been reared by wolves? And, above all, should we afraid of 'the big bad wolf' or simply consign such ideas to the scrap bin of erroneous stereotypes? *Howls of Imagination* reveals how folklore and myth can create and sustain misleading ideas while simultaneously offering a more factual understanding of this iconic animal of the wilderness.

Dr Paul Williams completed a PhD thesis on wolves in folklore in 2004 at Sheffield University. His short fiction and poetry has been published in magazines and anthologies such as *Focus* and *Roadworks*.

> "*Howls of Imagination* is a superb study of the fact, the fiction, the legend, and the mythology surrounding that most mysterious of creatures: the wolf. [...] *Howls of Imagination* was probably one of my most enjoyable reads of this year so far; and I can say for certain that in this concise-yet-packed [107]-page book, the author has revealed a wealth of hidden knowledge on this majestic beast, dispelled some myths, answered a lot of questions, and offered a rich body of data that is diverse, eye-opening, mysterious and magical in equal measures."
> Nick Redfern

ISBN 978-1-872883-98-4. 2007. 245 x 175 mm, 107 + vi pages, 10 b&w photos, 2 line drawings, paperback. **£12.95**

'Highly recommended'
Folklore Society Katharine Briggs
Award 2003

Explore Folklore

Bob Trubshaw

**'A howling success, which plugs
a big and obvious gap'**

Professor Ronald Hutton

There have been fascinating developments in the study of folklore in the last twenty-or-so years, but few books about British folklore and folk customs reflect these exciting new approaches. As a result there is a huge gap between scholarly approaches to folklore studies and 'popular beliefs' about the character and history of British folklore. *Explore Folklore* is the first book to bridge that gap, and to show how much 'folklore' there is in modern day Britain.

Explore Folklore shows there is much more to folklore than morris dancing and fifty-something folksingers! The rituals of 'what we do on our holidays', funerals, stag nights and 'lingerie parties' are all full of 'unselfconscious' folk customs. Indeed, folklore is something that is integral to all our lives – it is so intrinsic we do not think of it as being 'folklore'.

The implicit ideas underlying folk lore and customs are also explored. There might appear to be little in common between people who touch wood for luck (a 'tradition' invented in the last 200 years) and legends about people who believe they have been abducted and subjected to intimate body examinations by aliens. Yet, in their varying ways, these and other 'folk beliefs' reflect the wide spectrum of belief and disbelief in what is easily dismissed as 'superstition'.

Explore Folklore provides a lively introduction to the study of most genres of British folklore, presenting the more contentious and profound ideas in a readily accessible manner.

ISBN 1 872883 60 5. 2002. Demy 8vo (215x138 mm), 200 pages, illustrated, paperback **£9.95**

*Winner of the Folklore Society
Katharine Briggs Award 2005*

Explore Fairy Traditions

Jeremy Harte

We are not alone. In the shadows of our countryside there lives a fairy race, older than humans, and not necessarily friendly to them. For hundreds of years, men and women have told stories about the strange people, beautiful as starlight, fierce as wolves, and heartless as ice. These are not tales for children. They reveal the fairies as a passionate, proud, brutal people.

Explore Fairy Traditions draws on legends, ballads and testimony from throughout Britain and Ireland to reveal what the fairies were really like. It looks at changelings, brownies, demon lovers, the fairy host, and abduction into the Otherworld. Stories and motifs are followed down the centuries to reveal the changing nature of fairy lore, as it was told to famous figures like W.B. Yeats and Sir Walter Scott. All the research is based on primary sources and many errors about fairy tradition are laid to rest.

Jeremy Harte combines folklore scholarship with a lively style to show what the presence of fairies meant to people's lives. Like their human counterparts, the secret people could kill as well as heal. They knew marriage, seduction, rape and divorce; they adored some children and rejected others. If we are frightened of the fairies, it may be because their world offers an uncomfortable mirror of our own.

> '... this is the best and most insightful book on fairies generally available... ' John Billingsley *Northern Earth*

> '*Explore Fairy Traditions* is an excellent introduction to the folklore of fairies, and I would highly recommend it.' Paul Mason *Silver Wheel*

ISBN 1 872883 61 3. 2004. Demy 8vo (215 x 138 mm), 171 + vi pages, 6 line drawings, paperback. **£9.95**

The Enchanted Land

Myths and Legends of Britain's Landscape

Revised, fully illustrated edition

Janet and Colin Bord

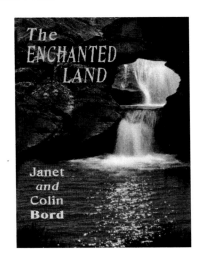

Britain's landscape is overlain by a magic carpet of folklore and folktales, myths and legends. Enchantment and legend still lurk in places as diverse as hills and mountains, rivers and streams, caves and hollows, springs and wells, cliffs and coasts, pools and lakes, and rocks and stones.

The dramatic stories woven around these places tell of sleeping knights, beheaded saints, giants, dragons and monsters, ghosts, King Arthur, mermaids, witches, hidden treasure, drowned towns, giant missiles, mysterious footprints, visits to Fairyland, underground passages, human sacrifices, and much more.

The 'Places to Visit' section locates and describes in detail more than 50 sites.

This revised edition is fully illustrated, with around 130 photographs and illustrations.

Janet and Colin Bord live in North Wales, where they run the Fortean Picture Library. They have written more than 20 books since their first successful joint venture, *Mysterious Britain* in 1972.

From reviews of the first edition:

'Janet's own enthusiasm for a number of the sites is conveyed vividly and lends credibility to the notion that Britain is still an enchanted land.' *Mercian Mysteries*

ISBN 1 872883 91 5. 2006. 245 x 175 mm, over 200 illustrations, paperback
£16.95

Heart of Albion

The UK's leading publisher of folklore, mythology and cultural studies.

Further details of all Heart of Albion titles online at
www.hoap.co.uk

All titles available direct from Heart of Albion Press.
Please add 80p p&p (UK only; email
albion@indigogroup.co.uk for overseas postage).

To order books or request our current catalogue
please contact

Heart of Albion Press
2 Cross Hill Close, Wymeswold
Loughborough, LE12 6UJ

Phone: 01509 880725
Fax: 01509 881715
email: albion@indigogroup.co.uk
Web site: www.hoap.co.uk